the LAST CANADIAN KNIGHT

the LAST CANADIAN KNIGHT

The Unintended Business Adventures *of* Sir Graham Day

GORDON PITTS

Nimbus Publishing Limited
3731 Mackintosh St, Halifax, NS, B3K 5A5
(902) 455-4286 nimbus.ca

Printed and bound in Canada

NB1296

Cover photo: Courtesy of Sherman Hines
Interior design: Peggy Issenman, Peggy & Co. Design
Cover design: Heather Bryan

Library and Archives Canada Cataloguing in Publication

Pitts, Gordon, author
The last Canadian knight : the unintended business adventures of Sir Graham Day / Gordon Pitts.

Includes bibliographical references and index.
Issued in print and electronic formats.
ISBN 978-1-77108-491-8 (hardcover).—ISBN 978-1-77108-492-5 (HTML)

1. Day, J. Graham (Judson Graham), 1933-. 2. Businessmen—Canada—Biography. 3. Lawyers—Canada—Biography. 4. Nova Scotia—Biography. I. Title.

FC2326.1.D39P58 2017 971.6'04092 C2016-908012-9
C2016-908

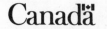

Canada Canada Council for the Arts Conseil des arts du Canada NOVA SCOTIA

Nimbus Publishing acknowledges the financial support for its publishing activities from the Government of Canada, the Canada Council for the Arts, and from the Province of Nova Scotia. We are pleased to work in partnership with the Province of Nova Scotia to develop and promote our creative industries for the benefit of all Nova Scotians.

CONTENTS

FOREWORD

It is truly an honour to introduce an individual I have been privileged to call a mentor, sponsor, and dear friend. Yet I do so with trepidation, as Sir Graham Day is not unlike the tweed sports jackets he favours: depending upon the thread your eye chooses to follow, a different pattern emerges. So how best to set the stage for *The Last Canadian Knight*? Thankfully, one of the first lessons I learned at the Graham Day School of Championing Young People is never impose your views upon someone through lecture when an anecdote is much more effective and charming!

The story begins in the spring of 2011. As a corporate partner at the law firm of Stewart McKelvey, I had worked as part of the team closing a transaction relating to the transformative reorganization of the Scotia Investments Group of Companies, the conglomerate built by the late Roy A. Jodrey. Graham was the chair of Scotia Investments Limited and I was its counsel. In effect, we crossed the Rubicon together—Project Rubicon being the name he had given the reorganization transaction.

Late in the day, my office phone rings. Seeing that it is Graham calling, I settle in for what I anticipate will be one of our comfortable and familiar conversations. I lean back in my chair, swing my legs up onto my desk, cross my pump-clad feet at the ankles, and hit the speakerphone. We have moved from general conversation to specifics relating to post-closing matters when John Rogers, the firm's CEO at the time, knocks and pops his head in. Well versed in Graham's keen sense of fun, yet strict adherence to the principles of decorum, John cheekily suggests to Graham that I might not be exhibiting the appropriate amount of deference that an "audience" with the chairman of Scotia

Investments would dictate. In short order, John captures my relaxed and unladylike pose on his phone's camera and shares my moment of impunity with Graham—pump-clad feet on the desk and all!

Fast forward to the spring of 2014. I am newly appointed to the role of Regional Managing Partner, NS, at Stewart McKelvey. This time Graham calls to advise that he and Ann are back from Florida and he would like to come for a visit. At the appointed hour, Graham arrives properly attired in a tweed jacket and tie with a present, the size of a shoebox, neatly tucked under his arm. He proceeds to explain that the present is a little token intended to celebrate my recent appointment, a role not previously held by a female. To my delight, the box contains a pair of shoes! At this point in the unveiling, with the formality that only an ace salesman schooled in the art of selling shoes could exhibit, Graham proceeds to kneel before me, remove the tissue and packing from each of the shoes, preparing them for me to try on, all the while with a twinkle in his eye and a smile on his face matching that of his generous spirit.

Just over a year later, on August 1, 2015, I assumed the mantle of CEO and managing partner of Stewart McKelvey. As I approached my first day on the job, I recognized it would be important to set the tone as to how I intended to lead. I knew I needed to signal that I was approachable and keen to meet all of the five hundred or so lawyers and staff, and, most important, that I could be trusted. I found myself recalling Graham's story of his first day in the shipyard of Cammell Laird and realized that I, too, needed to "walk the property." The Halifax office was familiar territory, so I decided to begin my first day as CEO in our Saint John, New Brunswick, office. Next pressing matter: "what to wear?" No deliberations required: I would "walk the property" in my Sir Graham "power pumps."

My story, like many in the book, conveys the essence of Graham. Graham's razor-sharp memory is a virtual library, cataloguing not only vast passages from his beloved classics, but also the minute details of every person, transaction, and situation he has encountered throughout his life. The photo of my "pump-clad" feet up on my desk was simply filed away until Graham found the appropriate opportunity to tie it to a career milestone.

Graham's ascension from corporate lawyer to Margaret Thatcher's "fix-it man" to corporate boardroom titan was meteoric. Yet his genuine interest in the advancement of others, particularly women in business, is apparent in my own experience. My elevation from corporate lawyer to regional managing partner of Stewart McKelvey's Halifax office was supported by his "guiding hand," as he put my name forward to take on client roles and corporate board positions that would expose me to Atlantic Canada's business elite—a tradition, I later learned, Graham carried on in honour of one of his guardian angels, Gordon Cowan, the managing partner of a predecessor firm to Stewart McKelvey.

Graham's own career took him to boardrooms around the globe, meeting with international business magnates. He was knighted by the queen in recognition for his service to British industry. Yet he has never lost the touch he learned from his introduction to business, selling shoes at Simpson's.

For those who know Graham, this book puts his many stories into context and validates what we already cherish about him. Like my story, it illuminates how many others have benefited from an individual so passionate and vested in the ideals of mentorship and sponsorship, long before those concepts were touted in business schools and leadership development curricula.

For those who have not met Graham, this book captures his place in the history of the Thatcher era and the evolution of corporate governance while revealing an extraordinary individual who has contributed unselfishly to the cultural, educational, and economic prosperity of our province and country.

Before being introduced to Graham by my good friend and former partner Mark MacDonald, I was counselled that I would never meet an individual quite like him. I never have. At his core is an unfailing belief in the duty of service to queen and country, yet he was raised and schooled in "the colonies." He is battle tested and at the ready to lend his steely determination and decisive intellect to a small business start-up or large multinational corporation, yet he carries himself with the bearing and charm of a learned British gentleman. Above all, he is a protector of the values of loyalty, equality, and respect: the epitome of a Canadian knight.

Lydia Bugden
Chief Executive Officer and Managing Partner
Stewart McKelvey

INTRODUCTION

It is a typical day in 1948 at Queen Elizabeth High School in central Halifax. Students are mingling noisily as they move from class to class. Far removed from this happy throng, a number of boys have gathered in the lavatory to play cards, read, and hang out. They are exiles, kicked out of their classes, and they have gathered as an irregular club of undesirables, labelled by the principal as the Shithouse Rats.

One of them is a tall lanky fellow named Graham Day, and he is typical of the group: aimless and angry, contemptuous of most of his teachers, whom he dismisses as incompetents. He seems to have raw talent—he can readily cite the history of ancient Egypt, he can sing beautifully—but the rest of his school work is alienating. So he has joined the Rats in their boys'-room pack. "I was absolutely adrift," he would recall in later life.

Flash forward forty years. The scene is 10 Downing Street, London, the residence of Prime Minister Margaret Thatcher. The Iron Lady is meeting with one of her most trusted lieutenants, the man she has mandated to turn around large state industries and transfer their ownership to the private sector. Privatization of Crown industries is a key thrust in the Thatcher Revolution that is shaking Britain in the 1980s by pulling back the role of the state in the economy. And that man beside her is Graham Day, the one-time Shithouse Rat.

By now, Day has established enough credibility to escape Thatcher's famously harsh grilling of subordinates. After the briefing, she asks a secretary how much time is left before Prime Minister's Questions in the House of Commons. Satisfied that there is an interval, she wonders if Day would like a little drink. He requests sherry, and she wets the bottom of her glass with a touch of Scotch. And in a moment of rare relaxation, Thatcher kicks off her pumps and leans back in her chair.

That simple gesture is a sign that Graham Day, once the ultimate outsider, once consigned to the boys' lavatory, has moved dramatically to the centre of power. He belongs to the elite of Thatcher's corporate managers, men she can trust to do the big tough jobs. He is a turnaround artist who would pull off the privatization of the shipbuilding industry, the Rover car business, and a big part of Britain's power generation infrastructure. He would be a trusted advisor to the National Health Service. He would head the board of one of Britain's signature companies, Cadbury Schweppes. He would be knighted for his services to Thatcher and to Britain—thus joining the ranks of that endangered species, the Canadian knight.

A British cabinet minister once told him that he was instantly expendable: the Brits would rather "shoot the colonial" than one of their own. In the sharp-elbowed world of British commerce, he would not only survive; he would play a key role in transforming the British economy—indeed, the global economy—and his impact still resonates. He is possibly the most important Canadian business executive ever to have graced the British corporate stage—perhaps the global business stage. And he took his act back to Canada, where he would become one of the best directors to inhabit a boardroom.

Oh, and there is another line in the Day resumé: as a young man, he was a singer and music director for *Singalong Jubilee*, one of the most influential career-making shows in Canadian television history.

How did this happen? What kind of miraculous conversion lifted Graham Day from angry boy to powerful adult who sips sherry with prime ministers? In fact, there was no wholesale conversion. The traits that alienated his teachers at Queen Elizabeth High—energy, tough-mindedness, stubbornness, a heightened sense of fair play—became the underpinnings of Day's success as a business leader. These traits just needed to be channelled. And something happened to Day that we all go through: he grew up.

The Graham Day journey is a picaresque romp through modern British and Canadian business history, with sharp turns, defeats, and triumphs. It reflects hard-knocks maturity gained in a stormy, but ultimately successful, stint at Dalhousie Law School, and then as a small-town lawyer in Nova Scotia's Annapolis Valley. It demonstrates the value of a sense of humour as a management instrument that can lower the temperature and raise the quality of conversation.

The breadth of the man is spectacular: a trouble shooter for Canadian Pacific, historically Canada's most important company; a musical talent who played a part in discovering Canadian songbirds Anne Murray and Catherine McKinnon; an auto executive who saved a legendary car marque; a trusted advisor for major Canadian enterprises, including Canada's most famous business families. It is reasonable to ask: could this all be the same man?

But it is. He is not widely known in Canada because so many of his triumphs were earned abroad. In Britain he was a capitalist hero, but in Canada he has been an adroit background player, influential as a mentor of people and a director for companies such as Bank of Nova Scotia, Sobeys, and Moosehead beer—the grey eminence to whom company builders and executives turn for wisdom. He has used the Atlantic law firm Stewart McKelvey as his base of operations, and has served his beloved Dalhousie University, which played such a role in his maturity, as chancellor and benefactor.

He could be viewed in the grand tradition of Canadian colonials who played starring roles on the British stage: brash entrepreneurs such as Sir James Dunn, Lord Beaverbrook, and Lord Thomson. But Day was different. He was the pioneer of a new tradition: Canadians who inject professional management into hidebound British institutions. Today, British recruiters pursue Canadians because, like Day, they bring an outsider's perspective, and they are not Americans. Graham Day's turnaround of a declining Liverpool shipyard paved the way for former Bank of Canada governor Mark Carney to take on the equivalent role at the Bank of England, and Moya Greene, Newfoundland-born former CEO of Canada Post, who moved on to head the Royal Mail and guide it through a difficult privatization. Each went to Britain to head a fundamental pillar of the economy and a legacy institution. Like Graham Day, they would work at the politically charged intersection of the private and public sectors. Their recruitment was based on track records of success in Canada, but also the knowledge that implementing change was easier for outsiders with scant ties to British entrenched interests. It is harder to slot them into a certain class, accent, or regional pigeonhole. That was one of Day's great assets.

But the truly surprising aspect of Day's story is that, at age sixty—still prime time for a business titan— and at the peak of his prestige in Britain, he gave it up, returning to Canada as part of a decades'-old pact with his wife Ann. His return was a gift to Canada and its institutions, from which they drew mightily.

Graham Day has really never slowed down. He has played the same role for Canadian businesses, large and small, as he did for Margaret Thatcher. He has navigated his way through the shoals of change and generational succession at supermarkets, banks, and breweries. He has not always been successful: sometimes wrong, never in doubt, he likes to say. He still painfully recalls the Hydro One debacle: the privatization he lost. But he has never wavered in his belief that government should do governing and business should do business—and the two should rarely commingle. I say "rarely," because Day's pragmatism is another crowning trait.

Now in his early eighties, Day says his was a career of serendipity, of being in the right place at the right time, of unintended adventures. Yes, but serendipity is what you do with it. As Napoleon allegedly said, bring me the lucky generals, not just the good ones. Luck is the product of the person and what he or she does with suddenly available opportunity. Sir Graham seized the day, and never looked back.

CHAPTER 1

Beginnings

Graham Day was born on May 3, 1933, in the Grace Hospital in Halifax. His parents, for reasons unknown, believed their first and only child would be a girl. Caught unprepared by this baby boy, they had to come up with a name. The presiding doctor was Judson Vye Graham, so the child would be Judson Graham Day.

The baby, who would have a secure but plain upbringing in North End Halifax, was the son of a Canadian mother and an immigrant father from the East End of London. At the time of Graham's birth, his father Frank worked in a furniture and appliance store owned by an uncle. Growing up in England, Frank Day had suffered from poor health since birth, including a bout of rheumatic fever. His family got him in a private school, giving him a better education than his siblings. When the First World War came, he attempted to join up, but flunked the medical. He found a job in the City of London—the financial district—as a runner, one of the army of messengers who delivered pieces of paper, including securities, among the banks and brokerages. He was in the employ of wealthy brothers, who took an interest in him and, aware of his health problems, offered him a job inside.

They liked Frank and felt he needed a healthier vocation, so they sent him to agricultural college. They saw he was not getting better, however, and in another act of kindness paid his way to Australia, with its lure of a better climate. He worked on a sheep ranch in the middle of the continent, where he encountered snakes. Frank Day hated snakes. Graham remembers a picture of his father on horseback, armed with a pistol and a rifle, on the job at the sheep ranch. He was posing beside a dead snake roped over a branch. This was not Frank Day's kind of life, and so that was the end of Australia for him. In Halifax, however, was this uncle with the furniture store. So Frank Day crossed the Pacific to Vancouver and made his way across the country to Nova Scotia.

Graham's mother, Edythe, came from a Nova Scotia family named Baker. Family lore has it that her grandfather, a young Dutchman named Willem Becker, from an affluent shipping family, had left home rather than accept his parents' career choice of the Catholic priesthood. His granddaughter Edythe (or Edie) was born in Herring Cove, a semi-isolated community south of Halifax that was largely cut off in winter and spring but is now part of the Halifax Regional Municipality. Her father was a harbour pilot who guided ships into the port. A boat would chug out from Herring Cove to put pilots on incoming ships. The pilots would arrange their own shifts, and one day a certain Captain Pelham offered to take Edie's father's shift. Pelham's pilot boat was cut in two by a large vessel and all hands were lost. Edie's father, probably haunted by the tragedy, couldn't go back on the pilot boats again, and found other marine jobs, such as navigating for the Portuguese fishing fleet and toiling for a ship supply company. Graham Day has a faded memory as a young child of accompanying his grandfather on the *Bluenose*, the famous racing schooner commemorated on the dime.

Frank and Edie met in the choir of St. Paul's Church, the old Anglican garrison church in Halifax—she was the soprano soloist, he the bass soloist, a predictor of the role music would play in their son's life. Choir practice was held on Saturday nights, but Frank Day had to work late those nights in his uncle's furniture store. (His uncle's inflexibility and skinflint ways helped build his reputation in the Day family as "Uncle Scrooge.") It was the Depression, and Frank was not going to give up the extra money from working late. Eventually, the rector at St. Paul's told him if he couldn't go to choir practice, he couldn't sing in the choir. Frank never went back to St. Paul's, and never sang in church again for the rest of his life. Perhaps the stubborn apple doesn't fall far from the tree.

Graham, born in the Depression to a lower-middle-class family, was in many ways a fortunate child, the only one in the extended family for a number of years. He borrowed and inherited clothes from a young uncle, common practice for kids growing up during the Depression and the Second World War. It was a close-to-the-bone existence: many in his family were jobless in the 1930s. A 1994 profile in *Financial Post Magazine* recounts a family story about how Day's parents would leave Sunday dinner at his grandparents' house with baby Graham tucked into a sled surrounded by turnips and other vegetables, concealed by his grandmother under the blankets to avoid embarrassing his needy parents.

Day grew up in a bungalow on Lawrence Street, a short shady road of tidy houses on the southern edges of Halifax's working-class North End, just before it gave way to the more affluent south. It was an appropriate setting for a family with aspirations. After Frank had laboured for years in Uncle Scrooge's store, the Days would venture out to open their own store, where they complemented the furniture business with sales of china and glassware. It was a small shop background that tended to breed upward strivers like young Margaret Roberts—later Thatcher—whose father was a grocer in the English Midlands.

As an only child, Graham Day was the focus of his parents' life. "He would deny this until he goes to the grave, but there was nothing he could do wrong in their eyes," Graham's son Michael says. Graham's father read to his son constantly, not just children's stories but tales of Arctic and Antarctic expeditions, deep-sea diving and salvage stories, yarns of submarines, and Dickens novels. His English grandparents would send books from the old country, including boys' annuals such as *Pip and Squeak* and *Tiger Tim's*, which he and his father would share. "My father had no desire to go back to England to live, but I think he was in part homesick for the rest of his life," Graham Day observes. And so he gave his son a *Boy's Own* upbringing.

One of Day's great aunts had married a Colonel King of the British Army, who had been an officer in the Gurkha corps and served on the staff of British commander Lord Kitchener in the First World War. (He was transferred off that assignment just before Kitchener put to sea in the ship that would blow up on a mine, killing the British military chief.) Colonel King retired to Herring Cove, where he spent time with young Graham, who passed his summers there. Regaling the boy with stories of derring-do and military life, at one point the colonel announced that his young protegé would go to Sandhurst, the British military college, some day. But then along came the Second World War, and life moved on.

The war was a very big deal in Halifax, a garrison town up close to the North Atlantic physically and emotionally. Halifax's 60,000 residents were haunted by a dark passage in their history.

People still had scarcely repressed memories of December 6, 1917, when a French munitions ship collided with a Belgian vessel, triggering a massive explosion that destroyed much of the North End of the city and killed 1,200 people—the greatest man-made disaster in Canadian history. Every time a couple of ships brushed close to each other in the harbour, the city gasped with trepidation.

With renewed hostilities in Europe, Halifax became a vital link in the convoy traffic to Britain. Ships would ease out of the harbour into the open sea, while German U-boats cruised nearby, sometimes picking off errant outliers, leaving their flaming hulks within full view of the port city. From his family's summer haven at Herring Cove, Graham could sometimes see burning ships just beyond the harbour.

The vulnerability of Halifax was underlined in late May 1943 when a German sub slipped undetected into the mouth of the harbour and planted fifty-six mines. As Stephen Kimber relates in *Sailors, Slackers and Blind Pigs*, his book about Second World War Halifax, "[l]uckily, a convoy escort vessel spotted one of the devices on the water just before a large convoy was scheduled to depart." That set off a mass sweeping of the harbour entrance, clearing a channel to allow the convoy to stream through. There was only one casualty, a merchant ship that strayed outside the channel, hit a mine, and sank.

Kimber also describes the tensions between the narrow-minded Halifax old guard and the diverse collection of soldiers and sailors—Norwegians, French, Belgians, Canadians of all stripes— bivouacked in the city. It was an uneasy cohabitation, and a breeding ground for prejudice, including virulent anti-Semitism. One young woman, Marjorie Whitelaw, recalled in Kimber's book that her crowd of young people was very liberal, but a number of their parents had laid down a warning: do not date Jews. In clear defiance, her social group included some young Jewish soldiers, including Len Kitz, an up-and-coming local lawyer. Kitz went overseas, had a distinguished war record, and served as a lawyer in Nazi war crimes tribunals. He would later become a key figure in breaking barriers in municipal politics, and he would play a critical role in the development of Graham Day.

The war would leave a deep impression on the boy, embedding a belief in the British Empire and its history and a feeling that many Maritimers shared—their fate was inextricably linked to the Atlantic. Young Graham was keenly aware of what was happening in the war's various theatres. "There were maps on my bedroom wall, and we listened to *This Is London Calling* on the North American service of the BBC."

Day was six when war was declared and Quinpool Road School and its principal, Miss Harlow, went on full alert. "We were hauled into an assembly room and told we should not worry about the war because the empire would win," Day recalls. "Miss Harlow would be giving us tasks to help with the war effort—[collecting] pots and pans and foil wrappers from cigarettes. We put war savings stamps in our little books; she was very keen on what she called 'our heritage.'" He remembers the day he and two of his peers, all in short pants—sons of British, Polish, and Greek immigrant families—stood together to deliver a stirring recitation of "Scots Wha Hae."

The Polish-Canadian boy, Irving Nudelman, lived with his family near the Days in Halifax. Now a retired Baltimore urologist, he had come to Halifax as a boy from northern Ontario as his father pursued his work. He remembers young Graham as a tall kid, very bright, and always in the middle of whatever the other children were doing. Frank and Edie were "fine people" in a neighbourhood where everyone knew everyone else.

That was the world of Graham Day in the early 1940s, replete with good friends, a high-quality education, the commitment of teachers, and a curriculum that included history and, eventually in grade eight, Latin. Teachers must have loved having this precocious, well-read boy in their midst. He was smitten with his grade one teacher, Mary McCurdy, fresh out of teachers' college, who had innovative methods of cajoling her charges into finishing exercises. She would sketch a brook on the blackboard and stepping stones across the brook. In spelling, arithmetic, or reading she would encourage each student to cross the brook, stone by stone. As each crossed, his or her name was added to the list of achievers. "She would whisper in our ears, 'Come on, you can do it.'" It was his first experience with a caring non-family adult who encouraged him to achieve.

By the time Graham entered grade eight, Earle Gordon Withrow was the Quinpool Road School's principal and the teacher of that grade. On the first day, Withrow told the class that, for the coming academic year, it would have the highest aggregate mark of all the grade eights in Halifax. He continued to remind them of that goal during the school year, and they were successful—a powerful example of group motivation that Day would appreciate in later years.

Unfortunately, that was the high-water mark of Day's pre-university schooling. He spent grade nine at Chebucto Road School, and moved up to rambling Queen Elizabeth High School for grades ten to twelve. That was when, as he says, "education started to go down the crapper." He had been a golden boy at Quinpool Road, but at Queen Elizabeth he was subject to mass schooling, often with larger classes and indifferent or harried teachers. Once praised, he now felt diminished. It would have been bad enough if the teachers had all been talented, but he found huge gaps in their learning. He once had to write a business letter applying for a hypothetical job, and addressed his missive to "Sun Life Assurance" because he had seen the company name on his father's life insurance bill. "I was told it was insurance, not assurance, and the conversation went downhill from that. The teacher didn't know the meaning of words."

He began to skip school, and was constantly disciplined. It was an old-school sanction that students would have to write out lines of poetry for being late. By grade twelve, Day could recite the entire *Rubaiyat of Omar Khayyam*. He devoured literature and history at home, but barely squeaked by at school. If someone wanted to talk about ancient Egyptian monotheism or the temples at Luxor, he was ready to participate. But then he would go to school: "A lot of the things that interested me had nothing to do with things I was exposed to in school." And so he became a Shithouse Rat. For boys kicked out of class, there was no other place to go, so he would drift down to the boys' room and play cards with the rest of the outcasts. The principal was a stern Second World War veteran, which meant Day had plenty of company.

His refuge was his life out of school—in music and, surprisingly, shoes. Graham Day became an ace shoe salesman. It started in the summer between grades eleven and twelve, when he secured part-time weekend and full-time summer employment with the Halifax branch of Simpson's, then a big national department store chain. He worked for the shoe department manager, Horace Campbell, for five years; in a struggling family, it meant he could make enough money to attend university.

Simpson's was his introduction to business. He was given courses in basic stock control, how shoes and shoe lasts were made, and when it was appropriate to sell off remainders of a line. Campbell knew he needed the job and found him other work. During the post-Christmas period, he worked every day on stock-taking in various departments. During his last year, he was paid extra if he met sales targets. "It was my first experience of working for a boss who actually managed," Day says, "who showed what and how he wanted things done and consistently trained and encouraged me." Day was a good shoe salesman, maintaining a log of customers' names, phone numbers, and shoe sizes so that, when a sale came up, he would contact the people on his list. He would continue in the shoe department until the summer after his second year of law school.

There was also the redeeming nature of music and, from his teenage years on, Graham was blessed with a powerful baritone voice. But, once again, this was a story of personal pleasure laced with the frustration of authority. The teenaged Day heard that an opera was being produced by the Halifax schools and, as an enthusiastic yet raw singer, he was keen to audition. In the end, there were no auditions: the director of music had decided in advance who was going to sing, and Day was not among the chosen. It angered him, but, as with most setbacks, it gave him a renewed purpose. He saved money from his newspaper routes to pay for voice lessons. One day, he skipped school in the afternoon, did his paper route early, walked down Spring Garden Road to the conservatory of music, and persuaded Audrey Farnell—considered the best soprano in Canada—to take him on as a pupil. His voice lessons with her continued through high school. Later, when Farnell left Nova Scotia, he continued the lessons with Teodor Brilts, formerly the leading baritone of the Riga Opera Company in Latvia. Day's mother insisted he also learn piano and the basics of harmony and counterpoint, which gave him a broad grounding in music. He was not as proficient on the piano as in singing, but it was all therapy in an otherwise unhappy life.

It helped, too, that he liked sports. The gangly kid ran the mile in track and field, and although he did not especially enjoy running, he liked the crowd he ran with. The sport he loved most was baseball, an affection that has stayed the rest of his life. As a player, he was just okay—what is known in baseball parlance as good-field, no-hit. But he understood the game, and was able to play "smart." He played ball in the small towns of Nova Scotia, including the coal-mining centre of Stellarton. As a right fielder, he would approach a fly ball hit in his direction, only to see the sky filled with objects—pieces of coal hurled by the rowdies in the stands to distract defenders. Later in life, Day would become a die-hard fan of the Toronto Blue Jays, and would conduct an annual pilgrimage to the Jays' spring training games in Dunedin, Florida. What attracted him was the blend of individual talent, the liberal use of data, strategic thinking, and tactical execution that can make or break a ball player. In those respects, baseball, for Day, has been a surrogate for business.

On the street, he played with a group of North End boys who ended up with very different lives, one as a Baptist minister, two as Roman Catholic priests (neither stayed with that calling), as well as a Halifax policeman and a medical doctor. Three or four collected criminal records, mostly for robbery; probably the most talented of them would edit the sports page of the prison newspaper at Dorchester Penitentiary for a while.

Day's school marks continued to suffer, but as far as he knew, his parents were unaware of the anguish he was experiencing. For a moment, the Korean War seemed to offer escape, and he thought about enlisting in 1951. But in that era, those under age twenty-one had to have parental consent, which was not going to happen. Then he considered joining the French Foreign Legion, but he somehow had to get to the Mediterranean port city of Marseilles. That wasn't going to happen either. It was the darkest time of his life. "In terms of fed-up-ness, my last two years in high school were the worst. I know now that it's not unusual for people in their mid- to late teens going through difficult periods. It's just that I just didn't see a way out."

He looks back with a bewildered perspective: who was that person? It is often a challenge for young people to move from a world where they are loved and even protected to a colder environment where teachers and fellow students do not treat them as special. It must have been extremely hard for an only child in a close family with a surrounding cast of doting uncles and aunts. And there was that streak of anti-authority that would persist. If he was pushed, he would push back.

As a boy, it looked like rebellion. As an adult, it was reflected in a sense of justice. Even when he had become one of the world's leading business figures, he had sympathy for the underdog and a hatred of bullies. He would stand up to restaurant patrons who abused waiters. He championed cleaning staff in businesses that dismissed those after-hours men and women as lesser beings. He stood up to chauvinist bosses who denigrated women. "If I thought something wasn't fair, and not necessarily just to me, then I'd push back."

It would be heartwarming to report that, when he enrolled in an arts program at Dalhousie University, things were miraculously fixed, but that was not the case—at least not at first. Dalhousie was better than high school, but there were ups and downs. Day began to develop a thick skin, and a new determination took hold that "I'll get through this."

One incident suggests the education of Graham Day was still a tortuous path. He spent two years in the arts program, which was a bit of a yawn but gave him time to mature. And the old frustration surfaced from time to time. A French professor, a former teacher at Queen Elizabeth High, was an old adversary.

The professor was constantly showering attention on one of the young women students, an attractive brunette. At one stage, another male student, Fred Hollett, made a gesture. Day is vague about its exact nature, but he thought it was funny and laughed. The two young men were kicked out of class and hauled before a disciplinary committee. Outside the meeting room, Hollett insisted on going in first. After a couple of minutes, he emerged to say he would be leaving school. Thoughts raced through Day's mind. He personally didn't mind being thrown out, but he pondered the effects on his parents, who struggled to make a middle-class living and to support their son's education. His graduation was a prime purpose of the Days' lives. They would take the financial leap into opening their own store only once they felt sure he would graduate. The committee told Graham he could be expelled, and asked him what he thought should happen. He did not want to rejoin that class, but he did want to write the exam. The committee decided he could stay on those terms. He wrote the exam and he barely passed. He was relieved that his parents would not have to know what happened.

Day's son Michael has come to realize the importance of these experiences. His father keeps coming back to the times in high school and at Dalhousie when people underestimated him and tried to dismiss him. "It's not quite a chip on the shoulder," Michael says, but there was "just this determination to prove himself, and to prove other people wrong."

Graham Day's career as a lawyer, troubleshooter, and global executive hung on a choice. He was twenty years old and running out of options. Three alternative paths formed in his mind. He could try to grind on in a ho-hum arts program, he could quit school and work full-time at Simpson's, which was eager to employ him, or he could go to law school. He did not have great marks, but he fulfilled the bare minimum requirements to get into Dalhousie Law School, benefiting from the then-prevailing philosophy that you put bums in seats first and then weeded out the ones that didn't fit. He filled out the forms, and was admitted. Thus, a great career was born—in desperation.

CHAPTER 2

Turning Point

Graham Day, first-year law student at Dalhousie University, was angry. He had failed his course in property law, and he was certain he should have passed. It was another chapter in a long-running series: the System v. Graham Day. He might have mellowed a bit, but the anti-authority fervour was still raging below the surface. He had finished the year at law school with marks down in the fourth quartile of his class, but the property mark of 45 was particularly galling.

He went to see the professor, a tall awkward-looking man named Graham Murray, to plead his case. Murray, an air force veteran of the war, said he didn't deserve to pass. His overall work didn't warrant it, and he explained why. "He went on to verbally kick my ass," Day says. The interesting thing was Day's response. A light went on, and he agreed with that judgment. It was an important moment in the making of the man. He wrote the supplementary exam, he passed, and he spent the summer thinking about life. His marks got a lot better the second year, and he had a great third year. Today he is asked why this transformation happened. "I think I grew up."

He took every course Graham Murray offered, and he kept getting better. Murray was not just a fine professor, a gentle man in the true sense of the words; he also became a quiet champion of this fiercely brilliant, sometimes angry young man. In fact, Day says, "I didn't think I had a bad teacher in law school; all were competent, some were inspirational." But what truly made the difference was that "Graham Murray cared." Murray became a force in Day's intellectual development. One of the professor's courses dealt with the law of evidence, which goes through constant transitions in terms of what is admissible in court. It can't be defined neatly by saying "this is admissible by this law or this regulation"—the law continues to grow. "I thought his course on evidence was inspirational," Day says. He saw the law not as a fixed canon, but as a living thing, and that appealed to the lover of history and the classics.

It helped, too, that Dalhousie Law School (now the Schulich School of Law) was the top incubator of legal talent in eastern Canada and going through a fertile period. In the early 1950s, it helped mould men and women who would change Canada. One of those in Day's class was John Crosbie, a brilliant student and multiple medal winner, but shy and withdrawn. In the future, he would find his voice as an eloquent, slashingly biting Newfoundland politician who was a giant in federal Conservative cabinets. Purdy Crawford, a year ahead of Day and a poor boy from rural Nova Scotia, would become Canada's pre-eminent corporate statesman and governance pioneer. (Indeed, Crawford and Day would have parallel careers, moving from law to operational business leadership and as formidable figures on corporate boards.)

Graham Murray, who suffered from multiple sclerosis, played a role in many of their lives—none more so than that of Bertha Wilson, a young Scottish-Canadian who came to Halifax with her husband, a naval chaplain. Enrolling a year after Day, Wilson would face resistance as both a mature student and a woman. It was the era. The law school dean at the time, Horace Read, recommended that she go home and take up crocheting. But, like Graham Day, she persevered, and found Murray's classes inspiring. She graduated as one of six women in a class of fifty-eight and went on to a stellar legal career, capped by being named the first female justice of the Supreme Court of Canada.

Graham Day was twenty-one when he got serious about the law. In his second year, he moved up into the second quartile of marks, obtaining four firsts, including one in Murray's course. In the third and final year, he finished in the first quartile, eighth in a class of forty-four. For a while he entertained the idea of applying at Dalhousie for a scholarship for a master's degree. The school administration did not seem to encourage him, however—perhaps there was still some scepticism that he had truly reformed—and he let it ride. He was proud that he had graduated from law at only twenty-three, the youngest in the province. This is a lesson to every teacher who has grappled with an underachieving student: sometimes the situation requires just quiet support until the person matures. When the light finally goes on, it is a transcendent moment. Professor Murray must have loved to watch his young protegé blossom.

Meanwhile, Simpson's offered a good job that paid money. In addition, Day got paid fifty cents an hour putting books away in the barristers' library, and he helped train the choir for a local production of the opera *Faust*, for which he also sang in the chorus. It was a chance to observe the celebrated Czech-born opera singer and actor Jan Rubes. In one scene, Rubes would leap up on the table and land on his toes. "That impressed me to no end," Day recalls. Rubes explained to the younger thespians how to cushion the landing. It is interesting to envisage young Graham's six-foot, two-inch frame flying through the air and landing gracefully. But one thing was clear: while the study of law was teaching him discipline, music was giving him the élan of a performer—and both were vital in the making of a leader.

There was a moment when his life almost took another course. At Dalhousie he was able to spread his wings in music. He got to know other young men with musical interests, people such as Jim Bennet, a fine singer, and Manny Pittson, a trombone player. In 1951 he auditioned for a role in a Gilbert and Sullivan operetta produced by a Dalhousie professor, and he was successful. He began directing and producing. He loved Gilbert and Sullivan, and was an avid member of any production that would have him.

Then he got an inquiry from an agent of the D'Oyly Carte Opera Company in London, the renowned specialist producer of Gilbert and Sullivan. It was a tempting offer, with the chance to move to London, become part of the arts community, and learn from great teachers. But Frank Day took his son aside and told him to look in the mirror. Just how good did he think he was?

He thought about it. At the time, he was still studying with Teodor Brilts. He was a baritone with lots of register down but not much up. Could he really stack up against the best voices in the world? He could see that Jim Bennet, for example, whom he came up against at Kiwanis music festivals, had a superior voice and was better equipped for a professional career. So he concluded the Gilbert and Sullivan career was not for him. But music would continue to be part of his life—an instrument of personal growth, a distraction from frustrations, and a source of pure pleasure.

And yet Day was still incorrigible, tilting at windmills. He had continual run-ins with the university administration, but the saving grace was that he truly liked his teachers at the classroom level. And after the French class incident, the administration was clearly still taking a wait-and-see approach to Graham Day. In 1956, his last year in law school, he had been training a small girls' choir, and there were plans to take it to high schools to encourage students to come to Dalhousie. Then, without explanation, Alexander Enoch Kerr, the president of Dalhousie, cancelled the trip. Day, indignant, drafted a letter to various parents explaining why they would not be doing the trip, referring specifically to Kerr. The president told him to withdraw the letter. Once again, the choice confronted him: fight or withdraw. He knew his parents would be shattered by the affair, even if he could prevent his degree from being withheld. So he choked back his pride and repudiated the letter. Again, more maturity. But there was perverse satisfaction when, that autumn, the administration asked him to return to produce and direct the 1957 university musical. And he was paid for it.

Even when things were hard, Day continued to find solace in his extracurricular life. According to a *Financial Post* profile, his lifelong motto, "I never lie and I never bluff," had its origins at this time. He told the interviewer about a poker game at Dalhousie with three other students—none of whom has the foggiest recollection of it, the article pointed out. Day's loss of five dollars because of a failed bluff later guided his approach to business, because, he explained, "to lie, you have to be able to bluff." One of those poker players was Roland Thornhill, later deputy premier of Nova Scotia. Interviewed for the *Financial Post* article, Thornhill said he had long forgotten that game, but distinctly remembered Day. "If you were going to choose some guy in the class who was going to be knighted by Maggie

Thatcher as the arch Conservative economic czar, Graham Day probably would have been the last one you'd have chosen. When someone's up on the stage in tights, you don't visualize them as having that kind of a career."

Day left Dalhousie in 1956 with a good feeling generally about the university. He did not realize it then, but he would keep circling back to the institution, which would continue to be his intellectual base camp. The law school had propelled him on his way to a legal career. Then he enrolled in the school of real life. In Nova Scotia, it was possible to complete three of the required nine months of articling between the second and third years of law school. Day had been fortunate to gain an unpaid articling position with a young Halifax lawyer named Len Pace, himself only a recent member of the bar and striving to establish a practice. During the summer and in the period after graduation, Day was involved in everything the office did, and became close to Pace, a future attorney general of Nova Scotia and later a justice of the province's Supreme Court. He learned a lot about law, but it was an experience outside the offices that left the biggest impact: he learned the importance of sacrifice for an important cause.

One day, as Day arrived at work, Pace told him he was closing the law office for a couple of days. The practice needed revenue, but there was a more important job to do: "We're going to get Len Kitz elected mayor," Pace explained. Kitz was that same young Jewish lawyer who faced the prejudice of wartime Halifax as he went off to serve in Europe. He had returned to Halifax after the war and opened his own law firm. In 1948, Kitz decided to enter politics, and he was an alderman for seven years before seeking the mayor's job.

In those days, there was an unwritten rule in Halifax municipal politics that the mayor's job would alternate between a

Protestant and and a Catholic. There was nothing in this rotation to include other religions until Len Kitz and his supporters decided to break the barrier. Day was part of the team that mapped out the city in a grid; he and Pace then took on canvassing of blocks in the North End, knocking on doors and introducing themselves, explaining why the city should elect a Jewish mayor. Kitz won the election, and the religious compact was broken. "I thought, 'This is a great thing we have done,'" Day remembers.

In his life, Day would have a lot of jobs, and some would pay him very well. But he always needed to know there was a greater cause than his own remuneration—whether working for a nation-building company such as Canadian Pacific or doing volunteer assignments for the British government in advising the National Health or setting teachers' pay-for-performance.

When Day graduated from Dalhousie in 1956, some of his class went west to Alberta, which was just exploding as an energy powerhouse. A number of classmates were members of legal families, and could count on a career in an established local firm. But Day would end up in a two-man practice in Windsor, in the Annapolis Valley, less than an hour's drive from Halifax. It was Len Pace's idea. In the Pace law firm, Day was the ever-available errand-runner, as he went through the hoops of articling for the Nova Scotia bar. One morning, Pace waved him into his office. As he sat down, he heard Pace on the phone telling someone "I think Graham will go to Windsor, sure." Day thought he would be doing a run to Windsor, where a friend of Pace had taken over a law practice. But the friend actually wanted to leave Windsor and practise in Cape Breton. There was an opening for a lawyer; all Day had to do was go. It wasn't a great practice, but it paid the rent. Although he hadn't yet been called to the bar, he could perform certain legal tasks—for example, becoming a commissioner of oaths to deal with documents to be sworn. Pace said, "I will take responsibility for everything you do. So if you can't cope, give me a call."

Day had no savings, and his days at Simpson's were over. He needed a car to get around the valley. The Royal Bank of Canada lent him $500, which in 1956 was a lot of money, and a sympathetic Halifax car dealer, Frank Zebberman, sold him a new basic Volkswagen, insured, with a full tank of gas, and the understanding Day would pay what he could in instalments. It was the beginning of a lifetime love affair with the tiny Beetles.

At twenty-three, Day became a lawyer in Windsor, population three thousand. He found a place to board with other men at Miss Marion Dill's house on College Road. Because Day was not yet a full-fledged member of the bar, he was limited in what he could do. It was part of his apprenticeship. And his attitude had changed. He got better every year, and became a very good small-town lawyer. He acquired a partner, Bud Kimball, who shared his love of music, and the two set up shop. He kept busy, and with Halifax just an hour away he could keep up his contacts in the musical world.

Day now realizes it was serendipity. But he also understands that serendipity demands action: here is the opportunity, but will you take the risk? You have to be open to change, imbued with the courage to move on and the willingness to experiment, especially early in life. Serendipity is a transferable thing: you try to create happy surprises for the young people who follow you. Some have a talent for serendipity, some don't.

This idea was explored in a *New York Times* essay by Pagan Kennedy. The term comes from an old Persian tale about three princes on the Isle of Serendip who possessed strong powers of observation. As eighteenth-century British essayist Horace

Walpole described it, they were making discoveries through accident or sagacity that they were not necessarily looking for; Walpole called this skill "serendipity."

Day had the adventurous spirit and observation powers that made him an artist of serendipity. A lawyer quits, another leaves to join the judiciary, a shipyard hovers on the edge of bankruptcy, a prime minister is desperate for help, and he is standing there, open to change and ready to act. Serendipity is no accident. In the words of the great baseball philosopher Yogi Berra, when you come to the fork in the road, take it.

Graham Day took it, time after time, seizing the opportunity when it presented itself. He quotes Brutus in Shakespeare's *Julius Caesar*:

> There is a tide in the affairs of men.
> Which, taken at the flood, leads on to fortune;
> Omitted, all the voyage of their life
> Is bound in shallows and in miseries.
> On such a full sea are we now afloat,
> And we must take the current when it serves,
> Or lose our ventures.

Tides of opportunity and tides of water: they would both play a huge role in Day's life. But he knew that such tides had human enablers and that personal relationships matter. After graduation, he kept in touch with Graham Murray. After the death of his old professor, Murray's daughter was going through her father's things when she happened upon a copy of a letter written by her father to Canadian Pacific recommending his former student Graham Day for a job in the legal department. Day never knew the letter had been written. He accepted it as a gift and had it framed—an enduring memory of a man who cared.

CHAPTER 3

Of Courts and Courtship

She was a nineteen-year-old fresh out of high school, living at home in Dartmouth, Nova Scotia, taking a few college business courses and recovering from a bout of mononucleosis. He was an older man—at twenty-four, all of five years her senior, but still a wet-behind-the-ears lawyer trying to learn the ropes of his profession in a small Nova Scotia town. Theirs was a whirlwind romance.

It started out as a lark on a June night as six young people poured into Graham Day's Volkswagen Beetle, off to see the sights in the Annapolis Valley. The son of Day's office landlady in Windsor had phoned Graham earlier that day to ask what he was doing that night. Windsor was home to two private schools, King's for the boys, Edgehill for the girls—and it was graduation weekend at Edgehill. A number of the recent "old girls" had come back for the round of events. Day had a car, so he got invited along on a group outing.

Day folded his lanky frame into his Beetle's front seat. His blind date, Sandra, sat beside him, while another young woman named Ann Creighton somehow squeezed in next to her. As the evening went on, he became more interested in the willowy brunette across the seat than in Sandra. He asked Ann if he could take her to lunch the next day. It was a busy weekend—her younger sister was graduating from Edgehill—and her mother was appalled that she would desert the family for a date with this overeager young lawyer. But they relented. The date went well, and he was deemed acceptable to her parents. Her father Jake quipped to her mother Ruth, possibly in jest, that "maybe we can get rid of her."

Day would later joke that the mono had left Ann in too weakened a condition to resist his ardent pursuit. "I drove down to see her [in Dartmouth] on Monday and proposed on Wednesday and we married a year later." The distance between "Can I have lunch with you?" to "Will you marry me?" was alarmingly short, but Graham Day, the king of serendipity, was not one to let an opportunity slip by. He was a consummate planner in business, but he made his most important life decision in a wink of an eye. In affairs of the heart, he knew what he wanted and he pursued it. In Brutus's words, "we must take the current when it serves, or lose our ventures."

Ann Creighton was swept off her feet. The young man possessed a decisiveness she had rarely encountered in the boys she knew. Did she know what she was signing on to? Probably not. She thought she was going to be the wife of a small-town lawyer, not the high-profile spouse of a transatlantic business figure. Even so, she knew there was something different about this earnest young fellow who had pursued her so vigorously and had won her heart.

Love trumps planning. Day was no doubt enchanted with this young but elegant woman, and it turned out he had found the perfect helpmate. Ann would be a witty companion, wise beyond her years, who could handle herself in any circumstance, who was willing to suppress her own ambitions to support his great adventures, but who exacted a high price: they had to have fun in whatever they did, wherever they lived, and she would have to come home to Nova Scotia eventually. And he repaid that bargain.

Ann quickly learned a central paradox in her husband's life. He revelled in planning ahead—he would never be happier than when he knew what was happening on a precise day in two years. Yet a lot of his major life decisions came in an instant. "To someone on the outside, these things happen very quickly, and yet he goes through everything in depth before he jumps," Ann says.

The whirlwind courtship and subsequent marriage were the highlights of Day's life as a young lawyer in the Annapolis burg of Windsor—along with, of course, the births of three children in quick order: Deborah in 1959, Donna in 1960, and Michael in 1962. And for eight years in Windsor, from 1956 to 1964, he grew as a lawyer. It was steady work, with the rural municipality of West Hants his biggest client. It was a time of school consolidation, as little red schoolhouses gave way to regional schools, and there were contracts to build new ones. The municipality had only two employees, so Graham picked up a lot of the work. He found at times that he was running the procurement function for supplies for new schools out of his office, with Ann testing reconditioned pianos and sewing machines.

Occasionally, a case would come along that would get his blood flowing. He remembers one early incident when a provincial Supreme Court judge, on his circuit through the province, arrived in town the night before court was in session. Whoever was low on the totem pole of lawyers got the pro bono cases dished out that night. And the judge said to Day, "I have a case tomorrow of attempted murder. And it is yours." He had never done this work before. His short legal career mainly involved dealing with trivial matters in magistrate's court.

The case before him involved a man, small in stature, who provided for his family by working in the woods, stripping trees as they fell. He had a double-bitted axe with a long handle. Food would arrive at the camp by truck, driven by a rather large woman who could handle herself in a man's world. The little woodsman was always one week behind in paying her, so she in effect was giving him credit every week. On this one occasion, he paid her for the previous week, but she then prepared to shut up the truck without giving him food for the following week. He began waving his axe and got the money back from the woman. No blood was spilled, but he was charged with attempted murder.

On court day, Day put the fellow on the stand to explain the financial arrangement. Then the woman painted a picture of being terrified of this man, despite her superior size. Day asked the judge to refer, in his charge to jurors, to the lesser charge of theft. The Crown was adamant that the relevant charge was attempted murder. He either attempted to kill her or he didn't. After some clarification, the jury went away. It then emerged to announce that the accused was not guilty of attempted murder, but guilty of theft instead. The relative sizes of two disputants no doubt affected the verdict. "Oh, God, I died ten thousand deaths in that case," Day recalls, "but then there was the sense of relief."

Other work was less dramatic but more influential in defining the thread of his career. He made connections that would last a lifetime. Atlantic Canada, then as now, was dominated by business families: the Sobeys in the north around Stellarton and New Glasgow, the Irvings and McCains in New Brunswick, the Olands in Halifax and Saint John, and the emerging Bragg lumber and blueberry businesses around Oxford. All would play a big role in his life, and none more so than the Jodreys, whose home base was the Annapolis Valley.

R. A. (Roy) Jodrey was an entrepreneurial giant. He had started off as a teenaged apple salesman and had parlayed that into pulp and paper mills, varied industrial holdings, a stock market portfolio, and one of the biggest personal fortunes in the Atlantic region. Based in the former shipbuilding centre of Hantsport, the Jodreys—led by Roy, his son John, and son-in-law Lovett Bishop—liked the young lawyer in nearby Windsor, and would give him bits and pieces of work. It was valuable work for a young attorney just getting started. "I look back now and know absolutely they were being kind," Day says. The Jodreys probably didn't need another lawyer. They already had a close relationship with the Halifax law firm of Stewart, Smith, McKeen, Covert, with brilliant business fixer Frank Manning Covert as its point man—a firm that would evolve into the modern-day Stewart McKelvey.

Day got to know Roy Jodrey, a fascinating blend of the sacred and profane, who could sing Baptist revival hymns at full throat while dreaming of business deals past and present. His teenage grandson George Bishop used to drive him around the Valley and remembers Roy's breaking into song with a stirring rendition of "Jesus Loves Me," then suddenly stopping in mid-verse at the memory of some exasperating business issue to thunder, "Hell and God damn." "It wouldn't take him a second to switch. It just broke me up," says George, who later became a key player in the Jodrey businesses.

Roy Jodrey was equally distinguished for his parsimony. He would rather give money away than spend it foolishly. On one occasion, Graham Day was in Jodrey's Hantsport office, reporting on a title search for a warehouse the businessman was buying for $25,000. They were preparing to close the deal. It was a time when, if you cut a cheque in one town and it was being presented in another, there was a hefty service charge. The cheque was to be drawn on the Bank of Nova Scotia in Hantsport but paid over in Windsor. Being a director of the bank, the tycoon phoned A. S. McKenzie, the manager of the branch in Windsor and said, "A. S., how much are you going to charge me to cash a cheque for $25,000?" Day couldn't hear the response, but Roy blurted: "You're not!" He paused, put his hand over the phone, and said to Day: "Are you prepared to take $25,000 cash and put it in your account?" Day nodded, and Jodrey roared, "To hell with you, A. S.," and hung up.

Day transported the cheque the full seven miles to Windsor to deposit it in his trust account. He drew a cheque on that account to pay Jodrey's bill at no charge—a saving of probably $100. It was his first insight into the world of Nova Scotia family enterprise. That little ride in the Beetle would be repaid over and over.

In Windsor, he was always open to new experiences that would enrich his life. He and his law partner became proud owners of a downtown bowling alley. Sadly, the investment was a dud, and he lost $15,000 in an era when that was a lot of money. As the West Hants solicitor, he got an education in financing capital spending through bond issues. He was instrumental in developing a new home for the fire department and town office, including rental office space. He moved in as the first tenant.

But just as important, he began an association with the Canadian military that continued through his life. When he launched his law practice in late 1956, one of his early clients was the local hardware merchant. The store owner was also a Second World War veteran, and the officer commanding the local reserve army unit, the 88th Battery, 14th Field Regiment, Royal Canadian Artillery. Four years later, Day joined and was commissioned in September 1961. He was awarded the Oland Cup for the "best lieutenant qualifier." In the mid-1960s, he taught military law to reserve officers.

The closest whiff of active duty came during the 1962 Cuban Missile Crisis when, as the threat of nuclear war loomed between the Soviet Union and the West, Day was seconded as a legal officer to the headquarters of the forces' local target area in Windsor. The assumption was that, if the army had to seize foodstuffs in the town, it would need a judicial officer on call. He was part of the judge advocate general (JAG) branch for a few days, until it became clear that, as the war threat subsided, his services were not needed. Following this experience, Day thought of joining the JAG branch and wrote to inquire. The answer was that recruitment was then limited to young, recent graduates. At age thirty, he was too old.

According to his son Michael, those experiences were formative. "That is what he cherishes. This is service before self, which he's all about. This is about something bigger than who you are. This is queen and country, and he is a monarchist at heart. He's all about giving back to the country."

Day was a conservative by instinct and practice. As Progressive Conservative premier Robert Stanfield prepared to contest a provincial election, Day was approached about seeking the Tory seat for West Hants. The sitting member was retiring, and three party contenders emerged: Day, then solicitor for the county; Norman Spence, a successful local farmer; and Stanton Sanford, a former country warden. Day finished "a pretty good second." Jake Creighton, his father-in-law, who had tried a number of times for a Tory seat in Dartmouth, asked Day, "Who was your guy at the vote count?" Day didn't have one. He was told, "Graham, it wasn't your turn." The fix was clearly in. Norman Spence became the member and, to Day's mind, he was a very good one. Day has often thought since about how fortunate he was to lose.

Whether teaching music to the girls at Edgehill or losing his shirt on a bad bowling alley investment, Day learned a lot in Windsor. Some colleagues believe he took on so many varied jobs in his small practice that he became well equipped to manage a complex company or troubleshoot a cascade of business problems. Bud Kimball, his Windsor law partner, later said the law gave Day a cool detachment that served him well in the business world. In the world of law, he told the BBC, lawyers would lock themselves into the adversarial process, but when they walked out of the courtroom, most lawyers would drop that attitude. Kimball said Day was the exception: he could apply that rational, analytical thinking outside the courts.

As a young family, the Days liked their time in Windsor, and they were attached to the community. After supper, Graham and Ann would often give the kids their baths and get them into pajamas, then the family would spend the evening sitting along the banks of the Avon River in Hantsport. They thought about building a house on the Avon and spending their later days in the pretty town, with its frame houses, quiet streets, and the mills of Roy Jodrey.

But Ann Day began to realize some things about her husband. He had huge energy and vast ambition, and he could get bored and twitchy if life became a grind. Ann could understand the frustrations of small-town law. Graham experienced a rare medical crisis in this period, an ulcer that caused him to be hospitalized. He clearly needed a release of some kind. And, she says now, "*Singalong Jubilee* was the saving grace." Indeed, music bailed him out again.

CHAPTER 4

The Singalong Redemption

Graham Day never met Pete Seeger, but the American left-wing protest singer played a pivotal role in the life of the future Thatcherite privatization kingpin. In 1960, the Canadian Broadcasting Corporation decided to produce a national television show out of Halifax hosted by Seeger, whose career was rising in the folk music revival then sweeping North America. It would be a thirteen-episode summer replacement for the legendary *Don Messer's Jubilee*, the showpiece of Down East fiddle music and old-time singing and dancing. Seeger even came up to Halifax for rehearsals with the producer—a CBC contract employee named Manny Pittson—and he was ready to go.

But Seeger was a former communist and, in a country still haunted by the McCarthy witch hunt, the US government had made it difficult for him to travel. No Seeger, no TV show. So the CBC told Manny Pittson to come up with something else. In the late spring of 1961, Pittson called his former Dalhousie musical cohort Graham Day, now practising law in Windsor.

The message was that Pittson had to put on a show, and there were only five weeks to get ready. "Manny had hired a couple of people and would I help to put a chorus together?" Days says. "That became *Singalong Jubilee.*" Day and his law partner, Bud Kimball, became members of the original chorus. For the first two seasons, he sang in the chorus and in a male quartet before stepping up to musical director.

Singalong Jubilee was remarkable for more than the entertainment: it made stars out of talented young people. These artists laid the foundation for East Coast music as more than a regional phenomenon but as an identifiable brand across Canada: the merger of traditional Maritime music, kept alive by people such as ethnologist Helen Creighton, and the folk revival wave that produced Bob Dylan, Joan Baez, and Gordon Lightfoot. The *Singalong* cast—people such as Jim Bennet, Bill Langstroth, Shirley Eikhard, Gene MacLellan, Fred McKenna, Catherine McKinnon, and, above all, Anne Murray—developed their own followings.

And there was Graham Day, who someday would be the biggest performer of all, but on a different kind of stage. *Singalong* made him comfortable with presentation. It underlined the value of being able to put on a show—of improvisation, dramatic ease, and communication. As he advanced in law and business, Day would never be shy before an audience. Business is performance, as well as strategy and people management. Running a musical production involves many of the same skills as herding a bunch of sensitive, talented managers.

At *Singalong*, Day was reunited with Jim Bennet, whom he had known as a teenager. They both loved Gilbert and Sullivan, and Bennet in particular embraced the folk revival with the Kingston Trio, Seeger, and the rest. For a while, Bennet had sung in a local country music group with Robert MacNeil, who would later become a television news reporter and for many years co-host of the US public broadcaster's *MacNeil/Lehrer Report*. Day always measured his musical talent beside Bennet's, and concluded that Bennet was by far the better singer. But Bennet observes that Day was strong in other areas: "He was a good singer, but he was a better director."

Singalong Jubilee would be Day's first management job, in the sense that he directed the marshalling of talent and resources to create something the market would value. It was purely an avocation, not a career choice, probably because of what his father had said to him: "Look closely at your abilities and where they can take you." But he was passionate about it.

The show put him in contact with handsome, charismatic Bill Langstroth, a Montreal boy who had attended Mount Allison University in New Brunswick and become a fixture of the burgeoning East Coast scene. He was a party guy, not in the debauched sense, but he could get a party moving like nobody else, Bennet recalls. He was the catalyst who would organize hootenannies at people's houses and had worked with Don Messer on TV. So when the Seeger deal fell through, Langstroth came on board, too. Bennet recalls that "the idea was for me to be the announcer and do occasional singing, but it came down to Bill and me sharing the host duties." He marvelled at how Langstroth would get up in front of the mic and just wing it. He was a superb improviser. "Graham was more disciplined," Bennet says, and Manny Pittson was not a musician—he played a little trombone—but he was a production genius.

Day remembers Langstroth as a good host, but not a student of music. The defining moment came early in Season Three, when the chorus was rehearsing to sing "The Battle Hymn of the Republic." To this point, there had not been a musical director. The rehearsal was not going well. Pittson asked Day what was wrong. "I replied that Bill was endeavouring to lead the chorus in two-quarter time when the piece was written in four-quarter time. For the balance of that season and the next, I was the musical director." Langstroth would go on to a sparkling career, and received considerable credit as *Singalong*'s creative force, an acclaim that Day insists should have gone instead to Manny Pittson. Pittson was a true television innovator. One of his ideas was filming his singers separately on location, with backdrops of beaches, forests, or city streets, where they would lip-sync the songs. Over these visuals, Pittson would play their studio-recorded voices. In Day's eyes, Pittson created the medium that became known as the music video.

The show could best be seen as a rare medley of talents: Pittson as producer, Langstroth and Bennet as announcers/performers, and, at least for a while, Day as the source of musical discipline. You can see him in the photos, a thin pole of a guy—six-two and 170 at his heaviest—clean-shaven in those days, sometimes serious, but with a confident near-smile, as if he was the one who got the joke.

While *Singalong Jubilee* was occupying his time—along with the law—Day got diverted into a local production of a beloved Gilbert and Sullivan operetta, *The Pirates of Penzance*, a charity production for which he had assembled a number of local CBC types and some Toronto imports. Bennet recalls that Day threw himself into it. "His reputation is he could be a pretty hard guy when it came to business, but he was very collegial as a director. He was not a mean-spirited man, but, my God, when he had his mind made up to something, it got done."

The *Singalong* experience meant recruiting people, and Day got his first taste of what would become a foundation of his managerial repertoire. The auditions were coveted by young musicians across the Maritimes. At one point, the *Singlong* brass auditioned a second-year phys ed student at the University of New Brunswick named Anne Murray, a native of the coal-mining town of Springhill, Nova Scotia. Murray, in her biography *All of Me* (co-authored with Michael Posner), recounts flying from Fredericton to Halifax with two girlfriends and competing for a job against about eighty-five hopefuls. She sang alto in a workshop, then returned for a solo audition, where she sang "Oh Mary, Don't You Weep," a black spiritual she remembered Pete Seeger singing. She thought she had done well, but on returning to Fredericton, she received a letter from Manny Pittson saying they had enough altos that year and her services were not needed. "The word devastated does not do justice to how I felt," she wrote. Later, she learned that the show's decision makers, including Graham Day, had agreed in advance not to replace an experienced known singer with someone essentially untried. Since no one was leaving the show that year, the entire audition exercise seemed to be a terrible waste of time to Murray.

But she had made a good impression. Day, now in his last year with *Singalong*, had been keen to hire her, and although it couldn't happen that year, he knew the show would take her on. According to Murray's account, that did happen two years later. She remembers Langstroth leaving messages at UNB that he wanted to meet her again. She ignored them. He managed to get a call into her dorm, and asked her to audition. Hearing the anger still burning from her first rejection, he assured her the audition would be a formality, and she was guaranteed a job. She sang "You've Lost That Loving Feeling," the white soul classic from the Righteous Brothers, and nailed it. She would join *Singalong* at $71.50 a show or, if she got to be a soloist, $99. It launched a superstar career—as well as a romance with Langstroth, who became her lover and eventually, after divorcing his wife, her husband.

Graham was also present at the audition of a raw talent, a young woman just out of high school at Mount St. Vincent Academy in Halifax. "She had hair down to her bum," recalls Day, and possessed only a rudimentary knowledge of music. The first task was to cut that hair and find her some appropriate clothes to wear on TV. Day was in the control room with Pittson and the guitarist Fred McKenna, when Catherine McKinnon got her shot at *Singalong*. They asked her what she knew, and it seemed she was only confident about singing the "Jewel Song" from *Faust* and one verse of the folk classic, "What Have They Done to the Rain?" What she lacked in repertoire she more than made up for in sheer talent. They put her on TV, and Day convinced her to sing "Plaisir d'amour," the first piece she sang on Canadian television. Catherine McKinnon went on to a long and glittering career, a star in the Canadian music universe, and Day helped her cut her first album. "She was very good—we rarely had to do a second take," he recalls.

Fred McKenna was, of course, a mainstay of the show, terribly overweight at 350 pounds, blind, and seated with his guitar in his lap, improvising ways of playing musical instruments that overcame his physical limitations. He was also a musical archivist and researcher who was the knowledge bank for the show.

Marg Ashcroft was a nurse who auditioned and landed a spot on *Singalong*. She draws a picture of a Graham Day who was very much at ease in the laid-back Nova Scotia of the 1960s. He knew Ashcroft was juggling a job with raising kids and appearing on TV. On show days, he would drive in from Windsor and pick up Ashcroft at her home and drop her off at night. Day had a big patch of rhubarb, and was always bringing her some. She never dreamt he would be a global corporate leader, but she did see glimmers of ambition beyond rural law.

David Sobey didn't see the big career coming, either. Sobey, the son of a grocer in Pictou County, had met Graham Day as a student at Dalhousie, where Day was taking some classes with Sobey's future wife Faye. Sobey couldn't believe it when he switched on the TV and saw his former schoolmate in the chorus of *Singalong Jubilee*. Day would continue to surprise David Sobey as he emerged in later years as an international business executive. Sobey didn't do badly himself. He and his brothers would take their father's grocery business and build it into a national supermarket force. They would call on Graham Day to be a steady anchor of wisdom on their boards. But, for David, that sober reputation was not what he expected when they first met in 1956: "He struck me more as a guy who I could have a lot of fun with."

For Day, *Singalong* was the great redemption that carried him above the otherwise mundane repetitiveness of law practice in a small town. "The work was fine, but a lot of it was quite boring," Day recalls. Then, one day in 1964, a manager at Halifax financial company Eastern Trust called Day to say the company would like to hire him. The salary would be around $10,000 a year. Day liked the idea. He had been a lawyer in Windsor for eight years, and had done about as much as he could with the practice. It was clear his life was about to change, but he had no idea how much.

In those days, older members of the bar served as guardian angels for younger members, particularly those who laboured outside of established firms. The esteemed Halifax lawyers George Robertson and Gordon Cowan used to send Day work to do. As Day prepared to join Eastern Trust, Cowan, the managing partner at a predecessor firm to Stewart McKelvey, phoned him up asking if Day could come see him.

The young lawyer was intensely curious as he entered the office. Cowan was, as usual, fastidiously dressed, with nothing on his desk but the paper he was dealing with. He got straight to the point: "I've been wondering how long you are going to waste your time practising law in Windsor." Cowan had heard that Day was contemplating going to work for Eastern Trust. "I don't think you should do that. I think you should go to work for Canadian Pacific in Montreal." Cowan said he should expect a call from CP's Montreal head office.

Day was thunderstruck. Here was the chance not just to be a corporate lawyer, but to be one for Canada's biggest industrial company, the company that basically built Canada through its coast-to-coast railway. Cowan had taught at the University of Manitoba, and among his students were three of the transportation giant's senior managers, including the executive responsible for the legal department, a rambunctious character named Ian Sinclair. A senior CP lawyer had been appointed to the Federal Court of Canada, and Sinclair needed a replacement. Cowan had someone in mind, and Day was that person.

He flew to Montreal for an interview with Sinclair and Jim Wright, who ran the legal department, the biggest corporate law contingent in the country. At one point, Sinclair asked him for the number of ownership shares in a ship. Day's response: sixty-four, except in the United States. That was the right answer, the product of a single elective course in shipping at Dalhousie Law School. Later, as the go-to lawyer on shipping issues for CP, he would appreciate the question even more. And Ian Sinclair would loom large in his career.

Canadian Pacific was now prepared to hire this young country lawyer whose biggest assignment had been saving a backwoods lumberjack from an attempted murder conviction. He had a wife and three children and a steady law practice and another job offer close to home. It was a risk for both sides. Day was ready to take it, but he had his conditions. He remembers telling Wright he couldn't do it for less than "twelve"—that is, $12,000 a year. Wright thought he meant "twelve" as in hundreds per month. So Day went to CP for $14,400 a year. It was the only salary discussion he ever had at CP. After that, his pay was reviewed annually and always increased.

With this lavish income in hand, he went home to tie up loose ends. He was ready to leave his safe, comfortable Nova Scotia life behind. His last task was helping record Catherine McKinnon's breakthrough album, *The Voice of an Angel.* "We finished very early Sunday morning, and I flew to Montreal that day to join Canadian Pacific."

CHAPTER 5

Troubleshooter

In 1964, at age thirty-one, Graham Day walked through the doors of Canadian Pacific's headquarters in that Romanesque shrine to train travel, Windsor Station in downtown Montreal. He was joining the most important company in the country—the largest Canadian-owned industrial business—which had built Canada's first transcontinental railway and, in the process, had acquired 25 million acres of land, including some of the most valuable in the country. Day loved the sense of working for a nation-building institution. He liked to use the adage, much quoted in histories and legal decisions, that Canadian Pacific took a geographical expression and created a nation.

By 1964, CP had amassed twenty-one thousand miles of track, but it was no longer just a railway. It was a vast shipping, hotel, and airline conglomerate, encompassing a telecommunications network, an oil and gas company, and much more, and with designs on further diversification. And there was all that land it continued to accumulate, including choice real estate at the core of the major Canadian cities. It was a conglomerate at a time when sprawling conglomerates were still very much in favour. In later years, markets would favour companies with a tight focus, but the fashionable thinking in the 1960s was that when one part of a conglomerate slowed down, other parts would offset that weakness with more positive performance. Wide diversification brought a margin of safety. In a landmark Supreme Court of Canada decision, it was deemed that CP could separate its expanding unregulated, non-rail businesses from the regulated, slower-growth railway part, thus augmenting the opportunities to add value.

Day's father was ecstatic about the CP job, because he saw working on a railway as a job for life, which would delight any hard striver who had carried his family through the Depression. And Graham did not disagree. He loved almost the entire time he worked for Canadian Pacific. He felt that, in the 1960s, CP was as important as the Canadian government—maybe more important sometimes. It was generally careful with shareholders' money and, for an employee, that stewardship was a motivation to do the right thing.

Since the last spike was driven to connect two strands of east-west rail construction in 1885, the company had been run by a series of individualistic, visionary, and often eccentric CEOs. When Day joined, the visionary tradition was continuing under Norris "Buck" Crump, a hard-nosed railway man out of western Canada who had reached the top of the greasy pole. Railroading was in his blood, but he also had a sense of his limitations, and was not afraid of drawing more talented people to his executive suite. He was the original practitioner of the management idea to surround yourself with people smarter than you.

Crump by then had found two talented seconds-in-command, both Manitobans, thus reflecting the value of that middle Canadian province for turning out people to excel elsewhere. They were a Yale-educated engineer, the highly professional Bob Emerson, and a 240-pound monster of a man, a hard-driving lawyer named Ian Sinclair. According to *Lords of the Line: The Men Who Built the CPR*, by David Cruise and Alison Griffiths, Crump managed amid creative chaos created by these two competing underlings. Crump, Emerson, and Sinclair would play big roles in Graham Day's life.

Day would become part of the legal department, and that was his official status for most of his eight years at CP. In 1964, CP's legal network consisted of its headquarters team and five regional offices, in Quebec, Toronto, Winnipeg, Calgary, and Vancouver. It employed some three dozen lawyers. The bulk of the work was domestic. The largest internal client was the railway, with hotels, shipping, trucking, the airline, and corporate activities making up most of the rest.

It was a terrific canvas for a young lawyer who had spent his career to that point doing real estate filings and other mundane tasks. But the family relocation to Montreal was daunting. The Days knew few people in the city. They moved in late fall, and didn't see many neighbours during the hard Montreal winter. But Ann sensed things would be better because Graham needed something interesting, and CP had so many different departments. There would be no boredom factor. He was lucky to be a lawyer, enabling him to work in every area of the company, and around the country—and the world.

He got a sense of his varied mandates in the first assignment, to prepare a report on regulated grain freight rates. In reading the file, he had not the slightest idea how to proceed. On day two, he was accosted by a young man from the research department who asked whether he had a certain file on rates. He did. The researcher then volunteered that Day would have to undertake a regression analysis to determine the range of appropriate track usage and the cost factor. Regression analysis—a statistical tool to investigate relationships among variables—was strange territory for the history and theatre enthusiast, but people such as Graham Murray and Earle Gordon Withrow had taught him how to learn. At lunchtime, he went to the nearest bookstore to find something on the subject. Then he hauled out a basic adding machine, and over the weekend he captured the essentials and proceeded.

It taught him the unspoken principle of Canadian Pacific: you were handed an assignment and expected to produce a result. It was up to you how it got accomplished. Don't kick problems upstairs, just go at it and get it done. It meant tremendous pressure on a still very green lawyer from the Annapolis Valley, but potentially great freedom. He learned to be a self-starter who didn't require a lot of handholding. His talent for improvisation would come in handy in his later role as a global troubleshooter who often found himself alone in a foreign country with no rule book.

After the freight rate analysis, Day's first truly big job was in shipping, where he would spend a lot of time. Canadian Pacific had its *Empress* suite of ocean liners, which it had accumulated during the heyday of transatlantic ship travel. But this world was fading in the 1960s, and Day got involved with selling off the passenger fleet (although CP would expand its commercial shipping). It was Day's job to close the sale of the *Empress of Britain* to a Greek shipping company named Goulandris Group. There were tricky financial issues, but CP emerged recovering its entire sale price. The ship was handed over to its new owners in November 1964. Two days later, it was renamed *Queen Anna Maria* and dispatched to Genoa for a refit.

After that, Day's jobs at CP were head-scratchingly diverse. A ship was lost at sea, and he would deal with it, as well as the hearings in Canada and the United Kingdom. He would contract the building of new ships in Japan and the Netherlands, and arrange for their charters. He established a Bermuda subsidiary for CP's bulk shipping activities. He would contract the purchase of aircraft, including the stretched variations of the Douglas DC-8, CP's workhorse long-distance carrier. He would take the lead in labour conciliation proceedings, and establish arbitration procedures. One big job was to arrange the acquisition by CP's trucking subsidiary, Smith Transport, of a US trucking company. It came at a time when the US Interstate Commerce Commission banned railways from owning trucking firms. So, to work around the US law, Day established a trust based in Houston that would buy the trucking company.

Such varied work gave Day a wide window on the company, but it also meant a gruelling travel regimen. "No one in the CP law department, or for that matter within CP, had anything like the varied assignments I was given, certainly none had the international exposure," he says. This was clearly not Windsor, Nova Scotia, and the life of a country lawyer.

For Ann, these were challenging times. After fourteen months in Montreal, the family moved to Toronto, where Graham became the regional counsel for CP's eastern division. After four years in Toronto, it was back to Montreal. All during the time in Toronto, Day was on the road 80 percent of the time—and in 1967 it was close to 90 percent. There was a family joke that Ann and the kids lived in Toronto, but Graham just travelled. Like many couples of that period, the two had made a pact: he ran his job and she ran the home. That was the only way the marriage would work. He had to have his mind totally focused on work. You did not whine, Ann says. You just embraced it and got on with it. Life in the Day household—whether in Toronto or Montreal—was hectic, but Ann kept things under control. When Graham went to the office in the morning, he did not know where he would be the next day. "Not infrequently, I phoned home on Friday morning to ask: what is the state of the laundry? Seven or eight times out of ten, I would be out of the country that night."

Meanwhile, Graham was getting an education in how a big company operated, as he observed the top CP managers. At the summit of the company, momentous changes were under way. Buck Crump, now chairman, had chosen Bob Emerson as his successor as CEO, so the issue was: what to do with Ian Sinclair? Big Julie—Sinclair's nickname, modelled on the gambler-gangster character in *Guys And Dolls*—was dispatched to create and run Canadian Pacific Investments, the holding company for the burgeoning non-rail assets, now hived off in a separate unregulated entity. Emerson officially became president of the core company in October 1964.

According to *Lords of the Line*, Emerson had the outward appearance of the cool professional, but possessed internal warmth and sensitivity. The railway was streamlining operations, and the hard decisions about firings, layoffs, and track abandonment began to eat away at him. As a service provider in the company, Day did a lot of work for Emerson and liked the man. On a Monday morning in March 1966, while still working in Montreal, Day arrived at the office. Crump's secretary phoned, asking him to come down to the chairman's office for a meeting. Emerson had been found dead on the floor of his garage by his driver, who had come round to collect him for the day's work. In the office, "everything went very quiet," Day recalls.

In fact, Bob Emerson had died two days earlier, on Saturday, but his wife had been out of town. Although there was a high proportion of carbon monoxide in his blood, *Lords of the Line* recounts, the coroner's verdict was death by heart attack. Because of the unrelenting pressures of work, some assumed suicide, but Sinclair insisted this theory was bunk. The two men had been working on an issue on the day Emerson died, and Sinclair observed nothing wrong with his colleague. Sinclair was shaken by the death because, for all their rivalry, the two men had respect for each other.

Emerson had been popular, and morale plummeted throughout the company. Crump briefly reassumed the presidency, and in time the directors—some of them reluctantly—approved the appointment of the larger-than-life Sinclair as the tenth president of CP in April 1966. For Ian Sinclair, there would be no Crump-like sharing of power, for it was one-man rule. Some CP staffers would privately describe Sinclair as the "beast that walks like a man." Newspaper columnist Allan Fotheringham once wrote that Sinclair was like "a linebacker who stumbled into the chairman's suite by mistake." *Lords of the Line* says, "Crump had been an all-powerful leader but a quiet and relatively self effacing one. Within a few years of succeeding Emerson, Sinclair's image overshadowed the company to the extent that many people believed he actually owned it."

Day, in Toronto, watched these events unfold from a distance, geographically and intellectually. There, he came under the spell of a man who would change his life: Leslie Raymond Smith, known as Les or LRS, the senior vice-president for the eastern region. Smith took to the young lawyer, and Day worshipped Smith, who became a mentor.

The son of a Scottish immigrant, young Les had left high school in the Depression and joined Canadian Pacific as a "spare board"—a work-if-available casual employee—thus beginning an improbable rise through the ranks to run the sprawling eastern region. Although Day had only a dotted-line reporting relationship—his actual boss was Jim Wright, the chief legal officer—the young man became Smith's sounding board. Smith would pop into the lawyer's office to ask: what about this? It would open up a long and exhilarating conversation—the kind of frank discussion Smith could never have with those who reported directly to him. "So I was second-guessing things at his request," Day says, "and he was teaching me. Lord knows what he got out of it, but I got everything."

Smith had assembled around him a group of young managers called "Les Smith's boys," and Day became one of them, an honour he cherished as the only member who wasn't an operating railway man. Smith paved the road from Day's being a big-picture lawyer to becoming an operator knowledgeable about the company's inner workings. He was getting the taste for management at the ground level, and he liked it. Smith would call him in to hear his speech to the new regional assistant superintendents. He would tell his charges that the burden of management would have to fall on them, and to take responsibility for their regions. He would leave them alone for six weeks, and after that he would be on their doorstep. Meanwhile, he said, "you have to cover every inch of track in your area and know everyone in your organization. And go buy yourself a hat so they will know you are the assistant superintendent. Above all, walk the property—you have to be seen." These words would echo in Day's mind for the rest of his life.

Later, a commerce degree or an MBA would become the standard ticket into corporate management, but in those days it was all about on-the-ground experience under a mentor. Day was fortunate in having a great one. Smith practised what management theorists today call "management by walking around." It would later be a fashionable theory, but in Smith's day it just made sense. Tom Peters, the management guru, would call it the science of the obvious. It was the only way to find out what was really happening in an organization and to build on that knowledge to create effective strategy. It was an opportunity to spread the company's values and to provide instant feedback and guidance.

From his first day in Toronto, Day found himself in a different world—in an operations environment, not a remote headquarters. He was included in operating meetings, and got to don a boiler suit to crawl around and underneath locomotives and cars. He rode in cabs running on the main line, and there were always ad hoc lectures by Smith about how to interact with employees and customers. But the critical part was watching Smith as he managed CP Rail's largest region. Later in life, Day found himself asking, "what would LRS do?" His mentor, he concluded, was "by no means a planner or strategist, but he was an extraordinarily effective manager and people motivator."

In recent years, Day has come to know about a TV show in which company bosses go undercover and infiltrate the front lines of their business, working unknown as clerks, cooks, or waiters, to discover how things really go at the sharp end. The whole idea of an undercover boss, however, drives Day to profanity—and he does have a salty tongue. He finds the concept distasteful, that a boss could possibly go undercover without his front-line people recognizing him or her. "The idea that employees don't know the boss—I mean, Jesus Christ, how awful is that!"

The Les Smith experience was part of a rich training in the complexity of management. He saw one man, Smith, who was a highly skilled manager of people despite a shortage of formal education. Then there was John Stenason, an executive vice-president who was well-educated but legendary for his terseness and lack of people skills. That made him the butt of jokes by Sinclair, who was brilliant, outgoing, and very funny, but also a bully. All of which provided lessons for the young Graham Day to absorb and store away.

To boil down the critical lessons from his on-the-job experience, Day summed up the art of management in four points. A manager, he concluded, must be able to deal with people, including through delegation, in a constructive and supportive way that enables them to perform and develop; learn quickly and deploy information of widely different kinds to "get the job done"; assess situations quickly, develop a preliminary plan, and modify that plan during execution as circumstances require; and take decisions and accept responsibility for them. This became his operating approach as he moved closer to the front line. As a quick study, he would come up with a plan, and start implementing it right away. But he continually reassessed, making course adjustments as necessary. He was never a weekend sailor, but he understood the sailor's method: have a chart and a plan, but watch the winds, and tack if necessary.

At this moment, Day's knack for the quick study was very useful to CP. Still a lawyer, he took on a broader mandate as troubleshooter. Over his time at CP, he appeared in court only once. He spent his time in labour negotiations and in an array of overseas assignments. "When a wheel fell off, I was the guy sent to put the wheel on," he says. "I was drinking from the proverbial fire hose."

CP's vast breadth meant there was much to do. The company was moving out of ocean liners, but expanding in merchant shipping, which required new deals, particularly in Asia. Railways were undergoing the switch to diesel, which meant new staffing and equipment requirements. There was a lot of abandonment of spur lines and small stations; airlines were moving to jet propulsion, and CP Air's reach was extending. With so many things in flux, Day couldn't really anticipate where the next challenge would come. "The old story was, if you get one deal done well, you go to the next and the next."

Day was not a one-man band. Very early, he realized he needed a trusted second-in-command or a team of them—what he later came to describe as his "sweeper." It might be someone to sweep up administrative details and potential operational issues behind him. Perhaps, it was to be as much a minesweeper as a broom-wielding sweeper. It was not the typical boss-subordinate role, but more of a partnership, and he was able to spot talented younger people to be thrust into this role. After the job was over, he would take a keen interest in their careers, making sure they did well in their post-Day periods.

His great talent was putting the right personalities in the right spots—strong people, not pushovers, people who would talk back and persuade him if they saw he was not getting things right.

David Gardiner was a young Montrealer, just out of Sir George Williams University (now Concordia University) and working as a researcher at CP. His work took him to Toronto to review the railway company's new properties in the eastern region; there, he attended a meeting that included a lawyer named Graham Day. Day seemed to be an interesting person, but also informal and friendly. Even though the two men had just met, Day invited Gardiner home for dinner. The three Day children were small at the time, and Gardiner remembers that, before the adults had dinner, Day disappeared into a bedroom to read a bedtime story. "He was a consummate family guy. You could see there were many sides to him right away."

Later, the two men would work together on setting up a holding company for CP's shipping interests in Bermuda, and eventually they would travel the world together. Gardiner crunched numbers and did research; Day provided the legal work, and he could call the shots on behalf of CP. The trips to Japan were memorable. The grand vision was that CP owned coal mines, it owned oil companies, it owned the rail system, along with terminals in Vancouver. So why not build ships in Japan and carry coal and other goods over there? There was a lot to do because they needed to negotiate contracts to build the ships and carry the goods. The tasks were varied and seemingly endless.

There was one marathon trip to Japan in 1967 to arrange shipping deals to carry resources from Australia to Japan. The two men waited and waited for meetings, but nothing was happening. Days stretched into weeks and months. At one point, after a month or two, a frustrated Graham Day was on the phone with Buck Crump in Montreal about the fact he was still sitting there. How long should he wait? Crump asked how old he was. Thirty-three, Day replied. Well, Crump remarked, "you still have thirty-two years to retirement, so settle in." "We just weren't allowed to come home until we had actually signed up something," Gardiner says. The targeted deal did get done, and then two more transactions were achieved on the same trip.

Day was learning what many North Americans did not yet grasp: the true test of partnership in China, Japan, and many other Asian countries is patience. He would watch others, especially Americans, arrive in Japan with the best of intentions, expecting to drive a deal and be on the next plane home. That would not happen. Their would-be Asian partners would ask themselves if these guys could be true long-term business partners when they were so impatient. For Day, the fortitude to wait out his hosts eventually resulted in big contracts, but it took time, and these lessons stayed with him, as Japan became a constant factor in his later careers in shipbuilding and automaking.

Gardiner was struck by Day's prodigious ability to read and absorb. When he went into a meeting, he had already researched the country and its history. He could talk knowledgeably about Japan's dynasties and about the cultural aspects of Japanese domestic life. Gardiner remembers being invited to a Japanese executive's home for dinner, which was very rare. "And Graham knew every one of the customs that were normal in that environment."

Gardiner also got some insight into Day's musical background as they visited Tokyo's karaoke clubs, with Day quickly becoming the star attraction at a couple of them. He kept being asked back to perform.

The flip side was Day's toughness in business. "He didn't suffer fools gladly, for sure," Gardiner says. "He had that kind of aw-shucks way about him at times, but he was hard. He knew his business."

The Japanese had a strategy to wear down the Canadians. Day and Gardiner kept getting triple-teamed. Three men would work with them all day, then three others would take them out for dinner. Three different people would be there to see them the next morning. "But Graham was on to that, and a couple of times we just took off, and weren't in our hotel for a couple of days."

Day gained an appreciation of Japan that continued through the CP deals and, as a British auto executive, in negotiations with Honda over new car models. He even learned to speak a little Japanese. On one trip to Japan, when Day was dealing with trading company Marubeni, one of its managers, who had become a friend, was entrusted with keeping him company on a long weekend. The two men visited the shrine at Nikko, formerly the treasure house of the Tokugawa Shoguns, war lords who ruled Japan for hundreds of years. His Japanese friend decided Day needed an *omamori*, or "body safe," a talisman for longevity carried by many Japanese. The friend bought one for him, and Day would carry the little silken bag with him always. When the first one wore out, he got another one. Decades later, in his eighties, Day would report that the bag was dog-eared, but still doing its work.

It was clear that Day was a comer in the CP organization. He was a manager who had been bloodied by battle, had carried the day, amassed varied experience, and proved he could deliver results. "I had been told, and I believed, that I was being prepared to be a contender for one of the top jobs," he says. He was also told that boss Ian Sinclair resented the support for Day among senior managers for whom he had performed. There was also a strong precedent for plucking CP's leaders out of the legal department. Sinclair himself had that background, and so did his number two, Fred Burbidge. According to Peter Mills, Day's colleague at CP, "the law department was seen within CP as one of the sinews that went around the whole empire and was a ground for talent development into very senior positions. You were either an engineer or a lawyer to be the CEO of CP in those days."

Mills became another of Day's sweepers. The recruiting of Peter Mills paralleled what Day himself had experienced, drawing on that extensive Maritime and Dalhousie network. Mills, a Nova Scotian studying at Dalhousie Law School, was a good student, recently engaged to be married, with the potential for postgraduate studies. One of his professors asked if he might consider a corporate law post; he knew a guy at Canadian Pacific who was looking for someone like him. The wheels started to turn, and within days Mills was being interviewed by Graham Day. Mills found that the older man had already done extensive due diligence. He knew about Mills's fiancée Lynn, his fiancée's family, his father, and what he did. "It was almost instant chemistry," Mill recalls. Soon, Day was making an offer for Mills to join CP in Toronto, promising interesting, challenging things to do.

Mills learned that among Day's talents were talent spotting and delegating. He drew people to him, and people could see he was on the move. It also meant he had occasional jealous competitors, although it was always very polite.

Later, when Day was transferred back to head office, Mills remembers him bursting into his office: "How would you like to go to Montreal?" By that time, they were very good friends, and their families were friends. "I always felt like it was an informal partnership. Graham was the senior partner, obviously, but our complementary skills made it very useful to him to have me bird-dog things for him."

Mills did a lot of the actual legal work, while Day took a broader focus. Day appreciated that Mills was a very good writer. The two confided easily in each other, and later, when they moved to England, they actually did each other's banking on occasion. "We were tight enough that I could tell him when he was just plain wrong," Mills recounts. It was not always easy—Day was physically tall, intimidating, and very forceful. Mills recalls there was a little joke in the company: really, it's not true that Graham was kicked out of the Mafia for excessive cruelty.

Mills saw another dimension to the man. When the two families moved to Montreal in 1970, it was a very hard winter, with huge amounts of snow. The Mills family lived in suburban Beaconsfield, about three blocks from the Days. Lynn Mills, pregnant, then contracted German measles, which meant there was a risk to the unborn child. The Millses had to get to the hospital, but they couldn't get their car out of the garage because of the deep snow. Day managed to get one of his trusty Beetles onto the street, plowed through the snow to the Mills's house, and got Lynn to the hospital. That was the kind of thing he would do.

Not that he had much time to be the good neighbour, because he was always on the road. He happened to be in Canadian Pacific's London offices on April 1, 1970, when he was called to a meeting. He was told that the parent company of Cammell Laird Shipbuilders, the Merseyside company that was building three first-generation container ships for CP, would likely have to declare bankruptcy. Day was told by Montreal head office to stay put and monitor the crisis.

Britain's Labour government had earlier formed an investment bank, the Industrial Reorganization Corporation (IRC), to intervene in situations like this. Within the next couple of days, Day was sitting down with a team from the IRC to try to arrange a rescue. The IRC team was led by another Gardiner, John (no relation to David), a fascinating character who would become one of Day's closest friends and fiercest champions. Whip-smart and boisterously opinionated, John Gardiner boasted a strong financial background, having been an analyst at the Prudential insurance company and later a financial journalist. He had been a writer of the widely read and rigorously reported LEX column in the pink-sheeted *Financial Times* before joining the government and getting involved in tight situations such as this. The two men were drawn to each other, no doubt because they were intellectual equals.

The upshot was that the British government, through the IRC, acquired half ownership of the shipyard's parent company, Laird Group. Gardiner became the managing director of the Laird Group, and the government agreed to be managerially passive. Day spent the summer working with Gardiner and his team to solve the crisis and ensure that CP would get its ships. Any rescue plan depended on the yard's customers kicking in more money. Most of the shipowners were balking, but Day stated CP was ready to step up and contribute to the interim funding. His comment to Gardiner was: "If you fly with the crows, you can expect to be shot with them." A plan was hammered out to keep Cammell Laird going.

Meanwhile, Gardiner had a chance to inspect close up the young Canadian across the table. He could see this was someone who wanted to be more than a travelling troubleshooter; he wanted to run something. Gardiner tucked that observation away. The two men, and that star-crossed Merseyside shipyard, would meet again soon.

CHAPTER 6

A Hard Day's Night

It was the dead of night in the old shipyard of Cammell Laird, one of the world's most venerable shipbuilding companies, directly across from Liverpool on the broad Mersey estuary. An almost completed Canadian Pacific container ship, one of three under construction in the yard, was floating in the wet basin, awaiting the final touches before edging out to sea. But a labour dispute had broken out in the yard over which workers got to do which tasks. It had blown up into a full-fledged strike that had closed down Cammell Laird. Throughout the day, pickets clustered around the entrances to the yard, and nothing was moving, in or out, including the CP ship trapped in the wet basin.

It was another job for Graham Day, the CP troubleshooter who in 1971 was charged with getting the company's ships built and out of the shipyard. The constant delays were costing his employer precious time and money. Day had an idea. He had observed that the pickets took the night off. He also knew there were two high tides in a twenty-four-hour span, one in the day and one at night. He instructed the Cammell Laird team to seize the nighttime window. In his view, "doing nothing is not a goddamn option." So, at the peak of the night tide, the gate to the wet basin quietly opened, and the nearly finished ship was towed out into the Mersey and the Irish Sea beyond. It ended up in a shipyard in Cork, in southern Ireland, for the final bits of work. The strikers arrived the next morning to see the wet basin empty and all their leverage gone out the door.

The mastermind of the nighttime caper was not on site to see the fruition of his work. Day had left for Canada the night before, and was sitting in Amsterdam Airport Schiphol, changing planes for Canada. He picked up an English newspaper to read about the release of the container vessel. The strike had run out of steam. The other two CP ships would get back on the construction track. "So, bugger the strike," he would gleefully recall a decade later. He didn't care about the wounded sensibilities of union or management. It was just another job for Canadian Pacific's ace troubleshooter. He always had a reputation for toughness and patience, and for seeing things that others couldn't. From that time on, plenty of people were watching worldwide. He became more than a crisis manager for CP—he became a hard-nosed operator who could get things done on the international stage.

The incident underlined the eternal advantage of the outsider: someone who was not part of the ingrained culture. In this case, it was a young Nova Scotian unencumbered by class attitudes or the management-labour stalemate that paralyzed British industry in the post–Second World War era. He was not impressed by the tendency in a strike situation to hunker down and slip into familiar patterns. Union and management would settle into a comfortable routine—and too bad for customers who were left waiting and absorbing huge costs. But this swashbuckling colonial could see a way out. The term "thinking outside the box" had not yet been elevated into the management lexicon. But Day was clearly operating outside the whole damn container.

By this time, he was tightly enmeshed in the long, once glorious but now tragic, tale of Cammell Laird. The previous summer, he had been part of a rescue effort to keep the shipyard alive. He knew the financial picture was still bleak, but he had come to appreciate this was an old and storied institution, a fixture on Merseyside since 1828, when Scottish steelmaker William Laird opened a shipyard across from Liverpool in the community of Birkenhead. In 1903, in one of many rescue efforts for the often cash-starved business, the Laird company found a merger partner in a Sheffield steelmaker named Johnson Cammell—hence the name Cammell Laird. Graham Day would become a major part of the story—he just didn't know it at the time he rescued the CP container ship in 1971. At that point, the future of the shipbuilding industry was not high on his priorities; he just wanted to get home. It was the latest CP crisis, and "whatever the international problem was, it was mine." His career had become the textbook case on how to be entrepreneurial within a large corporate superstructure. He officially worked in the legal department, but in reality he worked for whoever needed his services. His knowledge of the wider CP made him valuable, but also a bit vulnerable to empire builders who wanted to rein in his freelancing.

By that time, Ann had moved the family back to Montreal, where Graham would be "assistant general solicitor"—number three in the company's legal department. They thought this would be where he would retire, while serving as home base for interesting assignments across the company—and, perhaps, ultimately to rise to the top. There was one man who did not see it that way, however: Ian Sinclair, the bear-man who now dominated CP.

A brilliant corporate tactician, Sinclair's ego had eventually veered out of control as he amassed more authority. After Crump's retirement and Emerson's death, Ian Sinclair ruled with an iron fist, and he was not about to surrender an inch of authority. Day always felt Sinclair's great flaw was that he hung on to power far beyond when he had ceased to be an effective leader. In the 1970s, Sinclair was arguably the most fascinating and powerful executive in Canadian business, reflecting the overwhelming status of CP, but also deriving from the other boards on which he sat. At one point, twenty-two Canadian companies, including some of the country's foundation businesses—such as Royal Bank, Sun Life, and Seagram— claimed Sinclair as a director. He was the face of corporate power in Canada. Even if he could pay attention to all the issues on every board, which was impossible, he was at the centre of an interlocking power structure that made a sham of corporate democracy. "Sinclair rules every damn board he sits on," said a colleague on four of his boards, as quoted by Cruise and Griffiths in *Lords of the Line*. The challenge was that he actually knew more than anyone else: "It can be quite scary when you try to oppose someone with that much power and that kind of mind," the director said.

While Sinclair's influence extended to the highest levels of the Canadian economy, he continued to micro-manage deep into the complex company he ran. The managerial ethos of the Sinclair years was top-down interference. It got so bad that Bert Vandenberg, the respected finance vice-president, came in to see Day and informed him that he had just gone to Sinclair's office to resign. He was tired of being second-guessed, and if Day had any sense, he would follow him out the door.

Day was also disturbed by the increasing lack of focus in the company. As a transportation giant, it was very good at that business, but he felt it was on a track of reckless diversification outside its core competence. Here was one of the largest transportation businesses in the world buying pieces such as Syracuse China, a maker of fine dishes, and other businesses it knew nothing about. "Cobbler, stick to your last!" was the thinking of the old shoe salesman from Halifax.

Finally, Sinclair's lust for total control focused on Day. Soon after returning to Montreal from the Merseyside caper, the lawyer was walking down the hall of CP headquarters when he ran into the burly CEO. The message conveyed by Sinclair went something like this: "I'm fed up with you trying to organize yourself into another job. I will decide what your career is going to be. You'll stay wherever I want you to stay." Day's reply was that he had not approached people for assignments; they would just approach him. He referred Sinclair to Wright, his boss in the legal department. Then he went back to his office, his blood boiling.

Two days later he got a call from London. It was from John Gardiner, the young executive he had encountered during the Cammell Laird rescue. Gardiner had settled in as CEO of the Laird Group, the shipyard's parent. The UK government, now in the hands of the Ted Heath Conservatives, still owned 50 percent, but Gardiner and his team called the shots. Gardiner informed him that a first-class British Airways ticket was waiting for him in an office in downtown Montreal. The purpose: Gardiner and company wanted Day to come over to run the Cammell Laird shipyard. Fresh from his conversation with Sinclair, Day was receptive. Once again, he burst into Peter Mills's office: "Peter, are you and Lynn interested in moving to England?" Mills thought they might be. Day flew over that weekend to meet Gardiner and his people.

Of course, he had a conversation with Ann. They had been married thirteen years and had moved cities three times, not including the two homes in Toronto. She had handled everything connected with the moves. The children were still young—Deborah, the eldest, was eleven—and they needed close attention. Graham had been away constantly, and felt Montreal would be their long-term home. But Ann also knew he needed a challenge in his work. If they were to have any kind of family life, they just had to get on with it.

"I think it was pretty tough slogging for Mom in the early years because he is a guy who gets obsessed," says their son Michael. "He has a massive personal battery and a capacity to work a hundred-hour week, and he did. Of course, there is a toll on the wife and family and she kind of stuck through that." Michael points out that his father has a temper; he can be impatient, stressed, and frustrated at times. "She just has this ability to go 'Yeah, okay,' and ride through it," Michael says. "That's actually the story of Ann and Graham. It was her endurance and resilience."

Day was solving a big headache for the UK government and John Gardiner. They had struck out in attempts to find anyone seriously competent to assume the thankless task of shepherding Cammell Laird. Gardiner had remembered his conversations with Day and the Canadian's eagerness to step beyond itinerant assignments and staff roles to be an actual manager of operations. Might that apply to running a near-bankrupt shipyard, a company a fraction of CP's size, in a declining port city in the old industrial northwest of England?

Day, though, was a Maritimer, and shipbuilding was part of his cultural DNA. Liverpool loomed large in the story of his region. Nine million people had left the Merseyside docks in the late nineteenth and early twentieth centuries bound for the New World, many destined for Canada, and a good number of the ships on which they emigrated had docked at Halifax's Pïer 21. In the nineteenth century, an enterprising Haligonian named Samuel Cunard had launched the first regular steamship services between Liverpool and North America. The fabled Cunard Line revolutionized transatlantic travel—and a number of those Cunard ships had been built at the Laird yards.

Long before Graham Day's era, Cammell Laird was turning out big ships—1,300 over 180 years—from paddle wheelers for the Mississippi to aircraft carriers in the Second World War. During the American Civil War, despite Britain's official anti-slavery stance, there was considerable sympathy for the Confederacy in Liverpool, which benefited hugely from the cotton trade. The Lairds were very tight with Confederate agents in Britain, and their shipyard secretly built the CSS *Alabama*, the feared Confederate raider, masquerading it as a merchant ship before it was floated out to sea and outfitted for arms. The *Alabama* sank sixty-eight Union ships around the world before being sunk itself by a Union warship off Cherbourg. And then there was the *Ma Robert*, the doughty little steamer piloted by African explorer Dr. David Livingstone. And, as Day was pondering his decision, the shipyard was in the final stages of building HMS *Conqueror*, a nuclear-powered submarine that, a decade later, would sink the Argentine cruiser *General Belgrano* in the Falklands War with the loss of 323 Argentine lives.

Yet the shipyard had always floated precariously between prosperity and penury. It was busiest during the wars, when the production push was strongest and government money flowed into military production. During the Second World War, the yard spat out a warship every twenty days. Cammell

Laird was viewed as one of the cast of characters that beat Hitler, and when the economic tide turned in the 1960s and 1970s, it was hard to make changes in an icon.

Although warship building had periods of robust health, merchant shipbuilding mirrored the economic cycles and industrial dislocation. By the time of Graham Day's coup, the shipyard was on its knees, levelled by the industrial strife of postwar Britain, the sour mood of commercial decline and its constant companion, class warfare. Management and unions were locked in an eternal struggle for power in the yard. Communist agitators ran rampant, instigating work stoppages over issues big and small. There were constant turf wars over things such as who had the right to drill holes in sheet metal, and production was unreliable.

On top of that, the shipyard was the victim of industrial policies that saw ship construction deployed around the world as an economic tool. It had always been thus, going back to the late 1700s, when the British shipbuilding industry shifted from Britain to Canada in the quest for lower costs and proximity to the pine forests that were the major building material. In the era of wooden ships, a tiny Nova Scotia village such as Hantsport could become a major shipbuilding centre: the local Churchill Company constructed eighty or more ships in the early 1800s. One hundred and fifty years later, the materials were different, but the industry was still on the move. Enormous sums were pouring into capital investment in Asian countries such as Japan and South Korea, whose shipbuilding sectors were subsidized. "It was always an engine of development," says Roger Vaughan, a British naval architect who has worked around the world. And Britain was the loser in these global shifts.

Indeed, Britain in the 1960s and 1970s was moving from the old industrial country of coal mines, ships, and cranes to a swinging centre of music, the arts, and tourism, and London had become a financial services giant. Nothing symbolized the change better than four mop-topped lads who formed a rock group called the Beatles, right across the Mersey from Cammell Laird. They played in the Cavern Club on Liverpool's Mathew Street, in a building, like most on the street, that had once been a warehouse brimming with produce delivered by ships built at Cammell Laird. But even in Liverpool, few were talented or lucky enough to be a Beatle, or even a Pacemaker or a Searcher, and there were many who no longer could find work in the decaying industrial fabric. In singing, swinging Liverpool, an industrial underclass was being bypassed. So that made Cammell Laird's precarious manufacturing jobs even more valuable.

That was the scene as Graham Day flew to London on a weekend in 1971. John Gardiner picked him up at the airport, and whisked him off to see the Laird Group chairman at his golf club. They dealt with the details. Gardiner reminded him he had no job security except that the government wanted the shipyard to exist, given the otherwise dismal industrial scene in Merseyside. But why Graham Day? It was the UK government's desperation, of course, but also recognition of the Canadian's talent and ambition. Gardiner remembers saying his main strength was that Day lacked a regional British accent. Gardiner observed that, in all countries, including Canada, people identify strangers, and their positions in life, by their accents. Day's freedom from categorization would be an asset.

Day realized he owed Gardiner a lot—later, he would understand how much. "John gave me, an untried manager, an opportunity which transformed my career and which changed dramatically my life from 1971 onward."

For Day, there was one more stop. He had a meeting with the minister of state for industry, Nicholas Ridley, the younger son of a duke and member of a titled family that owned vast expanses of the county of Northumberland. Ridley was a talented water-colourist and fervent free marketer, with the classically careless grooming habits of a wealthy nobleman. Often caricatured in the satirical press for his chain smoking, on that day he was wearing a purple shirt with a white collar, and the ashes from his cigarette kept spilling onto the shirt. Ridley asked Day if he was prepared to take the job. Day said he was, but he had that same question gnawing at him: why me? Ridley had to be frank: "If you come and make a hash of it, it is easier to shoot the colonial than to shoot the natives."

It was not a lavish endorsement, but Day thought, "I have found an honest man."

CHAPTER 7

Miracle on the Mersey

Consider how far Graham Day had come when he landed on the Mersey in 1971. At age thirty-eight, he was only seven years away from a small-town law practice, enriched by the musical distractions of *Singalong Jubilee.* He had left behind a brilliant but stalled career at CP. Now he was running an entire company, and in a foreign country. Cammell Laird might have been a faded icon, but it was still a business with ten thousand employees—although down from more than fifteen thousand at its peak. It sprawled over many acres along the Mersey, and it was part of an industry Day had come to know and like.

He joined the grand tradition of "the Canadian in Britain." Then, as now, most globally ambitious Canadian managers ended up in the United States, drawn by the big money, but there has always been a group that gravitated to Britain. They tend to do well there because they provide an amalgam of skills: can-do management, North American style, but with an understanding and appreciation of British norms. For them, a career in Britain is the ultimate in having made it. There is something that inspires them in venerable British institutions, no matter how far past their prime, be it the Royal Mail, the *Times*, or a ragged shipyard in Liverpool.

Media barons Aitken, Thomson, and Black used newspapers as a lever into British politics and society. Newspapers offered a way to move British public opinion, to become a player in influencing the Mother of Parliaments. In particular, Max Aitken, the New Brunswick preacher's son who became Lord Beaverbrook, was ferociously driven to exceed expectations. A successful tycoon in Canada, he moved to Britain, got into politics, and became a sponsor of Andrew Bonar Law, the New Brunswick–born politician who was briefly British prime minister. After building a newspaper empire, Beaverbrook was minister of aircraft production for his friend Winston Churchill in the Second World War. Controversy followed him like a plague, and he resigned under a cloud. Beaverbrook, though, personified Britain's magnetic pull for Maritimers. Growing up physically closer to Britain than were other Canadians, for centuries they were also part of the trade of rum, fish, and industrial goods that flowed among the triangle of Britain, Canada, and the Caribbean. It was a more natural transition for a Maritimer than for someone from Toronto or Winnipeg to move to Britain.

Michael Donovan, a Halifax media entrepreneur who has taken up residence in London to pursue business opportunities, finds it a relatively seamless transition. "The British truly have no negative views about Canadians," not like they do about so many other nationals. They might on occasion portray Canadians as boring, but rarely are Canadians marked as people to avoid.

Graham Day was not boring. He could scarcely conceal his desire to run a company, to take what he had learned as a globe-trotting crisis manager and apply it to a real business.

But now he had taken on a crisis of mammoth proportions: a money-losing business in a sunset industry. You have to be crazy, some said. Certainly, his father thought so. Frank Day was always the barometer of his son's career moves. He believed that working for a railway meant, in hard times, your salary might get reduced, but you won't be laid off. "He thought I was absolutely bonkers leaving CP to run this shipyard," the son recalls. But Frank must have harboured some pride that, five decades after he had left England, his own son was going back to run a British company—not a household name, not a Royal Mail, but an institution of some weight in northwest England. The household names would come later.

As for Ann's father, Jake Creighton, he had his typical mordantly caustic comment on his son-in-law's wandering ways. "Can't keep a job," he would say, just shaking his head.

Jake was a constant sparring partner for young Graham Day. Creighton was the operator of a third-generation food brokerage business in Dartmouth. He was a larger-than-life figure, opinionated and combative, somewhat like his son-in-law. The competition was certainly a spur for Day. "For Jake, it was all about being the alpha male," Michael Day says, smiling. "It wasn't whether Dad was successful or not. Jake would grudgingly say, 'yeah, well, whatever, et cetera,' but Jake was the head of that side of the family, and Graham should get back in line."

Graham and Ann reaffirmed their pact: they would take the plunge, but they would come back to Nova Scotia. That was always the assumption in all their travels. As Graham told the *Times* of London in a later interview, he made sure he had a fallback position: "I'm not saying money doesn't interest me but it sure doesn't come first, or second or third or fourth. I work on a screw-you level. As long as I have enough resources to say 'Screw you' to anyone, that's fine." During the Merseyside period, the Days would build a cottage on North Canoe Lake in Nova Scotia, a handy emergency dwelling if they needed one. However, he had a sublime sense that everything would turn out. He once told a reporter, "I go through life with the sense that I'm fireproof." He knew he could always earn a living, even if it meant selling shoes.

Ann now realizes it was a risky move, but she became so immersed in the relocation that she scarcely had time to be afraid. There had been several moves already, and she and Graham had succumbed to a bit of superstition. They decided not to hang all the pictures in a new home, because whenever they hung the last one, they moved. So they always kept one picture behind her desk in the living room. "Where are you going to put that one?" people would ask. The Days replied, "We're not going to put it anywhere."

The other scary part was Graham Day's personal challenge. He had never run anything significant in his life, and he had never managed large numbers of people. He had managed projects, often negotiating an acquisition or divestment, or cleaning up a mess. "If the wheel fell off, I was the guy. If a ship went down, if an aircraft crashed, if there was a train wreck." He had dealt with artists, many of them with fragile egos. And at Canadian Pacific, he had conducted trade union negotiations. But that did not prepare him for Cammell Laird's remnants of old class and racial prejudices. That first morning, he went to work early at the Birkenhead yard. He had borrowed a big Austin car from the shipyard with the idea of being there at 7:15 to get a head start. As he drove, he could see the yard but couldn't find the entrance in the maze of unfamiliar roads. He spotted a pedestrian with a knapsack over his shoulder. Day rolled down the window, and said in his best approximation of a Birkenhead accent, "If you are going to Cammell 'Lerds,' get in and show me how to drive there." The man, a black employee of Cammell Laird, knew how to get there. Day let him off at the main gate, and then the word went around the shipyard. This new managing director was different, and not in a good way. Some of the talk was in the nature of, "He stops and gets a black bugger and drives him into the shipyard." Day had shed his first harsh light on the fear of change that was part of the culture.

His predecessor's secretary had been fired for removing items from the office safe, so one of his first acts was to retain the previous assistant, who was still working elsewhere in the office. Barbara Blackah became a loyal, dependable guide to Cammell Laird and its ways.

With the words of Les Smith ringing in his ears, he knew he had to walk the property. He immediately requested a hard hat and boiler suit. That in itself was revolutionary—his predecessor had never worn the clothing of the workplace. Suitably attired, Day started his walkabout. He immediately climbed on board a bulk carrier being fitted out. He approached the veteran worker who was fitting a sidelight on the ship.

Day said good morning. Not a flicker. The new managing director raised his voice, "Good morning!" The answer came back, "Are you talking to me?" Day pointed out there were only the two of them. The man said, "Oh, I know who you are. I've been here man and boy for twenty-eight years, and you are the first gaffer [boss] who ever spoke to me."

Suddenly, Graham Day had become the undercover boss, and he didn't like it at all. It went against his concepts of openness. "I thought, no wonder the yard has problems." The image of that worker stayed with him. "For decades, this man's labour was taken, paid for, but he was not part of the enterprise at all. He was not valued."

Thus began the transformation of Cammell Laird from a tired industrial relic to a modern organization. It was full immersion—a restoration of the physical plant, new technology, a change in management style, the introduction of training. Some senior managers had to go and new blood had to be injected. At the level of the industrial workers, there was no change to the numbers, but they had to become more productive.

So many issues were coming at him at once that "you had to rank the issues; otherwise you would get too dispersed." All the time, cultural change was a big part of it, as he tried to move from one based on status and religion to one of merit and democracy. You could modernize the shipyard, and he did, but you had to modernize human relations.

Day could count on valuable support. Peter and Lynn Mills came with the Days to Birkenhead, and Mills's sweeper role became more integral. Mills was Day's eyes and ears in the company, and what Mills saw was challenging: the plant was decrepit, the technology far behind best practice. "They were overmanned, they were essentially leaderless, and they were bankrupt," Mills observed. "They were insolvent again, and we were not sure they knew it. Graham's and my little joke was that we had inherited a one-star shipyard with five-star dining rooms." In fact, there were five levels of dining areas, depending on your rank. In the top two dining rooms, at lunchtime there was booze. So that had to change. In the Day era, "there was one dining room and you carried your tray," Mills said.

It was so bad that, as soon as Day and Mills arrived, it became apparent from the company's finances that it technically had lost its right to trade. The two Canadians rushed down to London to explain this to the government, which came up with standby support of £2 million. As it turned out, the funding never had to be tapped.

The other strong supporting character was Ann herself. She became a valuable part of the corporate team. Secretly, the Days laughed that Cammell Laird had thought it acquired just a managing director, but in fact it got a "two-fer": two for the price of one. She had a role—the Wife of the Boss—and it was very public. Cammell Laird had a sports club where people played darts and cards. The company owned the land and the building. Ann got a call and was asked if she would come and award prizes for competitions. She did, and it became a regular thing. "It took a while for both of us to realize what a departure this was," Day says.

There was a night shift, with a lot of jobs in steel-forming for people who were not part of the standard assembly sequence. When the Days were out for a night in Liverpool, they would drive back under the Mersey to Birkenhead and drop into the steel shops. "We'd go and talk to the guys on the night shift. It was just the humanization of the relationships."

All the time, they tried to avoid being slotted into categories. Everything about Merseyside was about slotting people—Irish or Scottish or Welsh, working class or middle class, Catholic or Protestant, white or black. Day had an advantage in that he couldn't be easily pinned down. In a place where religion mattered, his religious affiliation remained a mystery (it was Anglican). "They knew I was a lawyer, what the hell does that mean? They couldn't fit me socially. And they couldn't pin me down geographically." As John Gardiner had told him, his best advantage was his lack of an identifiable accent.

Ann remembers their being tested on local football teams: which side were you on, Everton or Liverpool? Supposedly, Everton was the team of the region's Catholic population; if you backed Liverpool, you were more likely to be Protestant. In fact, the religious lines of football had already become blurred, but for some hardheads this was another slotting opportunity. The Days never fell for it. Their answer was they were not football followers. Being Canadians, they could be excused.

With the unions he encountered, Day reached back to his poker-playing days to retrieve what became his pledge: I will not lie, I will not bluff. And that served him well. There were strikes, but nothing serious, and the unions largely bought into his vision because he delivered tangible improvements that made their members' lives better. It was not all positive. Union leaders said in media interviews that Day was essentially a lawyer who brought a cold legalistic perspective to the job. But there was grudging respect, says Peter Mills, partly because "the senior management leadership of the company was like night and day, pardon the pun, with what they were used to." Mills says, "We were there, we were visible, we were working hard. They recognized that the physical plant was dilapidated and obsolete and in some places falling down. When we were able to get them the latest technology, a much better plant, and greater efficiencies, it wasn't all roses. But all those ingredients together were enough of an enticement to gain some goodwill, which then led slowly to some improvements. And I think there was also a realization that they were lucky the yard was still going."

Jim Thomas, a trade unionist who got to know Day in this period, was quoted years later in *Financial Director*, a British publication, as saying one thing that helped Day was his co-operative, rather than confrontational, approach. Day recognized that unions had a purpose, and industrial relations generally improved under his oversight. "He's a bit of a sod," Thomas told the magazine, "but I like dealing with him because he's straightforward and I know if I get a deal it will stick. You have to impress the hell out of him with logic, but he certainly listens to ideas."

Indeed, in approaching government for funding, Day held some important aces. Cammell Laird was a key part of British warship production, and it had thousands of industrial jobs in a region undergoing massive deindustrialization. On most operational issues, he was given pretty free rein to do what he wanted, working with agreement from the board. It helped that, in year two, the yard was back in the black. With improved cash flow and government support, Day and his team were able to rebuild the yard. Day says, "When I arrived, the plant and equipment were, at best, circa World War Two, with some elements from the 1920s." The answer was to bring in a crack team of consultants to lead the redesign and rebuilding of William Laird's old shipyard.

Roger Vaughan was a young Lancashire man with a PhD in naval architecture, who, in his twenties, had co-founded a shipyard consulting firm that developed a worldwide reputation. He had studied shipbuilding in several countries, including Norway and Sweden, and brought an international perspective to the Mersey site. His company, A&P Appledore, had secured a major contract with South Korea's Hyundai Heavy Industries that helped elevate that country into the top ranks of global shipbuilders. He met Graham Day, and was impressed to find a man with an expertise and passion for professional management.

"British industry in those days was quite appallingly managed," says Vaughan, now retired and living in rural northern England after a career as architect, executive, business school head, and, at one point, shipyard co-owner. In building ships, teams were managed around a project. There might have been a managing director who had come up from the ranks, but rarely was there anyone qualified to run a complex business. "Graham was like a breath of fresh air," Vaughan says. Another innovation was bringing in a key lieutenant, Peter Mills, as an administrative director who could manage the critical staff side of the company.

One of the first things Day did was have the office block refurbished and painted in bright colours. Then symbolism merged with substance when Vaughan and his team redesigned the shipyard, which would include a massive covered production hall designed according to Swedish techniques. It was one of Vaughan's great achievements in a career littered with breakthroughs. It meant the owners had to commit £36 million, but it was the critical part of the turnaround in productivity. Vaughan says the Appledore firm had a bit of an international name, but the team was still considered a bunch of young pups. "Graham looked at a group of guys in their mid-twenties and gave us a huge contract. You give people their head and they get on with it. We couldn't believe our luck."

But all this new technology would be in vain if the workers lacked the requisite skills, and Day found there were great gaps in the British education system. As the company hired "school leavers" out of secondary school, they needed remedial training in the fundamentals, let alone new skills. Cammell Laird got into the training business, running an eight-room school where the basics were taught to skills-starved workers. The school had work areas where practical, hands-on training took place.

For Ann Day, the five years in Birkenhead were challenging, but they had a big advantage: her husband could come home most nights. The children found it hard at first, but eventually they settled in. It was stability after a time of upheaval—Deborah had been to six schools, but now settled in for four years in one place.

Still, there was some adjustment. Michael Day was a day student at the local Birkenhead School, and he stood out. First it was the accent, and then it was the fact that his father was running Cammell Laird. A large number of students were from families that were employed by or lived off some relationship with the shipyard. That made him a target, and he got into a fight the first week of school. One teacher would continually put young Michael on the spot by reminding him of who his father was right in front of the class. "He would say, 'Oh, I read about your father today. Don't think that that makes you important.' So I was very aware of it." At one point, one of the Day girls came home and said she was told by a fellow student that she would have to give up one of her new friends because the girl's father worked for Graham. Ann's response: Do you really need the person who said that as a friend?

There were also occasional flashes of a fading class system in words that might have come from the dowager duchess on *Downton Abbey*. In London one night, the Days were guests at the opera, part of an outing that provided dinner as part of the package. One woman heard Ann's name and said, "With or without the *e*?" Ann said "without," and the woman sniffed, "Below stairs." The whole place went quiet. "They couldn't believe she said that," Ann laughs today. "She had put me in my place. It had never occurred to me to think about the e or not. It is my name. But as colonials, there was not a lot expected of you. They were surprised we could eat with a knife and fork."

Ann found plenty of ways to keep busy. While Graham had the use of a big car and driver, she spent £800 on a Mini estate wagon of Dijon mustard colour with fake wooden sides. It could pull a sailboat out to the artificial lake on the Wirral Peninsula, which encompasses Birkenhead and its hinterland. And Graham continued to indulge his love of VW Beetles, notwithstanding the availability of the company car.

In time, Day came to appreciate the sense of continuity at Cammell Laird. Families had worked there for generations, and a job was a teen-to-death proposition. In the office building, elderly ladies cleaned the offices on a split shift, coming in after 5:00 P.M. and then early in the morning. And their forewoman, Nellie Smith, was a well-known figure in the company.

Smith and her fellow cleaners were very concerned about losing their jobs because of new working-age limits introduced by the government. The human resources records were in terrible shape, and Day made use of that fact. The head of human resources found a dog-eared little card that indicated Smith's advancing age. "So I got the ink eradicator, and changed her birthday on the card, and said to her, 'Nellie, as long as I'm here, you're here.'" And he did that for the other women.

Nellie Smith would become an important figure in Day's grand project. At one point, a shipowner from Newcastle was having three bulk carriers built, and he needed someone to christen one of them. It is a very serious matter, this christening of ships, with the ritualistic flowers, the smashing of the champagne bottle, and the celebratory lunch. The christener has to be an important woman, often the wife of the shipowner, a dignitary, or, for major naval vessels, the queen herself. The customer asked Day to find a senior woman in the shipyard to do it. So it was Nellie Smith who launched the ship, as a signal to the workers that they were valued in this business, too. Day suspects that "a number of them were saying, 'Oh, they won't do all this for Nellie.'" But Cammell Laird gave Nellie Smith the ceremony, and the lunch that followed. Years later, the BBC asked Smith what she thought of Graham Day. "Smashing," she said, beaming.

Other aspects of human resources were more painful. Day had a very talented number two manager whose shipbuilding prowess nicely balanced Day's business acumen. But he was drinking heavily, and this was having a marked effect on the performance of the entire shipyard. Day tried to get the man to seek help, but to no avail. Day had a very supportive non-executive chairman, Sir David Barrett, a man in his late sixties who had run a big engineering business and who would come in two mornings a week, stay for lunch, and talk things over with Day. This particular morning, Day told Sir David that he had no choice but to let his number two go. Barrett just said, "Oh, Graham, what took you so long?" It stunned Day, who asked why Barrett hadn't advised him earlier to dismiss the man. The answer came back, "What would you have learned?" Barrett went on to say, "You are the chief executive officer. I'm the non-executive chairman." It was a lesson in corporate governance. Managers manage; directors are there to support that endeavour.

The firing was exceptionally hard, and Day later learned the man's marriage fell apart. It taught him the importance of making tough decisions, but not to be cold or unfeeling. Day used it as a test in hiring senior people. He would ask, "How many people have you personally fired?" If the applicant had dismissed people, he would ask how it felt. If the response was a hard-hearted "piece of cake, I do what I have to do—not a problem for me," Day would seldom be interested in hiring that person. One applicant confessed, however, that he had gone to the men's room and thrown up after firing someone. "I thought, that's the person I'd prefer to hire. You do what you have to do, but you can't not care."

At Cammell Laird, Day began to develop a reputation as someone who could make hard decisions. But the job cuts were almost entirely on the management side, and he changed about a third of the team. Mills noted that "there was a huge amount of talent there just looking for leadership, and Graham was that breath of fresh air. He got rid of a lot of senior deadwood, appointed a lot of really bright people who should have had the leadership jobs, and we also recruited from outside."

Mills could see his old colleague changing during the five years at Cammell Laird, as he slowly brought the shipyard back to positive cash flow. He had been impressive at CP, but in Birkenhead, his confidence blossomed. "He was a mover and a comer at CP. At Cammell Laird, he was it. He was the leader, he was the guy; it was all on his shoulders. And he just responded to that challenge."

Few Canadians knew about the miracle on the Mersey, unless they were part of the global shipping business. While Day was turning around Cammell Laird, a young Montreal businessman named Paul Martin was a rising executive at Power Corporation of Canada, the holding company controlled by master corporate builder Paul Desmarais. The son and namesake of a federal Liberal politician, Martin was taking a leap into the shipping business as the new president of Power-owned bulk carrier Canada Steamship Lines. His new focus took him to industry meetings in Britain, where he would learn about Graham Day, the shipyard turnaround star. Day was not a big name in Canadian business circles, but in the marine world he was golden, and that lustre would only grow. Martin remembers, "You cannot exaggerate the reputation of Graham Day as a Canadian who had made it in the biggest play of all."

That name would stay etched in Martin's mind as he led a buyout of Canada Steamship Lines and later stepped back from the company to pursue a political career, rising to become the Liberal finance minister and prime minister. His sons took control of the company, and two of them were directors. They told him later that they had recruited a strong board member, name of Graham Day. "I was delighted," Martin says.

CHAPTER 8

Best of Times, Worst of Times

Brian has worked in the Cammell Laird shipyards for half a century. This morning, a sunny Sunday in March 2016, he is manning the security gate, and he takes time to chat with a journalist from Canada. Yes, he remembers Graham Day and the time, forty years ago, when Nellie Smith was chosen to launch a ship—a role unheard of for a cleaning lady. Nellie's family had worked at Cammell Laird for generations, and she was as much a fixture as the Mersey itself.

The shipyard is busy this morning as men in hard hats come and go past Brian's security station. In the background there is a glimpse of the wet basin where the container ship was liberated in the nighttime coup that made Graham Day's career. Brian smiles as he remembers that incident, too. There were always strikes at Cammell Laird. They were a fact of life, he shrugs.

It is a much smaller yard now—the main building of Day's era is gone—and yet it survives and even thrives, and that is part of Day's legacy. But what Brian remembers best is the style of the brash young Canadian, compared with previous managers: "He was more open."

That comment would please Graham Day, who regards the Cammell Laird tenure as his best job ever. He was able to put into practice the things he had learned at Canadian Pacific. He liked and respected the people, some of whom became lifelong friends. He was able to blend his own knowledge of commercial shipping with Cammell Laird's technical expertise in building commercial ships. The company reaped the benefits by amassing the largest order book in the world for petroleum tankers. Graham Day was lauded as the great turnaround manager who changed an insolvent business into one with a positive cash flow.

His performance stood out because the world shipbuilding industry was in woeful shape, and it got worse through the 1970s as the Arab oil embargo, the OPEC supply squeeze, and rising oil prices undercut the demand for shipping. Entire shipyards were wiped off the map and national industries eliminated. In the mid-1970s, for example, Sweden had the second-largest shipbuilding industry in the world; a decade later, the entire industry was gone. The British industry, too, was badly affected, and the country was sharply divided on how to respond. The opposing views were summed up in a 1966 task force on the prospects for the industry: "On the one side were those people who, aware of the geography, history and pride of craft, believe it unthinkable to be without a strong shipbuilding industry. Preserve at any cost. Others, viewed as more realistic, see ships as a product that developing countries could make more economically. They see shipbuilding as a relic of the first industrial age, now due to decline."

It was a natural breeding ground for partisan politics. The opposition Labour Party was on the side of preserving, and nationalizing, the industry, which would be heavily concentrated in working-class Labour-dominated areas such as Liverpool, Newcastle, and Glasgow. The Conservative government, meanwhile, was sharply divided. When Day arrived at Cammell Laird, Ted Heath was prime minister. Faced with deteriorating economic prospects, Heath flirted with free market economics, but in his heart was a one-nation Tory in favour of governing by consensus. His cabinet was polarized between Heathites who inclined to the status quo and an impatient cacophony of radicals led by Keith Joseph, the intellectual force behind a free market U-turn. Joseph was a mentor for Tory insurgents such as Norman Tebbit, Nicholas Ridley, and a rising star, Margaret Thatcher, who was sympathetic to the new ideas but far from a raging radical at that time. They were champing at the bit to enact structural reforms, reduce the power of the trade unions, and, in their view, liberate business from the chains of government.

This was Day's introduction to the politics of industrial policy, and it would be a major factor in his life. He always worked at the confluence of public and private enterprise. He was a conservative—both small and large *c*—but he was pragmatic and sensitive to political nuance, never letting ideology get in the way of his primary purpose, which was to restore companies to health. He believed nationalization should be avoided, if at all possible, but in the event he could live with it for a while.

During his Cammell Laird period, Day actually had a very brief flirtation with becoming a partisan, big *c* Conservative. The party had an opening in a constituency in nearby Chester, and a party official brought the message that there was interest in having Day offer his candidacy. Day said he would think about it, but concluded he wanted to finish the Cammell Laird job. Besides, he was seen as a Canadian. Instead, Peter Morrison stood for the seat, winning in 1974 and becoming an early Thatcher backer, a minister of state, and parliamentary undersecretary for the prime minister.

The Heath government of the early 1970s was reeling from the economic pressures of skyrocketing inflation and a currency under pressure. In fact, its only major success was finally getting Britain into the European Community in 1973, after years of being blocked by France's former president Charles de Gaulle. Even then the party was divided on Europe. Other combustible issues took centre stage, including the demands of the powerful miners' unions to exact higher pay raises in the face of savage increases in the cost of living. It was an issue that would roil British politics for the next decade and more.

Heath called an election in 1974, and was edged out of power, allowing the return of Labour leader Harold Wilson to the prime minister's job. In a leadership challenge to Heath, the Tories rebuked their long-time leader. Keith Joseph was considered a leading candidate to replace Heath, but he stepped aside, opening a window for his protegée, Margaret Thatcher.

Day didn't really know her—they had met briefly when she was education minister. She had taken a terrible beating in the controversy over eliminating free milk in state schools. "Thatcher, Thatcher, school milk snatcher," a Labour member had chanted, and the phrase caught on. But she survived to join the leadership challenge, and won the leadership on the second ballot, humbling Ted Heath. The Tories knew they were getting a right-leaning leader, but they were not expecting a revolution. They might have taken their cue from her first press conference. As she posed for a picture, she said: "I am now going to take a turn to the right, which is very appropriate."

Labour, too, was in the throes of change. Wilson resigned abruptly, officially because of ill health, although the motivation remains a bit of a mystery. As his successor, he endorsed sixty-four-year-old Jim Callaghan, a Welsh union man but a pragmatist who, in early April 1976, suddenly found himself thrust into power as prime minister. Callaghan, with his stellar war record as a chief petty officer in the navy and a charming style, was someone Day could like. In the darkest of hours, he would be Sunny Jim.

Callaghan and his Labour cabinet certainly noticed Graham Day. They had commissioned a consultant's study of the shipbuilding industry, and the report showed Cammell Laird as the only yard with a serious strategic plan that it was actually implementing. Cammell Laird had become the role model of the industry, and so Graham Day, at forty-three, was invited to lead the nationalization organizing committee with the idea that, when legislation passed, he would ultimately serve as the CEO of the massive state company.

To work on the committee, Day plucked Peter Mills as his second in command. "Neither of us wanted to do [the nationalization]," Day says, but after the OPEC energy crisis, shipbuilding was cratering. "We rationalized that at least we would get an industrial organization that was sustainable." Forty years later, Day could see the irony: the man later charged with privatizing big parts of British industry was originally tapped to be the nationalizer. He had beliefs that were strongly free market, but he was also a pragmatist who knew that you worked with the hand you were dealt. He had just come off what he later viewed as his best job ever. Now he was going into what he later described as the worst year of his working life. He got a great education on the industry and its players, but he quickly despaired of the company that would emerge and of his role in it.

In 1975, he felt that nationalization would give the industry some breathing room to restructure. He found, however, that this was not the plan. The government's real aim was to embed nationalization as a permanent solution. As the year progressed, he learned that the process was all about ideology, not about strategy and rebuilding. The government benches were dominated by people who wanted a passive administrator in charge, not someone who would direct change. "It was clear that we were not going to be permitted to actually do the job commercially," he says. Instead, it would be a political solution. The government had a board in waiting, but he took it as a negative sign that at least three of the members could not even get security clearance. Like Groucho Marx, he didn't really want to belong to this club.

As tension grew between Day and his Labour political masters, his personal stress level rose to the boiling point. It was exacerbated by long delays in getting the nationalization bill passed by the House of Commons, and there were challenges in the Tory-dominated House of Lords. If the industry was to be sustained, there must be action and soon, but all that happened was paralysis.

It got harder and harder to suffer fools. He and Peter Mills would spend their week in London and head back to Birkenhead on the weekend. One night they were in a London restaurant, when, two tables over, a diner said something entirely inappropriate to the waiter. Day swung around and harshly rebuked the man, ending with the warning: "Don't you ever say that to these people again." Here were two aspects of Day on display. He was always sympathetic to those in the low-level services jobs—from cleaning staff to labourers—who kept an enterprise going. And he was extraordinarily stressed at the time.

A decade later, he told Hazel Duffy of the *Financial Times* that he was proud that no minister of his had ever been bounced in public by something he did or failed to do. But relations were difficult in 1976 while the shipbuilding bill was dragging through

Parliament. The relationship between Day and the junior industry minister, Gerald Kaufman, was exceptionally strained. Later, Day would say he disliked the man for his rudeness, "his wilful ignorance of commercial realities," and his constant undermining. Kaufman was the only cabinet minister in Day's British tenure he could not abide.

"When I took the job on, I felt without a doubt that I could do the same for the industry as I had done at Cammell Laird," Day told the *Financial Times*'s Duffy. It took him just two months to change his opinion, Duffy wrote, "and he now admits he should never have taken the job in the first place."

Yet through it all, he retained a warm regard for Jim Callaghan, a man of integrity thrust into an impossible job. Day was willing to go the extra mile for him, whatever he thought of his politics. At Easter, the Day family had gone to Italy during one of Britain's periodic economic crises. He got called back to London because there was an export opportunity the government wanted to explore.

Callaghan had received a message through the British ambassador in Kuwait saying the Kuwaitis, who previously had ships built in Britain, were interested in ordering four more cargo ships. The Kuwaiti ruler remembered earlier satisfactory discussions with Callaghan in a meeting in the desert. No one was supposed to know about this new opportunity. Day took one shipbuilder with him, the head of the Glasgow yard that had earlier built ships for Kuwait. The man was told he could tell only his wife about the trip and that he should bring his passport and the outline drawings for the earlier ships.

The two went off to see the Kuwaitis, who had hired a Palestinian businessman as a go-between. It was a strange meeting. There were uncomfortable moments as the Kuwaiti delegation tried to pigeonhole Day. They asked about his religion, and he said Church of England. But when did he change from the religion of his father?—for some reason, the Kuwaitis were convinced Day was Jewish. Then they shifted gears: "Why are you working for the British? You are not British." Day said the ambassador could speak to his status as a British citizen, but as to why he was doing this, "I am a mercenary." He worked for a living, just like the Palestinian who worked for them, he said. The Kuwaitis got the idea, and the deal moved ahead. Day and his Scottish shipyard companion returned to Britain with a draft for 25 percent down-payment for four ships. "That was the thing I did for Jim Callaghan," Day says proudly.

Meanwhile, the privatization bill was a sprawling piece of legislation that covered not just shipbuilding, but also ship repair and engine building, as well as the big aerospace industry. It touched ideological nerves on both sides of the House, and conflict broke out.

The fate of nationalization and the career direction of Graham Day were largely determined on the night of May 27, 1976, when the House of Commons met to debate the bill and hold a vote. Day was not there, but Peter Mills was. As a policy advisor to the government, he was sitting in the "Strangers'" bench on the floor of the House and could see the dramatic tableau unfold. The scene comprised a number of people who would shape Day's future, including Margaret Thatcher, the new leader of the opposition, and Michael Heseltine, an intensely charismatic Tory MP with a fabulous golden mane. Passions ran high, as the House prepared to hold the key vote. The Labour government was intent on adding to the number of state-owned industries to preserve jobs, many of them union jobs. The Conservatives under Thatcher were moving towards a denationalization strategy.

The vote was expected to be a stalemate, but the government squeaked out a single-vote victory. The Tories cried foul, charging that a Labour MP had violated the pairing convention, whereby an absent member could balance his non-vote with an agreed abstention on the other side. This time, the Labour member broke the deal and voted. Welsh Labour MPs stood up and sang the socialist hymn, "The Red Flag," which further inflamed the opposition. Some MPs began jostling, and one took a swing at another. Heseltine rushed over and seized the mace, the ceremonial symbol of authority in the House. "He started swinging it over his head and pointing at the other side," Mills recalls. It was a serious breach of parliamentary decorum.

Heseltine's action had parallels with the physical intervention of Prime Minister Justin Trudeau, when he made contact with opposition MPs during the assisted-dying debate in the Canadian Parliament. Trudeau's actions were much less menacing, but the circumstances were similar: a bill in trouble, a heated issue, an obdurate opposition, and tired and angry MPs. Heseltine apologized, as Trudeau did, but the British MP would never lose the nickname "Tarzan"—someone who would swing from the trees.

The fiasco set off a long procedural wrangle that stopped the nationalization bill in its tracks. In the end, the bill was deemed a hybrid that mixed private and public implications. As a result, the legislation was broken up, and the ship repair industry was removed.

The shipbuilding turmoil set the stage for a more fundamental shift. In time, Heseltine would emerge as a key figure in the battle for the soul of the Conservative Party. As the 1970s rolled on, it became clear that Margaret Thatcher was a new kind of political leader who would not protect or defend nationalized industries, but expose them to the market. Thatcher would give rein to a breed of liberalizers, including Nicholas Ridley, the "shoot the colonial" advocate, who authored a key party report on state-owned companies.

According to the Thatcher biography *One of Us* by Hugo Young, Ridley believed that nationalized industries were, from every point of view, deplorable. Oversubsidized, uncompetitive, and monopolistic, they could not but be inefficient and underproductive. His report proposed a strategy for dismantling them, or at least for removing their offensive dependence on subsidies from the taxpayers' bottomless purse. The other bonus was undermining the power of the industrial unions, which were dominant in the state-held industries.

At that time, the Tory terminology was "denationalization." It would take a while before the more explicit "privatization" became the battle cry. In the future, Graham Day would play a key role in this war of ideas, not as a doctrinaire ideologue, but as the implementer of privatization. In November 1976, however, he was more interested in action, any action at all, to save the shipbuilding industry. But the much delayed nationalization bill died on the order paper, and thus so did his committee's terms. A revised bill eventually would be introduced and passed, but Day had seen enough. So had most board members, who declined to be reappointed.

For Day and Mills, it was a parting moment, the end of their deeply trusting and highly effective professional partnership. The two Nova Scotia boys would remain friends as Mills moved on to new jobs, including a long tenure as an executive in the Thomson organization based in Toronto. On news of their resignation, there was recrimination on both sides of the House, with the Labour government charging Conservative obstruction and the Tory opposition railing about Labour's high-handed mishandling of the bill. They all agreed, however, that it was a tragedy Day was leaving. The House heard from Eric Heffer, the Labour member from Liverpool and a tradesman who was a kind of conscience of the party's working-class wing. Heffer asked if the industry minister was aware that, "on Merseyside, particularly in the trade union movement and in the shipbuilding and repair industries, regret will be felt at the decision of Mr. Graham Day to resign? He was well thought of on Merseyside, particularly in Cammell Laird. He did a first-class job." The minister, Eric Varley, agreed that Day had done a magnificent job. "I understand his frustrations and why he was worried about the bill getting on to the statute book." Varley also agreed to ask Day to reconsider. But there was no turning back for Graham Day. He had made up his mind.

Roger Vaughan, too, had joined with a couple of colleagues in writing to beg Day to remain in Britain. He was personally saddened that Britain was losing an exceptional manager. Vaughan knew Day was not perfect, but when he failed, it was usually because "everybody had high expectations of him and sometimes they were unrealizable."

The facial hair styles of Graham Day reflect the phases of his career. There was the clean-shaven young singer on *Singalong Jubilee* and the rising lawyer of Windsor, Nova Scotia. In the Cammell Laird era, he took on sharp sideburns that arched menacingly across his face. Then there was the beard. As he once told the *Times* of London, its origins could be traced to November 1976. "On the day the shipyard nationalization bill failed," he said, "I said to myself, sod it, I'm not going to shave today." "The not-shaving was a rebellion," Ann says. "The kids couldn't believe it—he always had a heavy beard and he had shaved twice daily if there was something on."

The beard was born, and the British chapter of his career

seemed over. In June 1977, with the school year ended for their children, Ann and Graham Day returned to Nova Scotia, not knowing what lay ahead.

CHAPTER 9

The Interregnum

Maritimers come home. No matter how high or how far they fly, they return to the nest. The homing instinct brought the Days back to Canada in 1977, with Graham still smarting from the nationalization debacle. He and Ann were holed up at their cottage at North Canoe Lake, marking time, waiting for their new house to be built in Hantsport, along the Avon River, just as they had dreamed fifteen years earlier. Ann Day fully expected they would spend the rest of their lives in Nova Scotia. The question was, doing what?

The answer was, as always, serendipitous—or, as the Days call it, "happystance." Day was driving out of downtown Halifax, heading over to the city's Northwest Arm area to pick up Ann, who was spending time at the home of a friend. Commandeering Ann's pickup truck, he was taking his customary shortcut through the Dalhousie University campus. As he passed the arts administration building, he caught some movement out of the corner of his eye. Andrew MacKay, then the university's executive vice-president, was waving at him to stop. MacKay had estimated that Day would be driving through the campus at about that time. MacKay breathlessly explained that he understood Day was in the process of moving back from England. The university, he said, had some problems he might be able to help solve.

One issue was that some members of the law faculty had applied for government grants to look at transportation and ocean law. These were the early days of ocean studies as an academic discipline, arising from the United Nations' interest in the Law of the Sea. MacKay hoped Day would help Dalhousie write a fresh proposal. Also, one of the business professors (in what is now the Rowe School of Business) was facing a heavy load teaching all the strategic planning, and he would like to share it.

Day demurred, saying he didn't have any qualifications to teach strategy. But MacKay felt it would be refreshing to have a non-academic with rich experience teach business courses. And if the grants came through, the university would form a marine transportation centre, and he could run that.

Thus, a new chapter opened: Professor Graham Day. He liked research, understood business, and would have a more practical perspective than his fellow professors. It proved that the job always seemed to find him; he didn't go looking. He settled into life as a university teacher and director of the new Canadian Marine Transportation Centre. He loved the teaching and the students. It gave him time to consolidate his thinking based on his experiences. For a moment, there was the thought he might make a life of it. Ann thought so, too, but now looking back, she knows he would not have been content. He was a thinker, yes, but he also had to be making things happen.

He was a fresh breeze in the business faculty. One of his students was Mary Brooks, a former occupational therapist working in a Halifax hospital who wanted to try something new and applied for an MBA. She had heard that Graham Day's strategy courses were essential. She got into his class, and she enjoyed it. Here was this young man in his forties who had such relevant experience, who had run a major shipyard, and he was telling students about how the world worked. Yet she failed the first term. Coming from the non-profit sector, she was having trouble navigating around the idea of profits. "I was struggling a bit." But by the time she got to the end of the second term with Day, the light had come on. She got the highest mark in the final exam.

She thrived on his style of teaching: real-world experience combined with positive reinforcement. Some events stick out, like the time a team of British bankers came to class. The bankers had been visiting Day, and their flight was not due to leave until after the class, so he invited them along. There was a case study, and the class got animated talking about solutions. In the next class, Day confided to the students that the bankers had been blown away: "You guys were just simply wonderful." University students didn't usually hear that from professors in those days. There was not that positive reinforcement. But, says Brooks, "he was always really, really good at being positive and making us all feel like we were first class."

Brooks is now professor emerita at Dalhousie's Rowe School of Business, having spent a career studying transportation. She took home classroom lessons from Graham Day, but the life lessons stand out. One, in particular, was the longstanding Day motto that you always need drop-dead money. It was a wisdom learned during Day's British sojourn. It's the idea that, if you ethically can't live with the job you're doing, or if it starts to fall apart, you can walk away, that "you aren't so dependent on the job that you have to continue [to] do something that you personally can't do." She has told all her classes this should be a constant theme in their lives.

Brooks also recalls Day's views on the need to promote women in management. Part of it reflected respect, but for the hard-nosed industrialist there was also practicality. He always said that hiring women was a high-return investment. "He meant that, when you hired a woman, she was going to work harder because there was something to prove. They had to prove that they could do the job."

Finally, she kept another gem from someone who had spent his British time in a declining industry. Day felt that anyone can look good in an industry that's growing quickly, but it takes real intelligence to do a good job in an industry that's mature or stagnating. Day himself would make a career of working in embattled industries. Brooks got into the transportation field as a researcher, academic, and consultant. "This is a mature industry. We've been putting stuff on railcars for more than a hundred years. Even the airplane industry is maturing. Shipping is really mature. And so how do you solve the strategic problems?" Shipping appealed to her because it's a global industry and highly mobile, which makes it difficult to regulate internationally. By the time she had done a shipping consulting project and studied some marine transportation, she was hooked on the industry. She found the same combination of romance and hard realism that Day found so fascinating.

No doubt influenced by his own university experience, Day had a huge tolerance for people such as Brooks, who didn't fit into the classic mould. Another of his projects was Steve Acker, a young Halifax man enrolled in the MBA program at Dalhousie. Acker came from a business background—his father was a senior manager at the Shaw Group, a venerable Halifax company in the building materials trade. While he went to school, Acker earned money working on seagoing ships. He wanted a permanent job after graduation in the marine industries, and heard there was this fellow at the Marine Transportation Centre who helped graduates find employment. So he walked in on Day and said, "I hear you get kids jobs in the ocean industries." Day's response was in the nature of, "And just who are you? Don't let the door hit you on the way out." Acker departed, but left his resumé.

Two weeks later, Acker went back. Day had gone over the resumé, found it desperately wanting, and told Acker to rewrite it—a process repeated over and over. "I ended up in my graduating year taking three classes from him. Those were the best grades I had in graduate school, and the best professor I ever had." In time, Graham Day became a mentor. "I don't think he was grooming me for anything in particular, but was trying to make me realize I had some modicum of intelligence and it would be a waste not to use it. I think he just saw a kid who had no direction whatsoever, some reasonable level of intelligence, and enough gumption to say 'I need some help or direction.'" A bit like Graham Day at that point in life.

Day meanwhile was keeping a toe wet in the business world. He served for four years as a director of a private shipping company owned by the Misener family from St. Catharines, Ontario. It gave him some early exposure to the thorny issues of family business. The company had been started by entrepreneur Scott Misener, who, in the 1920s, operated ships on the Great Lakes and later on the newly built St. Lawrence Seaway. The business had been inherited by his son Ralph, who, when Day joined, was endeavouring to hand it down in turn to his three sons. Ralph Misener had hired a Harvard MBA, a smart and competent man, to guide the enterprise. The sons were good people, Day recalls, but not up to the task of running the company. In fact, Day arranged for his old sweeper, David Gardiner, to join and manage the fleet. There was a board, but its members were not all intent on providing the required oversight. When the

Harvard-trained professional manager left, the businesses had to be wound up. It was a situation Day would encounter time and time again.

Meanwhile, Day was becoming restless in the university setting of the 1970s. The Dalhousie faculty was being unionized, and Graham Day was not a man who took easily to constraints. He had known union leaders, liked many of them, and worked with them, and he appreciated that they were often people with whom he could do business. But he wanted to negotiate his own path in life. It was not that he was an enemy of unions, but they were not for him.

Yet, he was a paradox. Even as he grew restive under academic unionization, he was considering plunging more deeply into academic life: he would go to Wales for a PhD. The thinking was that the University of Wales, a centre of transportation scholarship, would admit both him and Mary Brooks. It is hard to imagine what he would have become had he pursued that course: a distinguished university professor? A thought leader in transportation? Or perhaps a caged lion?

Then, in 1981, a call came, as it usually did for Graham Day. This time it was Dome Petroleum, a venturesome energy company based in Calgary and a huge player in the exploration of oil and gas in the frontier areas of the Arctic. It had become the repository of Canadian hopes—and public incentive money—for tapping frontier sources. And it needed shipping and shipbuilding expertise to get the energy out by tanker.

Graham Day was a natural fit—he had already done some consulting on Dome's effort to find a site for a new shipyard. The appeal was not just the job description—vice-president, shipbuilding—he also bought into Dome's national dream, a Canadian champion bringing oil out of the Arctic. This was Day's next Canadian Pacific, a company he could love for turning a geographic expression into a nation. It reflected the ambition of Dome chairman Jack Gallagher, a charming visionary known as Smilin' Jack, and everything in the company was subjugated to that vision.

Steve Acker remembers that he and Day had discussed how Dome had become the most interesting Canadian company in the marine field. Then, out of the blue, the young man got a call from Dome inviting him to Calgary for what turned out to be, in his mind, a disastrous job interview. But he got hired anyway, and ended up in Dome's offices, sitting around with nothing to do. Suddenly, "there's a knock on the door and I look up and there's Graham. And I said, 'What the hell are you doing here?' And he says, 'Do you think I was going to come out here by myself?'" For Day and Acker, it was mentor and student again. At first, they didn't work together, but Day knew he eventually could call on Acker.

At Dome, Day found a company where everything was sacrificed for the dreams of Gallagher and his president, Bill Richards. Day had a front-row seat on how the place operated, and he could see that Gallagher, like Icarus, was flying close to the sun. That became clear when Dome made its fateful $1.7 billion purchase of a controlling interest in Hudson's Bay Oil and Gas, a deal that expanded the company greatly but stretched its finances.

On one occasion, Day and a group of executives were accompanying Bill Richards in the company's plane to Ottawa. In the air, Day and another senior executive spent the whole trip trying to persuade Richards and his team to pay for all or part of Hudson's Bay with Dome shares, instead of borrowed cash. Richards and his team seemed determined to borrow because the money was in the bank in terms of potential borrowing power. They resisted financing any portion by issuing paper.

The Hudson's Bay deal became part of the crushing bank debt that eventually took Dome down, turning it into one of the classic failures of the Canadian energy industry.

The Dome management style was a concern to the very exacting Graham Day. The people worked long, hard hours, and on the whole were very competent. But he noticed that, if you scheduled a three o'clock meeting with a senior officer, you might get him by five. A lot of these people could not manage their own time. His own superior would have subordinates lined up outside his office doing nothing, waiting their turn for their appointments.

"There wasn't a sense that what I'm doing right now with you is so important, everything else is subordinate. It was dysfunctional in that sense, although, at the sharp end, they were very good people." He had no sense then that this was a company that would fail—except he thought the Hudson's Bay deal's structure was "wrong and stupid."

The dream of building a shipyard had brought Day to Dome, but the company was overstressed. Day was back in familiar territory, travelling to Japan, where they were converting old ships into drilling rigs for the Beaufort Sea. That was proceeding very slowly, however, and the shipbuilding dream was slipping farther away.

Dome already owned the Davie shipyard in Quebec, but didn't know quite what to do with it. Davie was Canada's oldest and largest shipyard, founded 150 years earlier. It was a classic Canadian institution, teetering on the edge of bankruptcy and tossed in the wind of political calculation. Dome acquired it for one purpose—building Arctic-class ships—but that idea was looking more remote. The Davie yard, in turn, was having problems fulfilling contracts, including some drilling rigs for Mexico. There was also a leadership crisis in the shipyard. A number of the key officers Dome had taken on when it bought the shipyard were exiting the company, leaving a big hole. After fourteen months in Calgary, Day agreed to run Davie, and he would take Steve Acker with him. In Quebec, they rolled up their sleeves to solve the array of immediate crises and shore up the order books.

There was much that Day liked about Davie. It had amassed a contingent of outstanding welders who did very good work. So, under the Canada-US military equipment agreement, Davie bid on a bunch of sonar domes. Then it contracted to build Newfoundland ferries. What's more, it sorted out the Mexican imbroglio, and got paid.

Acker was now reporting directly to Day, and he thrived. He became one of those in Day's life who could say, "Graham, if you want to do that, you know I'll bust my ass to help you do it. But I do think we should sit down and talk about this again." Acker could see the different sides of Graham Day. One side was the Graham Day who took pride in seeing the people he liked do well in life. He backed them to the hilt. At the same time, Acker says, he was not always easy to get along with. "He has an ego, he makes his mind up extremely quickly. He just happens to be, like most good gamblers, more often right than wrong. I've seen him offend people, I've seen him make decisions that I didn't agree with, but I've only had two bosses in my life who, if they called me today and said they needed me to do something, I would do it." Those two are Graham Day and Howard Macdonald, the last president of Dome, who cleaned up the mess and negotiated the sale of the former Canadian energy champion to the US giant Amoco in 1988.

By the fall of 1982, Day had fixed the Davie yard's problems and restored it to positive cash flow. There was nothing left to do, and he did not want to stay. Davie was a shipyard, like

Cammell Laird, but it was only about a twentieth the size of the Birkenhead operation. Meanwhile, the Dome dream was receding in the rearview mirror. Acker would be moving back to the Dome head office in Calgary, and Day told Dome he was pushing off. He did not worry about his future. He could go back to Dalhousie—he loved working with students—or something else would turn up. It always did—after all, he was fireproof. "It never ever occurred to me that I wouldn't be employed. Now, you may say that's arrogance, but I work hard and I generally produce the results that have to be produced, so I figure guys like me can get jobs."

The Days had just returned to their flat in suburban Quebec City after spending Christmas in Hantsport when Day's mother called from Halifax with a message: "John Gardiner wants you to phone."

It was a replay of 1971, but Day was older and had accumulated more scars and more seasoning. Much had happened since he had left the United Kingdom. In 1977, Parliament had finally passed the bill nationalizing the shipbuilding industry, and British Shipbuilders had emerged as the repository for most of it. But it was a troubled albatross right out of the chute, as the financial picture worsened—in the industry and in the British economy.

And there had been a tsunami of political change. After a winter of discontent, when labour troubles brought the country to its knees, a desperate electorate had turned to Margaret Thatcher's Conservatives in the national election of 1979, defeating the Labour government of Jim Callaghan. It was, Thatcher believed, a mandate for change.

The Cammell Laird yard was part of the nationalized company, but John Gardiner was not involved. He was building the non-shipyard assets into a successful conglomerate under the umbrella of the Laird Group. One day, he was chatting with a senior public servant who had known Graham Day during the difficult year of the nationalization committee. The bureaucrat asked, "Where is Graham Day?" He added that he thought Day was a very good man. Gardiner, noting that British Shipbuilders was in dire straits, suggested he ring up Day that afternoon and ask him to fly to London.

Gardiner called his old friend's number and urged Day to come and hear what the government had to say. The idea was that he would clean up British Shipbuilders, then privatize it—a project perhaps better suited to Day's economic world view. Day proved receptive. He recalls saying to Gardiner, "It's like chicken soup—it can't hurt." Graham Day was soon on a plane to London, primed for his next adventure.

CHAPTER 10

The Privatizer

Colette Bowe was a fast-rising young public servant entrusted with the care and feeding of Britain's ailing shipbuilding industry. In the early 1980s, she led a team in Whitehall—the nerve centre of the British public service—working on a bill to privatize the sprawling, industry-encompassing octopus known as British Shipbuilders. One afternoon, suddenly appearing at her office without an appointment was a tall man with a North American accent, tinted glasses, and sporting what one journalist called "his misleadingly sinister Mephistophelian beard."

"Hi, I'm Graham," he said, pleasantly enough.

People were shocked. This kind of drop-in meeting was just not done in Whitehall, where formalities were the way of life. Here was this informal guy wanting to say hello to the team he would be joining as the newly minted CEO of British Shipbuilders. Bowe, still in her early thirties, already knew a little about Graham Day: that he was a prominent industrialist and a Canadian who had rescued the shipyard across the Mersey from her hometown, Liverpool. But that was about it. So there was this moment of shock, until they learned he had a particular style of working: unstuffy charm mixed with steely intelligence.

It was the beginning of a beautiful relationship. The bureaucrats of Whitehall learned to like the Canadian's mien, which was midway between British and American—informal like the Americans, but respectful of how things were done in Britain. He admired the pomp and circumstance of British public life—as long as it didn't get in the way of decision making. There were elements of British society he understood as a Canadian and a former lawyer with CP—a significant labour presence, a large and powerful public service, regional inequity, and with it a degree of condescension—but there was also the added obsession with status, schooling, and class. It never wore him down—rather, it constantly amused him and Ann.

Bowe became the point person in Day's dealings with the government. She already had a reputation in the macho world of shipbuilding as a young woman of grit and elegance, impeccably coiffed and stylish, who would climb over ships in various stages of construction. She was irreverent, a Liverpudlian with a loyalty to the Beatles and a deep appreciation of Cammell Laird's tradition. People like her gave Day his strong regard for British senior public servants: well educated, well briefed, well prepared, who ably served their political masters no matter of what political stripe. He also tended to like the cabinet ministers he worked with, save for one or two.

Another embodiment of the professional public servant was Peter Carey, permanent secretary of the Department of Trade and Industry, with whom Day had a history going back to the nationalization committee of 1975–76. It was Carey who set the ball rolling for Day's return to Britain and who conducted his first interview. It went well.

Next up for Day to see was the secretary of state for industry—the minister, in Canadian parlance. Norman Lamont was a fervent Thatcherite and part of a clique of Cambridge whiz kids in cabinet. It was a bizarre discussion. Lamont kept pressing to know what classification of law degree Day had obtained at Dalhousie—1, 2.1, 2.2, or 3. It was terminology used at Oxford or Cambridge, but not in Canada—and besides, Day's performance in his early years of university had been undistinguished, to say the least. Again, an attempt to pigeonhole him failed—as a Canadian, he defied categories.

It was a relief to get down to brass tacks with Colette Bowe, who negotiated the precise terms of engagement. Day asked, "Do I understand absolutely that Mrs. Thatcher, whom I only met once, wants me for this job? She doesn't know me from a hole in the ground." Bowe responded, "That's true, but she thinks she does."

Day and Gardiner had discussed the high risks involved with British Shipbuilders. It was not a long-term job, and failure was a definite possibility. The industry was in a mess. He had been a board member for a Canadian company, Misener, that had ships on order from a Scottish yard—which meant he had some knowledge of the problems.

So Day made demands that became central to his privatization dealings from that time onward. He told Bowe it would work only if he had dictatorial powers. He must be able to hire and fire everybody, with no exceptions, including the board. "I will decide who stays or who goes. The only remedy you have is you can fire me," he said. Day would be happy to keep the government informed, but there would be no second guessing. He expected ministers to stand up in Parliament in the face of opposition criticism and say they had hired him to do the job, they had confidence in him, and they would let him do it. And he wanted those assurances in writing.

All that sounded reasonable to Bowe and her political masters. It became the Day formula: if he did not perform, his political masters could fire him, but they should not undermine him. The job of turning around and privatizing an industrial giant required political will. In Britain, under Thatcher, he had that political will behind him, from Day One, so to speak. Later in life, in Ontario, he did not have it, and it went very badly.

Bowe asked about timing, and Day responded that he would have the timetable the next day. "At Shipbuilders, the government was not spoiled for choice," he acknowledges. "They had to get it done. This thing was hemorrhaging cash." The job, he decided, would take three years, and some insiders thought that was wildly optimistic. But the government agreed with his terms, as outlined in a two-page contract he drafted.

Bowe had a favour herself: she wanted to lend him a young public servant named Peter Thompson, an energetic Whitehall operative whom Bowe trusted. Day would come to trust him, too. Thompson would become the next sweeper, the new Peter Mills.

Day needed all the help he could get, given the state of the company. Here he was, fifty years old, a former railway and shipping lawyer, recently boss of shipyards in Quebec City and Liverpool. He now found himself heading thirty shipyards, with sixty thousand workers—down by about twenty thousand from 1977. The overall business was losing close to $250 million a year. It was a tall order, but he felt he could do it. He had a continuing romance with shipbuilding; he knew the industry and its people. A shipbuilding job could lure him like no other assignment. Years later, retired and living in Nova Scotia, he drove by the Halifax shipyard and told Ann that he missed it. What was it that roused those feelings? The smell of the welding. This olfactory connection was like none other Day experienced.

Little did he know, but there would be more jobs to flow out of this one at British Shipbuilders. It would be the launching pad for the Decade of Graham Day. From March 1983 to July 1993, he would be a force in changing British corporate life. He wasn't the only one, but he was instrumental. There are physical monuments to Day's tenure—the Mini car, the recovery of British carmaking ability, and a number of operating shipyards—but he also left a new way of working. He loosened up British industry, fostering a style of management that was funny, irreverent, casual, yet professional—a lot like Les Smith would have wanted.

It was the most successful decade ever for a Canadian executive on the British stage—better even than the performance of Beaverbrook, who was prone to overreach. Day ran big companies, bigger than most in Canada, to positive reviews. Yet he operated largely below the radar in North America, except in his native Maritimes. He was probably the best Canadian crisis manager ever in his ability to put out fires, turn around moribund industries, and retain the confidence of shareholders. In this case, it was usually one shareholder, the UK government, personified by the prime minister.

Thatcher needed problem-solvers like Graham Day. "At that time, the government was in search of heroes," says Graham's shipyard ally, Roger Vaughan. She had risen to power after the so-called Winter of Discontent of 1978–79, which saw 29 million working days lost to labour strife, with bodies left unburied following a gravediggers' strike and uncollected rubbish piled high in the frozen streets when garbage workers walked out.

Sunny Jim Callaghan's Labour government had bet that things would get better, and lost. It would pay the price.

Margaret Thatcher became prime minister, armed with a fierce enmity towards socialism, communism, and trade unions in general. For many, the monetarist ideas that seized the Thatcher government—high interest rates and a laissez-faire industrial policy—were not only disastrous but sadistic in their uncompromising application. But she was tossed a lifeline when Argentina invaded the faraway Falkland Islands in April 1982. The British responded with a counterpunch that recaptured the islands and set off a wave of patriotic good feeling. Day was hired to return to Britain just ahead of the election of June 1983. Canadian friends thought he was mad—Thatcher might not be re-elected. But in the wake of Falklands enthusiasm, she won a landslide victory, and Day looked very smart, even if he didn't appreciate it at the time.

The victory gave Thatcher renewed confidence to pursue her radical agenda. By 1983, she was fully committed to returning publicly owned companies to private hands. Her memoirs indicated that privatization "was fundamental to improving Britain's economic performance. But for me it was also far more than that: it was one of the central means of reversing the corrosive and corrupting effects of socialism." Through privatization, she said, "particularly the kind of privatization which leads to the widest possible share ownership by members of the public—the state's power is reduced and the power of the people enhanced." She concluded, "Just as nationalization was at the heart of the collectivist programme by which Labour Governments sought to remodel British society, so privatization is at the centre of any programme of reclaiming territory for freedom."

Thatcher's sermonizing would be greeted with cheers in many quarters, but jeers as well. Privatization was one of the central polarizing issues in British public life for a half century, and the battles are still raging. Some of the best known state-held enterprises—British Telecom, British Airways, Jaguar—were removed from public ownership. And no one knew the history better than Graham Day, the would-be nationalizer under Jim Callaghan, now the arch-privatizer under Margaret Thatcher.

Day was hired about the same time as Ian MacGregor, a tough Scottish-born American executive who had come back to run British Steel. Day was told privately that the feeling in government was that at least these two outside appointees wouldn't make things much worse. Andrew Fisher of the *Financial Times* noted in March 1983 that, "Mr. Graham Day, who takes over as chairman in September after returning from Canada, will have an awesome task in keeping the corporation afloat."

By the time September rolled around, British Shipbuilders was in even worse shape. The company encompassed illustrious names: Govan on the Clydeside, Swan Hunter at Newcastle, Vickers, Scott Lithgow, and, of course, his beloved Cammell Laird, the company he once headed and now one of the healthier yards, thanks largely to his work. Not all yards were part of Shipbuilders—Belfast's Harland & Wolff had been hived off separately—but they were all hurting. Merchant shipping was in free fall, and the yards tried to survive with military contracts. The global industry was in gaping overcapacity, and some countries continued to support their yards with massive subsidies.

Colette Bowe knew it was very challenging. The United Kingdom had once been enormously dominant in shipbuilding, and there was the feeling that it was still important. There were attempts to keep it alive through warship contracts, but there had been a failure to invest in new technology, and labour practices were out of date. Like coal, shipbuilding was a bastion of traditional working-class jobs. And, Bowe recounts, there was deep suspicion that privatization was part of a great plan to close down the industry. Her job was to get legislation in place and make sure the privatized company was properly led.

Day was central to that. The advantage was that he loved shipbuilding and he understood the challenges. He was going into an industry and a country that he knew and understood.

In Canada, Day's new job was interesting, but hardly front-page news. One of the few who covered it, the *Globe and Mail*'s London correspondent Jeffrey Simpson, noted that Day was the only Canadian running a nationalized industry in Britain and perhaps the only one running any British company of significant size. He was also the best-paid chairman and chief executive officer of a nationalized industry, earning £80,000 ($152,000) a year. Simpson noted that three thousand more jobs had recently been cut, and Day predicted another six thousand would go soon. The new boss faced more grief ahead: "A rundown in capacity, further job losses in the industry, a desperate attempt to identify those parts of the company that can survive, the probability of strikes—with headaches ahead like these, no wonder there were few shrieks when Mr. Day's salary was announced."

Day's predecessor, sixty-seven-year-old Sir Robert Atkinson, had been making only £52,000, but Sir Robert, although a great soldier in the Second World War and a patriot in his continuing service, was not a professional manager but more of a top-down martinet. He spent his years at British Shipbuilders bad-mouthing the industry, the unions, and specific troubled yards, perhaps hoping that approach would elicit more government money, but it only contributed to sinking morale and a sense of defeat.

Day had the right management resumé and some experience in British public life, but he was still a relative initiate to the corridors of power. Peter Thompson became indispensable.

At an early stage of his career, Thompson had been private secretary to Tony Benn, the dynamic radical Labour politician who was industry minister in the Harold Wilson government. Thompson loved working with Benn, just as he would love working with Norman Tebbit, the Rottweiler of the right and a fervent Thatcherite.

Thompson found unlikely connections between the two politicians and Graham Day. All had people skills and that knack of remembering the last conversation they had with someone—that maybe their mother had been ill—and they would ask about her. "They were people people, simplifiers, communicators."

Day's success was built on a lack of public ego. He was always careful to credit his ministers for the success of a plan, even when they in fact had played a less significant role than they trumpeted. And he did not centralize decisions. Thompson had worked in a structure that was hierarchical; suddenly, the new CEO was saying, "Here, Pete, you do it." (Day was the only one he permitted to call him Pete.) The company was constantly in crisis mode, and Day realized he could not put out all the fires at once.

Day valued civil servants. A lot of industrialists—those raging bulls of finance—would demand direct contact with the top, the minister. Day, however, recognized the proper channels of communication; he understood he should talk first to the senior bureaucrats whose job was to advise the minister. For their part, Thatcher's ministers wanted to see things happen in a hurry, and were impatient with the elongated deadlines of privatization. In winning over ministers, "it was not all sweetness and light," Bowe admits. "It was not a case of 'Oh, Graham Day is here and all is fine.'" Day understood that ministers sometimes would say no to his ideas, but he also talked to them in a way they had never heard: informal, direct, and funny.

Once, Day was sitting with a minister and the two were locked in an intractable discussion. "Well, Graham," the minister said, "there are a lot of balls in the air." Day shot back, "Sure, and yours and mine are up there with them." The comment defused the tension. Bowe recalls, "To this day, Graham is a revered memory for those young public servants he worked with in the trenches of privatization."

It helped to be an outsider, to be able to give this "aw-shucks, I'm just a Canadian" disclaimer, along with "you will have to explain this to me." It was a fairly novel idea that a major industrial leader would be a foreigner—even a Commonwealth foreigner—and, for God's sake, a Canadian with that infernal beard.

Unlike blockbuster stock flotations such as British Gas and British Telecom, British Shipbuilders was a one-by-one selloff of a diverse bunch of yards. Thompson remembers Day setting a strategy that, in previous years, would have led to a fight with the government. Instead, it was managed quietly behind closed doors. The government's preferred approach was to get early wins by selling off the best shipyards first. But Day insisted on keeping the best for last and packaging them up with the ones that wouldn't sell as readily. The desirable yards would be a kind of lifeboat for the ones that didn't float as easily.

He pushed this plan through the proper channels. Says Thompson, "I got officials to see that that was the right strategy. Then the officials persuaded ministers that it was the right strategy."

The temptation might have been to try to fix everything at once, but Day developed a practical approach. He made a list of things to do, then focused first on the three most important of them. When one job was done, he would move another one up to the top three. Some things he could not defer were assigned to other people. "He didn't abdicate decisions, but he empowered you to get on with it," Thompson says.

Another thing Thompson learned was to take time every day to reflect. "Are we going in the right direction? Are we focusing on the right things? If you were firefighting fifty things at once, you wouldn't necessarily have time for reflection, so he would build it in."

The firefighting started early enough. In November 1983, the *Financial Times* outlined the challenges, pointing out: "It was shaping up as a tough week for Mr Graham Day, the blunt-spoken extrovert who runs British Shipbuilders." Just two months after Day took over as chairman, the industry was threatened with a national strike over pay, and an oil rig order worth nearly £90 million also seemed set for cancellation. But after fourteen hours of talks, Day announced that the strike threat had been lifted by the promise of extra pay in return for improvements in productivity. It was a breakthrough, and it was followed by a couple of big ship orders. In gaining the deal, Day told the *Financial Times*, "confrontation is non-productive. I've never felt any need to make any macho gestures." If the talks had broken down and a strike had been called, he would have had to respect the unions' decision.

Through these talks and others with unions, one of his strong supporters was his old colleague, Roger Vaughan, now a senior manager in charge of productivity for Shipbuilders. Vaughan was no great fan of Thatcher—he found her cruelly heedless of the value of industry in the nation's fabric—but he hailed the return of Graham Day.

"It was a question of getting [union leaders] on board because their heads were where the industry had been," Vaughan says. The goal was more flexible, multidisciplinary work that broke down barriers between trades. One turning point was taking a group of labour leaders on a study trip to Japan to see the competitive challenges from the new flexible workplace. It was a case of adapt or die. "They fairly quickly saw the light, and we got a new deal with them," Vaughan says. "The problem then was getting existing shipyard management to take advantage of what they could do."

Day also had to talk tough with some customers. Within the first week, he undid some of the decisions his predecessor had taken the week before. He told customers that they should tear up the agreements and sign new ones or he would walk away. The company simply could not avoid it. He knew his mandate—the government was the owner, but the government couldn't afford shipbuilding anymore. It wanted to take some cash from privatization, but the essential task was to staunch the bleeding from high costs and heavy losses.

The mechanisms of privatization were straightforward. Day's team would develop offering memorandums, which provided the details of the shipyard or plant for sale. But he did not trust the usual suspects to prepare the documents. The auditing firm, for example, would be very defensive about the financial numbers it had signed off on. "I believed that they had taken a more generous view of outcomes than I would have taken," Day says. Because they had too much credibility at stake, Day concluded that the auditors should not prepare the offering memorandums. Instead, Day reached back into his Canadian network. He remembered that, at Davie shipyard, he had been impressed by the Quebec accounting firm they had used, so he phoned its affiliate in London and set up a fast meeting. The firm was on the job the next day. "And so they tackled the privatization's offering memorandums, yard by yard by yard."

Similarly, Day looked to hit the ground running with financial advisors. He retained Lazard Frères, whose chair was Sir John Nott, secretary of state for defence during the Falklands War. Day did not seek competitive proposals; he simply picked the firm he wanted, knowing it lacked conflicts and could do the job. The approach performed well.

Meanwhile, Colette Bowe and her colleagues admired Day's easy way with people. He was a storehouse of great quips, gleaned from a combination of an education in the classics and history, modern pop, and sports allusions, and an agile memory. John DeMont, a Halifax journalist and author, once wrote that Day in his conversation "peppers his words with the thoughts of English viscounts, Harvard psychologists, hard-eyed trade unionists and steel-spined generals."

Some of the Whitehall dialogue had the sense of being lifted from the scripts of the hilarious British TV series *Yes, Minister*. Bowe remembers a meeting she had with Day and Norman Lamont in which a difficult decision was being hashed out. Day wanted to keep the conversation on track, and commented, "You know, Norman, sometimes when you are up to your ass in alligators, you forget you are here to clean out the swamp." A senior civil servant guffawed, leaned back in his chair, and fell back on the floor, splintering the chair beneath him. The aphorism became legendary in the halls of power.

But Bowe also got a view of the self-discipline. On one trip to Clydeside in Scotland, Day's perpetual dislike for clutter was on display. As he was looking around the Yarrow yard, he saw a pile of rubbish and asked why it was there. It turned out the guy who was supposed to clean it up was absent that day, and it wasn't anyone else's job. Day's response: "Give me the goddamn broom." He promptly swept up the mess.

He made allies in unexpected places. Costas Grammenos is a Greek-born academic who grew up in a family of army officers but went to work for a bank in Athens. He became a specialist in shipping finance and, in the early 1980s, having shifted to academia, was pioneering a new program in maritime finance at City, University of London. Someone said he should meet Graham Day, the boss of British Shipbuilders. It was a fast friendship. Day could see the value of Grammenos's fledgling program, and the young academic could count on Day's support at fundraising gatherings and conferences. "He was good with implementation and action," Grammenos says. "There was not a lot of discussion; once he said 'yes,' it happened. In my view he was one of the very influential people in creating this program."

Day was unfailingly polite most times, but he had a way of cutting through the underbrush. He was different from many of the Britons Grammenos had encountered. He was straightforward: in the middle of one public meeting full of posturing, the Canadian suddenly interjected with "horseshit." The room went silent. He had made his point.

The City, University of London program has attracted students from 155 nations, and its 3,700 graduates include many of the world's top shipping people. One is a son of Paul Martin, the Canadian politician whose earlier business career was highlighted by his acquisition of Canada Steamship Lines.

Not all Britons were impressed with the Day persona. Some union leaders found him cold-blooded, as reflected in Hazel Duffy's profile in the *Financial Times* in February 1987. "Graham Day? He's a dessicated calculating machine," said one shipbuilding union leader, borrowing the words of the Labour Party's firebrand Aneurin Bevan describing a more moderate colleague. The unionist said, "You can have a perfectly pleasant chat with him, but I think he looks at everything in purely arithmetical terms."

Despite, perhaps because of, the progress on labour-saving productivity changes, union leaders continued to take an adversarial stance—no surprise in an industry under attack and in which job numbers were declining. A BBC-TV documentary quoted Jim Murray, head of the union negotiating committee, describing Day as "secretive and aloof." The unions, he charged, were kept in the dark about his plans for the industry. The BBC filmed the response from Day, looking rather severe with his heavy, grey-flecked black beard and shaded glasses. "Horseshit," he retorted, once again using that epithet, but now on national TV. He said he had told the negotiating committee shortly after his arrival about his mandate for productivity and privatization.

Day was never able to shake the perception, held by many unionists, that he was a cold fish whose only passion lay in bottom-line numbers. Some labour leaders also grasped, however, that a technocratic professional manager would be a considerable improvement over the incompetent amateurs who had made a mess of their industries. Day once told the *Times*: "I've always had difficulty saying 'Here's the line: we're the good guys and you're the bad guys.' The trade unions were absolutely essential to this country." He also felt that "there are no bad soldiers, only bad officers. When business is bad, always start weeding out at the top."

Day ended up touching a lot of people. He helped Peter Thompson make the leap from civil servant to businessman by backing Thompson's attending the Harvard Business School executive program. After a sterling career in business, Thompson became a successful executive coach, building on his experience of leading under pressure. In 2016, he was approaching retirement and looking forward to his new role as expert garden composter.

John Gardiner had a great career as one of the less heralded business heroes of the Thatcher era, one who did not get knighted but probably should have; Graham Day would join the board of Gardiner's Laird Group. Costas Grammenos went on to be a thought leader in shipping and ship finance.

Colette Bowe became an interesting footnote in the history of the Thatcher era. By 1985, she had become the information officer in the Department of Trade and Industry, headed by Thatcher favourite Leon Brittan. At the time, the government was embroiled in a crisis centring on a familiar topic, the country's commitment to Europe. It involved a small military helicopter company called Westland, which was about to be acquired by US defence interests. Michael Heseltine, then defence secretary, was an ardent Europhile who wanted the deal squelched. The issue split the cabinet as Heseltine pursued his vision with messianic zeal, pitting him against Thatcher and Leon Brittan.

The Thatcher team quietly commissioned a legal opinion on the role of the defence minister from the solicitor-general, whose status was somewhat above the fray of politics. The opinion was framed in the form of a letter from the solicitor-general highly critical of Heseltine, which was leaked to the press. The aim was to humiliate a government colleague. In the uproar that followed, Bowe took the fall, identified as the person who leaked it.

More than thirty years later, Bowe—now Dame Colette Bowe—is still a disciple of Graham Day. She long ago shrugged off her moment as a sacrificial lamb and built an impressive resumé as a financial and commercial regulator. In 2014, she became the chair of Britain's Banking Standards Board, which aims at improving the culture of banking to serve the public. She once told a newspaper that she did not believe in management gurus, but that she did have a management hero: Graham Day. That view never changed.

The Thatcher government was impressed with Day's progress at British Shipbuilders. He was far ahead of schedule in cleaning up and selling off the yards. The selloff had reduced the nationalized company to a shadow of its former self. Then Day embarked on a series of cryptic meetings with Minister of State for Industry Peter Morrison, the MP for Chester—the seat Day had once been approached to contest. Thatcher had two big problems in state-owned industries. One was coal—a nasty labour situation; the other was cars—also difficult, but not as bitterly contested. Day remembers Morrison saying, "She wants to move you." Morrison asked, if Day were to leave Shipbuilders, would it be in good hands? Day said privatization was on target after two years, and he could be replaced with a capable executive who could finish the process. But Day warned that his wife would not live with him if he were to end up trying to sort out the unseemly coal mess.

So cars it would be. Ian MacGregor moved from British Steel to British Coal, which, as Day expected, turned out to be a dark hole of pain and strife. Day left British Shipbuilders a year ahead of schedule and, on May 1, 1986, moved over to the state-controlled automaker British Leyland. Asked by a reporter why the government was always tapping him for controversial assignments, Day quipped, "I am not sure whether I attract them, they attract me, or we simply find each other in the dark."

This time, emotionally, politically, economically, the stakes would be even higher. But, as one public servant told him, he was now considered to be "safe hands."

CHAPTER 11

Rover Unleashed

Graham Day had scarcely arrived at British Leyland's head office in May 1986 when his public relations manager remarked, "You have to go to Paris for a car show." A what? "An automobile trade show."

So the newly installed CEO hustled off to Paris to show the flag, press some flesh, and get to know his French managers. Immediately, the head of Leyland's French operations said he had a beef with him. "Why are you cancelling the production of the Mini?" he asked Day. "It's the one thing we're doing well with here."

Day was flabbergasted—he knew nothing about it. The Frenchman indicated it had been in the cards for a couple of months. "Didn't Musgrove tell you?"

"Musgrove" was the imperious Harold Musgrove, one of the legends of British carmaking, the hard-bitten chairman of the Austin Rover Group and a man who now supposedly reported to Graham Day. And the Mini was the little box-like car that, as Day knew, was a bestseller not only in France, but also in far-flung markets such as Japan, where its agility in small spaces was desirable. (Day used to say that *Parisiennes*, who loved the Mini for the city's congested streets, were particularly attached to it. In Paris's overpopulated *rues*, people didn't so much park the car as abandon it, he said.) The Mini was a British icon, one of the most popular cars the benighted national automaker Austin had ever produced. Day had a soft spot for small, odd, cult-inspiring cars, such as the Citroën *deux chevaux* and his beloved VW Beetles. And there was a special family connection with the Mini: Ann Day had owned a Mini estate wagon for knocking around Birkenhead.

However, there were design headaches involving a new engine and challenges on the panel fit, and, apparently, unknown to the new CEO, the whole car was on the chopping block.

Day returned to the Leyland head office and contacted Musgrove, who had started working at Leyland as a fifteen-year-old on the production line and now, in his mid-fifties, was head of Austin Rover and famously protective of his turf. Day recalls asking Musgrove what the big state secret was about the Mini. Musgrove dismissed it as an operational matter that the new CEO really didn't need to know about. Day recalls saying, "Harold, the Mini is not being cancelled." When Musgrove protested that Day didn't know what he was doing, Day again insisted that the Mini was not to be cancelled, adding that the next move would be to go to the design studio and start on a new version of the car.

The survival of the Mini is one of Day's most visible accomplishments. BMW, the car's current manufacturer, sells more than three hundred thousand Mini Coopers a year, up from forty thousand in Day's era. Most of the cars are built in the Oxford-area factory where Austin Rover models were once built. The redesigned Mini is still that cube-like cult vehicle, now beloved of urban hipsters. Since Day saved the Mini, millions have been sold worldwide—not a mass market success, but a niche car aimed at an upscale market.

The incident spoke to a deeper cultural problem at British Leyland. The company was run by a cabal of entrenched senior managers who, he believed, concealed information from him, intentionally deceived him, and failed to tackle the essential issues that dogged Leyland. At British Shipbuilders, Day had had instant credibility because in a way he had come from the industry. But at Leyland, there was downright hostility towards this Canadian outsider who allegedly knew nothing about cars. There was a feeling of "we know best" and the lawyer-executive at the top of the company should just keep out of operations, out of marketing, out of engineering—basically, out of day-to-day management. But that was not how Graham Day, that disciple of Les Smith, ran a company.

The passive-aggressive resistance by senior management was Day's first big test on taking the CEO's job on May 1, 1986. In an interview with the *Financial Times* on his first day, he refuted suggestions that he was a hatchet man: "I think in the past I have been able to save jobs—although never as many as one would have liked. I also think that what I have done, wherever possible, is to preserve the preservable jobs." Questioned about the possibility of changes within Leyland's senior management, Day said, "We don't have to like each other, but we have to have an effective working relationship. I look for professionalism and confidence." He did not find it. On September 25, less than five months after Day joined, Rover announced the departure of Musgrove and two other senior executives. Another two had exited earlier. The surgical decapitation of senior management was known in the press as "the Night of the Long Knives."

It's a wonder it took so long. The company Day joined was a mess, the product of a clumsy merger between truck company Leyland and carmaker Austin Rover, which turned out a stew of brands from Leyland trucks to the venerable Land Rover and Range Rover to mass market Austins and the precious little Minis and MGs. There was no clear strategy of brand building, and the company was seeing its share of the British auto market eroding away. Owned almost entirely by the government, the company was being kept alive by public money, but lacked the necessary investment in technology, including robotics, that was revolutionizing the global car industry. Its labour practices were outmoded, but its prospects for change were being blocked by obdurate unions and uninspired management. It had swallowed up well over £3 billion of government funding, and more probably would be needed. Prime Minister Thatcher wanted desperately to staunch the flow and get it off her hands. In her memoirs, she concluded that "[t]he company had become a symbol of Britain's industrial decline and of trade union bloody mindedness." About the only thing that seemed to be working for Leyland was a burgeoning alliance with Japan's Honda to co-develop car models.

Day arrived in the middle of a crisis for the Thatcher government, when Leyland was negotiating to sell its car division to US automaker Ford. The news leaked, causing a storm of protest against selling to a foreign buyer that would strip away British production and jobs. Tory MPs, particularly in marginal ridings in the West Midlands, where Leyland had a factory presence, rebelled and forced the government to walk away from the Ford deal. Also under attack was another negotiation to sell the truck and Land Rover business, potentially to General Motors. And yet, there did not seem to be any alternative to a foreign buyer to secure the company's future. When the government backed down under this onslaught, the *Times* commented that "the government has run for cover, leaving the state still owning, in this seventh year of Thatcherism, a car company which continues to make losses despite £3.8 billion in subsidies from the taxpayer."

Could Graham Day pull off a recovery at cash-devouring Leyland? He gave no hint of a lack of confidence. As he said to a Canadian journalist, "I must tell you, and I wouldn't want to give an impression of arrogance, I actually don't contemplate failure."

As he sized up the situation, Day pledged Thatcher that she would need to put no new public money into Rover, although she still had to deal with the company's historical debt, including government-guaranteed bank loans. He hoped Rover could fund future capital needs on its own, and pay down bank loans as profits and asset sales materialized. And he succeeded.

A big factor was the shifting labour scene. Day actually would benefit from the spadework of Musgrove and other senior managers under the previous CEO, South African Michael Edwardes. In the 1970s, the vast British Leyland factory at Longbridge, Birmingham, had become a byword for wildcat walkouts, union militancy, and industrial chaos; indeed, its dysfunction had helped clear Margaret Thatcher's path to political power. For many years, the factory was in the grip of radical agitators led by Derek Robinson, nicknamed Red Robbo, signifying his reputation as an unregenerate communist. Robinson was a union officer at Longbridge and a troublemaker. The BBC observed that, between 1978 and 1979, Red Robbo alone was credited with causing 523 walkouts at British Leyland, at a cost of an estimated £200 million in lost production.

In 1979, Edwardes and his managers had averted what would have been a damaging strike, but Robinson continued to attack management in a pamphlet he distributed. The communist organizer was promptly sacked. When a strike ballot was held on the issue, his dismissal was upheld by an overwhelming vote of unionists. It signalled the end of communist domination at the plant and the rise of a new generation of union leaders at Longbridge and elsewhere who were more realistic about what could be achieved and more committed to improving, not impeding, the production process. Day would benefit.

After Edwardes left Leyland in 1982, he wrote a memoir about his time there called *Back from the Brink*. But it was not back far enough: the company was still losing truckloads of money, and the team he had left in charge was ill-equipped to change that. After Musgrove was dismissed in September 1986, Malcolm Brown of the *Times* observed that he was "one of the headbashing school" whose talents had been sorely needed in the late 1970s when the biggest challenge was taking on Red Robbo. But times had changed, Brown wrote. "[Graham] Day may look and even sound like an autocrat, but behind the tough words is a very shrewd strategic thinker." Brown concluded with a harsh judgment: "Musgrove's problem is that behind his autocratic mask is an autocrat. He was the man for the hour, but the hour has passed."

This set the tone for change as Day pulled the company out of the clutches of the old guard—some of them engineers and deeply protective of their status and their knowledge—and put it in the hands of professional managers who took their cues from the customer. He opened the doors to new ideas about quality, training, and technology, and he made it a marketing company, flourishing on the basis of its best brands. Concluding that he could not compete with the international auto giants on price, he moved the company upmarket, betting its future increasingly on high-end consumers, not the mass markets of the past.

There were still valuable pieces—not just the Mini, but also the much admired Land Rover and Range Rover lines.

Another venerable brand, Jaguar, had already been spun off in a management buyout under the direction of Thatcher favourite John Egan. But inside Rover, that left the dinosaurs of unloved Austin cars and factories that were almost untouchable because they sat in these marginal constituencies.

Fortunately, Day was able to bring with him from British Shipbuilders a couple of loyalists in Peter Thompson, his latest sweeper, and John Pullen, an ex-RAF fighter pilot and capable public relations man. He also found the equivalent of Colette Bowe in Catherine Bell, a bright senior civil servant with rich experience in the car industry. Bell recognized that Day had the advantage of sensitivity to British politics and a clear direction from the prime minister's office. "He had a sort of baton in his hand from Mrs. Thatcher to be as radical as required—to take this Leviathan off the taxpayers' hands and move forward."

Day's reputation began to grow, and both friends and enemies helped it along. Shortly after the Night of the Long Knives, Labour MP Ronald Brown rose in the House of Commons to say, "Surely it has to be admitted that Graham Day, the slick lawyer from Canada, the undertaker of British Shipbuilders, was brought in to destroy the [auto] industry rather than to build it up. That is the real issue that is at stake. Let us admit that Mr. Day is a hatchet man for the Conservative Government." Paul Channon, the Tory industry minister, noted that Day was first employed by the Labour party when it was in government in the mid-1970s. He had a sheaf of quotations containing glowing tributes to him, including some from leading Labour politicians. "If the House wants me to do so, I can read out those tributes." That thread of opposition questioning was dropped.

With the government's backing, he looked at Rover with a fresh eye. The truck and van business would go; after some dallying with GM, it was the Dutch truck maker DAF that bought the unit. He sold off a dozen businesses that he felt were extraneous to Rover's core business. But what about cars? Market share, particularly for the mainstream vehicles, was under attack, and the factories were wallowing in massive overcapacity. Day needed a rethink, and approached the company's ad agency to analyze how the brands fared with customers.

The analysis complete, Day's team attended a briefing where they received a summary. The ad man flashed some slides on a screen. When the beleaguered Austin cars came up, the conclusion was: "If you're between fifty-five and dead, you are a customer or a potential customer." That said it all. It was not a brand with a lot of growth potential. As for the MG, it was much loved, but a niche product only. It was much the same with the Mini: a loyal following, but nothing you could take to the bank.

Then came the 4 x 4s, Land Rover and Range Rover, the parts of the company making money. The more utilitarian Land Rover had two basic markets: the wealthy farmer group and military customers, including a kind of vehicle you could drop by parachute into a war zone. The Range Rover was a premium, higher-end vehicle. The Rovers came out as "middle-class aspirational" brands in the survey. That was what Day wanted to hear, and he switched the focus of the company over to Rover, including the introduction of new models under the Rover name. The company was no longer Leyland—now shorn of its Leyland truck baggage, it would be the Rover Group.

Day saw changes he could make right away. You could sell only so many Range and Land Rovers domestically. To raise production volumes and gain market traction abroad, he needed a line extension. That became Discovery, an SUV that was slightly below the market niche for the Land Rover, and it provided the necessary volumes. "We made money from day one on Discovery," he says, and it remains a mainstay Rover product.

Graham Day, student at Quinpool Road School, 1940s.

The thespian Graham Day, left, in the Dalhousie theatre production of *Iolanthe*, 1952.

JUDSON GRAHAM DAY
Halifax, N. S.
"Ambition has not any risk."

Graham came to Dal in '51 from Q.E.H.S. and after spending two years in an attempt to become liberally educated, entered the Law school in '53. He has sung major roles in four Gilbert and Sullivan operas, been Secretary and President of the Glee Club, directed the music for three Glee Club revues and the radio program "Music from Dalhousie". This year Graham succeeded to the position of Musical Director for the Glee Club, taking over from Prof. Hamer. In this capacity he produced "The Mikado."

The ambitious graduate of Dalhousie Law School, as chronicled in the 1956 yearbook.

The young troubleshooter takes over Merseyside's Cammell Laird shipyard in 1971. The ship in the background, *M. V. Letchworth*, launched on October 5, 1971, the first merchant ship in ten years to make money at Cammell Laird.

Mrs. Ellen "Nellie" Smith, Cammell Laird's longest serving female employee, has the honour of launching a ship, with Day as escort.

The Rover mission, as seen by Colin Whittock, cartoonist, *Birmingham Evening Mail* in May 1985.

Margaret Thatcher reviews the latest Rover while her husband, Denis, inspects the wheels before taking it for a test drive at Chequers.

Guiding His Royal Highness the Prince of Wales (second left) on a tour of the Longbridge Rover plant, 1987.

Dr. Day, upon receiving his honorary degree from Dalhousie, 1987.

A newly dubbed Sir Graham with Lady Day outside Buckingham Palace, 1989.

Edie and Frank Day at Herring Cove, 1930.

The Day family at Pink Beach, Bermuda, 2001. Left to right: Graham, Ann, Michael, Deborah, and Donna.

A man of many hats: Sir Graham reviewing officers at the Royal Military Academy, Sandhurst, United Kingdom.

Day's installation as Chancellor of Dalhousie University, with Allan Shaw (right), chair of the board of governors, 1994.

Day (right) signing on with West Nova Scotia Regiment, 2005.

A pilgrimage to the East London house where Graham's father, Frank, grew up.

Catherine Bell says that, in the marketing of Rover, Day brought an international perspective that included knowledge of North America, where Rover would make inroads. The industry had been run, she says, by enthusiastic engineers, and it is vital to have great engineers, but Day was a professional manager who could see the bigger picture. He could envision where the 4 x 4 market was going. "We saw muddy Land Rovers in farmers' fields, but look at it now," Bell says. More Land Rovers can be spied in the posh lanes of London's Mayfair and Belgravia than in mucky barnyards in Yorkshire and East Anglia. Day grasped that trend and ran with it.

As at Cammell Laird, Day discovered a woefully underskilled workforce. Many employees needed skills upgrading in areas such as calculus in order to be retrained in new technology and, at the other end, there was a need to remediate the poor quality of school leavers. "You faced a situation in cars where you were trying to get a fifty-year-old man to understand the calculus that is driving a three- or five-axis milling machine. That is a challenge, but you have to try," he recalls.

Rover sent qualified employees into schools to teach subjects the schools had difficulty handling. It embarked on in-house instruction to enable employees to secure nationally recognized qualifications. Rover and Rolls-Royce Engines built a dedicated manufacturing engineering building on the University of Warwick campus, and the university worked with the two firms to deliver a master's degree in manufacturing engineering. Rover, for several years on a per employee basis, was the largest spender on training in the European Union.

This is where Day was grateful for a new generation of workers and their union leaders, who would accept and even embrace training changes. "The Second World War union leaders with Marxist leanings were being gradually replaced by a younger, better educated, more pragmatic leadership." As a result, Rover was able to move its basis for pay to skills acquired, rather than skills deployed. Over time, as individual employees expanded their skills and their pay, Rover could deploy them on a variety of tasks.

In all he did, Day tried to advance women to supervisory and leadership roles. The media became interested in Day's improvements, and the company would give tours. On one occasion, reporters came upon an area where workers were involved in the process of stuffing engines in cars. A reporter looked at his watch and noticed a young woman standing there: "Excuse me, are you providing the tea?" Day remembers the scene. "This big guy had his head inside an engine compartment and he looks at this guy: 'Tea, my ass. She's the boss.'"

Day realized that a key to the turnaround was for Rover employees to regain pride in their business. He talked with one woman on the trim line who was embarrassed by the Rover image. She and her husband would walk down to the pub on a Friday night and face a barrage of snide remarks. The joke was that Rover employees just clocked in—they might as well have signed the visitors' book.

But the new marketing push was turning opinion around. One Christmas, the company released an ad showing a stately house with guests arriving for a Yuletide party. Two parked Minis eye each other and come together, their bumpers just about touching. The romantic message: "Minis have feelings, too." The day after the campaign launched, Day walked out to talk again to the woman on the trim line: "Did you see the new ad?" She had. On Friday night, as usual, she and her husband had gone to the pub. "All our friends were all talking about the ad. Do you have any idea what that means to me?"

Day paid a lot of attention to production values. One inheritance from the old management was a new saloon car model under development called the Sterling. The launch was approaching, and a television ad shoot was scheduled for beautiful, barren Iceland. But Day was not impressed by the producer. He knew someone who could make this work. He put through a call to Toronto and got in touch with Manny Pittson, his old producer at *Singalong Jubilee*. Pittson flew to Iceland to produce the ad. Gillian Perry, who was dating Pittson at the time, remembers that Pittson had just proposed to her, but he dropped everything to help out his old friend. She forgave Day. The wedding happened, and she found Day to be "a very interesting man."

Day told the British crew and ad agency that Pittson alone had the production authority, and when shooting went ahead, he would come to London and decide what footage to use. The car took longer than expected to get right—a full eighteen months—but the ad was highly successful. (Manny Pittson died in 2013.)

Early in his Rover tenure, Day announced he would set up with a small team in central London, although the rest of the corporate group would remain at head office in west London. The core group bonded as it suffered the ups and downs of running Rover. When things were going badly, they gathered for lunch at a fish and chips place behind nearby Victoria Station. When they were going well, it was the posh dining room at the Goring Hotel. Day, Bell says, "had the ability to make the very difficult into fun."

Shortly after joining Rover, Day got a call from a senior bureaucrat, offering to lend him a mid-ranked young woman manager for six months. Her name was Frances Elliott, and she had worked in the Irish Office, had been through a stressful situation, and needed a change. Elliott came with great credentials, including a double first in languages from Oxford. She would become a key part of Day's small chairman's office. She decided not to return to the bureaucracy; instead Day sent her to INSEAD, the Institut européen d'administration des affaires, in France for a crash course in finance and accounting. She became the key negotiator when Rover finalized its joint venture arrangement with Honda. The Honda people in Japan referred to her as "your Frances," and in an unusual tribute to a woman gave her a pearl brooch at the deal's closing dinner.

After two years, when it was clear Elliott enjoyed business, Day told her she should work for someone else, and arranged for her to join Thorn EMI, the big music company, where he was a director. Later, she was recruited for a top public affairs job at Tesco, the supermarket chain. Day kept tabs on her after he returned to Canada. She had married a prominent journalist and was doing well. Then he learned she had been diagnosed with motor neuron disease. She declined rapidly, and died at age forty-six. Day chokes up today as he describes how she remains a stirring example of the young people, including many women, he encouraged in their careers. Her death "left a mark on him," Ann Day says.

As with previous assignments, Day worked well with the cabinet ministers he served, including Paul Channon and Lord Young, an affable former businessman who was another Thatcher favourite. Day knew when to advise, when to step back, and when to duck the limelight, giving the minister the opportunity to take credit. The *Financial Times*' Hazel Duffy noted that Day's critics emphasized the cold mathematical manager, but she wrote that "it is difficult to reconcile this characterisation of Day with the polite warmth—familiar, but not cringingly chummy—which he extends to the media, and, it is said, to ministers." Duffy quoted an unnamed observer who said that Day "weaves a web of charm" around cabinet ministers.

That web extended to the most important minister of all, the one who occupied 10 Downing Street. His relationship with Margaret Thatcher would be the ultimate test of what he had learned in Canada and the United Kingdom about leading and following.

CHAPTER 12

Mrs. Thatcher and Mr. Day

"Now, Mr. Day, you sit here."

Graham Day remembers those words from one of the first times he was summoned to 10 Downing Street. He had regularly met with the prime minister during his stint at British Shipbuilders, but the meetings would be more frequent and intense at Leyland. It represented, to Thatcher, the failure of top-down British industrial policy and labour intransigence. Leyland also had large implications for British trade and employment and, until Day's arrival, had been a money pit for the government. So she paid a lot of attention to it.

They met in her sitting room, and Thatcher pointed to the chair at her left. Henceforth, he would sit in that chair. She proceeded to grill him on his plans to turn the auto company around. The questions were very specific, but he was new in his job and he had to give general answers: "I don't know about that yet." "Here are the things I think are the most important." "These are the things I'm drilling down on." But she was impatient, pointing out that Leyland's previous bosses had constantly asked for money for things that never panned out.

He admitted he wasn't sure where the exact truth lay. Maybe in the next couple of months he would know, and then he would tell her. "Whatever I tell you, even if I'm wrong, it will be what I believe to be the truth," he remembers saying.

He came out of the session shell-shocked. About a month later, there was another meeting at No. 10—the same tough questioning about detailed projections. Emerging from the relentless assault, Day asked the civil servant accompanying him if he would face this kind of beating every time. The bureaucrat doubted there would be another meeting like this. Day should understand, he said, that her greatest fear was that he would tell her what he thought she wanted to hear, not what Day believed. "She may not agree with what you believe, but she is desperate to know what you really believe."

He passed the test. He never faced another grilling of that intensity, and Thatcher came to appreciate the wry Canadian who told the truth. It was a durable relationship of mutual admiration and respect that continued through the most important decade of Graham Day's life.

They were an odd couple: a shopkeeper's daughter from the Midlands who had taken chemistry at Oxford and been drawn into Conservative politics; and a shopkeeper's son from Halifax who combined a smooth baritone voice with a love of opera and the arts. But to the British establishment, he was, like her, an outsider. The upper echelons of British government and business were dominated by old boys from public schools (private schools, in Canadian terminology), graduates of elite Oxford and Cambridge, and members of the best clubs. She was an Oxford grad, but not one of them. And he was a rough-hewn colonial.

The men Thatcher enlisted to run the state companies often hailed from outside the classic establishment mould. John King (British Airways), Ian MacGregor (British Coal), John Egan (Jaguar) were bootstrap business people, not to the manor born. And she trusted them to run their companies. Whereas she was often a micro-manager of government decision making, she stayed mostly out of Day's way once he had won her trust.

Day had spent his life looking for a leader like this, someone who would assign him a task and step back to let him accomplish it. To be a good leader, you must also know how to be a follower, and he got very good at managing up. He could put her at ease. He was not her most high-profile industrialist—King and Egan shone a bit more brightly—but perhaps that is what she liked about him: he did not screw up, and thus avoided embarrassing headlines.

Not everyone found the Thatcher style to their taste: the great head of hair, the withering contempt for fools, the high-pitched voice, sometimes grating, sometimes inspirational, the tendency to ream someone out with exquisite brutality. She always carried a handbag, so a verbal attack by the prime minister became known as handbagging. Yet there was something seductive about her. Thus the famous quote, "She has the lips of Marilyn Monroe and the eyes of Caligula." The line was attributed to French president François Mitterrand, who understood the politics of power, in government and in the bedroom.

Thatcher could be extraordinarily kind to underlings, but she could turn on her closest cabinet colleagues. In the end, she drove many of them into the arms of party rebels, which helped spur her downfall. The image of heartlessness—deserved or not—was one that lingered. Even people who liked her general thrust felt that the monetarist policies of the Conservative government had unduly savaged manufacturing, leaving a wasteland in the old areas of the Industrial Revolution. And she didn't seem to care. Anyone who resisted her radical prescriptions was dismissed as "wet." Her judgment of individuals often came down to one question: "Is he one of us?" Day became "one of us."

Her stubborn refusal to bend was infuriating to her detractors. The miners' strike of 1984–85 was a major test, and she would not budge. The miners capitulated and returned to work, leaving a bitter taste that still lingers. The musical *Billy Elliot*, the tale of a plucky miner's son who overcomes his mother's death and class prejudices to become a ballet dancer, became a hit movie and, as a play, ran for eleven years in London's West End. Even in 2016, audiences cheered its anti-Thatcher sentiments, still applauding the lyrics: "Merry Christmas Maggie Thatcher / We all celebrate today / 'Cause it's one day closer to your death."

Day appreciated that Thatcher could mete out rough justice, test people for their judgment, and, if they fell short, cut them down with a comment. Day saw this happen with a member of the Policy Unit, a group of people recruited from private industry to advise the prime minister on policy. A stunningly confident and well-educated young man had just been plucked out of the mining industry to join the Unit. New to his job, the fellow was preparing a briefing file on Rover before a meeting with Thatcher. Catherine Bell, an official from the Department of Trade and Industry with deep expertise in the area, offered to help prepare the file. No need, the young man huffily declined. He had it all in hand.

The day of the meeting, Day took his customary seat; the young man sat opposite. The prime minister, as was her custom, zeroed in on one item in her new policy advisor's briefing. Turning to Day, she said, "Now, I understand you want to spend £25 million to do this." Day replied that, no, he did not want to spend it for that particular purpose—he was intending something entirely different. Day calmly explained how the money was being generated and how it was being spent. Thatcher looked at the young man, closed the file, and disdainfully let it drop to the floor. She said to him, "You can leave." According to Day, "I never saw him again."

Day enjoyed the execution because he had such a strong regard for public servants, and he abhorred the arrogance of refusing the offer of help. "Why would you not have someone else give you their comments, even if it were horseshit?" he says, bewildered.

As time went on, he would be called in to advise Thatcher just ahead of Prime Minister's Questions in the House. Often, the conversation ranged beyond Rover to his views on industrial and economic policy. The nature of the relationship changed, reflected in her willingness to kick off her shoes and have a drink. Whatever the issue, she might ask what he thought of it. One day, near the beginning of their relationship, she began by saying, "Now, Mr Day." He suggested that he call her Prime Minister and she call him Graham. She smiled broadly, saying that would work. At that point, he felt the relationship was one with a future. Although she was disdainful of lavish ceremony, he treated her with a certain courtliness that she found appealing.

His role was to keep her and her office aware of any events that might end up in the public domain. For example, there was the launch of that Rover saloon car, the Sterling. Day was asked to bring a model of the car to No. 10 so that Margaret and Dennis Thatcher could look it over. She wanted to drive the vehicle to show confidence in a revived Rover, but there was a problem. As revealed in Thatcher's private papers, her aides were agitated because she had not driven a car for years. Imagine the indomitable prime minister crashing this symbolically important car in Downing Street. So Day had a couple of professional drivers quietly take the car down to the prime minister's country house, Chequers, where she was able to test it out. The Rover drivers were given a tour of the estate, and she served tea. Two weeks later, as crowds watched and her staff sweated, she drove the car a short distance on Downing Street and then reversed it. No crash occurred, and cameras captured the event. Aides breathed a sigh of relief, and Rover gained valuable publicity.

Day would later tell Canadian journalist Rod McQueen, in a *Financial Post* profile, "I'm an unabashed admirer of Mrs. T. and I've had all four sharp sides of her tongue, particularly in my early dealings with her until I understood why. My admiration is not founded on the fact that she was always right all of the time, none of us are, but because she was steadfast.... Right, wrong or indifferent, she was a politician of conviction, not consensus." Once a topic had been fully thrashed out, the prime minister might wrap up by saying, "Can you deliver?" or, "Then we are agreed, are we not?" He came to understand that was his last kick at the can, he told McQueen. If he said yes, he knew that, as long as he delivered his part of the deal, she would deliver hers.

From time to time, civil servants would phone Day to say that, although they knew he was determined to follow a certain action, could he, in fact, "trim it a bit?" That was shorthand for being more flexible—delaying the action or dulling some of its sharp edges. Day would ask whether they wanted to speak to Thatcher or should he. There were never any takers.

As the relationship strengthened, he would end up at Downing Street, sometimes at a working dinner, where people from various corners of business would come in to discuss a topic she needed to know about. The formal occasion that stands out was when Prime Minister Brian Mulroney landed at No. 10.

There was a dinner followed by a reception for the Canadian leader, and Day was standing there with a drink when he heard her voice at his side, "Graham, come and meet your prime minister." Without even thinking, he said, "Prime Minister, you are my prime minister." Indeed, she was.

He knew he had truly arrived when he attended an agricultural fair one day. There was a luncheon in a canvas tent, and Day was called over to join Nicholas Ridley, now secretary of state for trade and industry. Ridley mentioned there was a takeover offer for Jaguar, and Day agreed he had heard about talks between Ford and Jaguar, now a publicly listed company. The government held the "the golden share," a residue of the former state ownership that gave it the right to veto any sale. Selling Jaguar to a foreign buyer would be controversial. Ridley asked for Day's opinion on what to do with the golden share. Day recommended against exercising it, arguing instead for confidence in the market. Then Day added, "I assume you're going to tell the boss that, aren't you?" And Ridley grinned, "Oh, yes." Within a couple of days, the government announced it would not deploy its golden share. Ford bought Jaguar for £1.6 billion. Ford would later write off its entire investment, but that is another story.

One of Day's most powerful impulses is loyalty. He sticks by people, sometimes to a fault. He steadfastly defends the Thatcher revolution, and sees the justification in the turnaround in Britain's economy during her tenure. He hears critics who decry the era's creation of crass millionaires. His riposte: "Millionaires were created but they took enormous risks, they paid tax on the money, and they created jobs. The tax rate came down and that helped create jobs, too. Did the government and the bureaucrats get everything right? Of course not. Policy, yes, but execution didn't always happen that way."

For Day, his support of Thatcher was not about simply earning a living; "I believed I was doing something which had value. I was a little cog in a series of cogs that was making that economy better and stronger." He was often called Thatcher's hatchet man, but while he was cleaning up state-owned companies, he insists he cut only about ten thousand jobs, and these were shed through attrition. That compares with the more than one hundred and fifty thousand workers who were employed in various companies he led. He can't speak, however, to the fate of jobs after he had sold the privatized companies. Take, for example, Cammell Laird. Cut loose from British Shipbuilders, it was merged with another privatized organization, and by 1986 was reduced to fourteen hundred jobs, down from ten thousand a decade earlier; about thirty years later, the shipyard, though still in operation, would employ a core workforce of about a thousand people. But Day always argued he would preserve only the preservable jobs. He was best known for taking out managers he thought were surplus or unable to do the job. This is what truly earned him the hatchetman label. "Were there things I wish I hadn't had to do?" he asks. "Yes, and if a lot of my predecessors had done a better job, I would not have had to come in to clean it up."

Ann Day understood that there were two strong women in Graham's life, and although she was clearly pre-eminent, the lady at No. 10 held a particular status: "He would have gone through fire for her," Ann says, "and he did."

In January 1988, Day came home to make a speech at the Empire Club in Toronto. Hailed as something of a conquering hero, he delivered a progress report on the Thatcher privatization efforts and his role in them. Although Day had not been involved in the big flashy public offerings, he had done a lot of deals, including a selloff of parts of Rover Group. But there was more to do: "During 1988 we will start to plan for the return of the group to full private ownership," he pledged.

It couldn't happen soon enough for Thatcher. Her memoirs reflect her concerns at the time. By the late 1980s, she observed, "Rover had by now a superb chairman in Graham Day, who had been making great efforts to do what I had always hoped would be done—dispose of surplus assets and increase the drive for higher productivity." But she was not happy with the numbers. "It retained an apparently insatiable appetite for cash."

Thus the pressure intensified as Day faced a barrage of competing interests: hyper-anxious MPs, hovering global car companies, and a trade and industry minister, Lord Young, with a can-do reputation who wanted to reap the political credit for finding a solution. And there was one very impatient prime minister. A buyer had to have the essential attribute of being British, while guaranteeing the security of the Rover workforce. There were not many companies with that kind of profile.

At that time, Geoffrey Owen was editor of the *Financial Times*, and he wrote a lot about industrial policy. He knew Graham Day—and he was knowledgeable about the Rover Group's challenges. On March 1, 1988, he attended what was heralded as an important news conference involving the Rover Group and major defence contractor British Aerospace (BAe), the big conglomerate that also managed Britain's stake in Europe's Airbus passenger jet project. It turned out the two British companies were entering exclusive talks towards a merger. On hand were Graham Day and Professor Roland Smith, BAe's larger-than-life chairman, plus the ebullient Lord Young, who would later call it "the deal of the decade." Owen wrote in the *Financial Times* that the merger would at last move Rover out of the public sector. He added that "the deal will be expensive to the taxpayer—the purchaser will press for substantial debt writeoffs—but ministers will see this as a price worth paying. What is far more open to doubt is whether the deal makes industrial sense for the two companies."

Whatever those doubts, Thatcher was pleased. She argues in her memoirs that there was, in fact, "an industrial logic" in BAe's eventual acquisition of Rover Group. She said the car business—if relieved of debt and provided with substantial new investment—would complement BAe's defence and aerospace business. Cars were a steadier business than a few huge defence contracts. And, of course, Rover would stay British.

But, almost thirty years later, Geoffrey Owen, now retired, is even more sceptical of the industrial merit of the deal. He says the discussion of the merger's great synergies was "rubbish." The sale to British Aerospace was all about getting Rover out of public ownership, while solving a problem for Thatcher. He asserts, "it was a blot on Graham's reputation to have overseen a merger with no logic whatsoever, except for a political solution to an awkward situation."

Graham Day strongly disputes Owen's allegation that the BAe deal made only political sense. Day argues that the transaction was, at its core, commercial. He repudiates any suggestion that, in this and other privatizations, he was essentially a political fixer, not a genuine business leader. Thatcher was consistent, he says, in seeking two possible outcomes from the privatizations. In some cases, she expected large financial proceeds from the flotation of profitable companies such as British Telecom. In others, she sought the elimination of state money flowing into cash-strapped companies. Shipbuilders and Rover fell into the second category. "After the sales of several subsidiaries, including trucks and vans, Rover became profitable with positive cash flow which made the sale to British Aerospace possible," Day argues. BAe also acquired employee training practices that far surpassed its own efforts. His critics might have smelled politics at work, but for Day it was business.

For insiders to the deal, the sale to British Aerospace was never seen as the end of the story. Five years later, BMW, the upmarket German automaker, paid £800 million for the Rover business, beating out Honda, which many felt would have been the best owner, based on its long association with Rover. Day argues that the £800 million was a tangible tribute to his team in making Rover a desirable property to own.

What he could not foresee was that the BMW purchase would be a disaster. Day believes that the Rover workforce culture, so strengthened during his regime, clashed with the new German management. By 2000, BMW was racking up massive losses, and it sold Land Rover to Ford for £1.8 billion. Eventually India's Tata acquired both Jaguar and Rover from Ford. Today, Britain's auto industry, thanks to an influx of foreign investment, is no longer British owned, but it is a productive, competitive industry. That is not entirely Graham Day's doing, but he was a critical part of getting there.

Catherine Bell credits Day for taking the long view at all times. He was able to balance the government's fiscal imperatives with driving Rover's strategy. "It was rare to see someone step into a company like Shipbuilders and then into something difficult like cars—and remain the golden person," she says. His strength, she believes, was the courage to say, "This is what I believe in." Indeed, he could feel comfortable telling Thatcher the truth.

CHAPTER 13

A Knight in the Boardroom

Graham Day did not look for baubles to repay his loyalty, but in time Thatcher and her government recognized his work in dramatic fashion. It was not straightforward, however. The knighthood of Graham Day serves as a small case study of the constantly evolving, always awkward dance of two sovereign nations, the United Kingdom and its former colony Canada, whose citizens are still subjects of its queen.

In late 1985, as Day was successfully privatizing British Shipbuilders, a senior civil servant asked to borrow his two passports, Canadian and British, for a day. When they were returned, he was told confidentially that the government was trying to determine his citizenship eligibility for an "honour." He interpreted that to mean a potential knighthood. But it took a full three years before he received a letter from Thatcher's assistant private secretary indicating it would finally happen.

Apparently, the delay had been in securing the agreement of the Canadian authorities. He was later told by a senior British official that the prime minister's office had spent two years securing the "permission" of the Canadians. Earlier, he had heard that Thatcher had spoken with Brian Mulroney, Canada's prime minister, and had received his agreement. But before the recommendation could go to the queen, she had to be assured that, in any action taken, her role as monarch of the United Kingdom did not conflict with her equivalent role in Canada.

The queen must have been given the required assurance, because Graham Day was included in the New Year's Honour List of 1989 and, in spring 1990, he was dubbed Sir Graham. Day was immensely proud, as was his English patriot father, who was too feeble to travel to London but who shared in the moment. Sadly, his mother had died by then. For Day, it was an honour to be part of the eight-hundred-year-old tradition of Knights Bachelor, his particular category of knighthood, whose members have included Sir Thomas More and Sir William Gilbert, of Gilbert and Sullivan fame.

Day's service as a knight has been routine. He became a member of the council of the Imperial Order of Knights Bachelor, a registered charity in Britain. And he could proudly wear the insignia of a "Knight Bachelor" as honorary colonel of the West Nova Scotia Regiment and as colonel commandant of the Judge Advocate Branch of the military. In his appointments to the Order of Nova Scotia and as Queen's Counsel, he was addressed as "Sir Graham Day." But there is a postscript.

In 2014, Governor General David Johnston phoned to say he was being appointed to the Order of Canada in the rank of officer. Day received the information package, addressed to "Mr.," and a questionnaire. Among the questions was an inquiry as to his "form of address." He filled in "Sir." Thus began a long series of exchanges that concluded with a letter indicating Canada's Chancellery of Honours—the office of the governor general that deals with such awards—could not address him as "Sir." Day conceded the point, but he believes his lengthy exchanges with the chancellery had an unintended consequence. The governor general's website, which lists all appointments to the Order of Canada, has removed the knighthood appellations of the few appointees who had also been knighted. This is unfortunate, Day says, because the names affected by the removals include Sir Ernest MacMillan, Canada's greatest orchestra conductor, and Sir William Stephenson, Britain's US-based spymaster in the Second World War, who was a Canadian citizen. "'I suggest that the Chancellery may be of the opinion that British titles, even in retrospect, threaten Canada's sovereignty,' Day wrote to me in an email message, a bit mischievously. However, I doubt that either Sir John A. Macdonald or Sir Wilfrid Laurier are in any danger, as their knighthoods predated the formation of the Order of Canada!" Day is now convinced that there are no circumstances in which Canada will support the queen's conferring knighthood on a Canadian—even a dual national. Nor is it likely that the UK authorities would seek such permission from Canada.

This reality was underlined in 2001 when Welsh-born high-tech entrepreneur Terry Matthews and academic leader George Bain, both dual nationals then living in Britain, were put forward for a knighthood on the queen's honours list—without Canadian government approval. That triggered an angry letter of protest from Prime Minister Jean Chrétien. Emotions were still raw from the controversy over Conrad Black's pursuit of a British peerage and the Chrétien government's opposition. One scholar argued that Canada was playing politics with the new knighthoods, and pointed to three dual nationals so honoured without controversy in the previous fifteen years: heraldry expert Conrad Swan, sugar executive Neil Shaw, and Graham Day. The UK government said it was sorry, and went ahead with the Matthews and Bain knighthoods.

As a Canadian born and residing in this country—and who was knighted without objection from the Canadian government—Day feels he is the survivor of a proud line. In his view, he is "the last Canadian knight." Some might question his exclusive claim to that title, but not his reverence for the tradition. No one alive is more passionate, and combative, in defending this proud legacy, part of two countries' shared history, but now sadly abandoned in the fog of politics.

"Crotchety "—*Independent*

"Charming, warm and straightforward"—*Financial Times*

"A very shrewd strategic thinker"—*Times*

"A dour Nova Scotian"—*Sunday Times*

"The country's most ruthless crisis manager"—*Daily Mail*

If Graham Day's British adventures were a movie—perhaps a biopic titled *The Iron Man*—you might say he got positive reviews, but the critics never seemed to figure out what show they were watching. Was this the tale of a cold-blooded hit man? Or of a charming man of the world? Or the quixotic adventures of an upstart colonial, a kind of Mark Twain–like fantasy, "A Nova Scotia Canuck in Lady Thatcher's Court"?

Of course, they were all correct. There are many Graham Days, depending on the job to be done. Like the musical stage director he once was, being a senior manager in a corporation meant playing many roles. They all drew on parts of his personality.

The UK media was fascinated with his unprepossessing background. BBC-TV labelled him "the onetime cornpone country singer," while running clips of him singing "Little Bo-Peep" on *Singalong Jubilee*. The press jumped on his Canadian roots, suggesting that Thatcher had a weakness for North American executives—after all, Ian MacGregor had built his career in the United States. Day insisted that performance, not birthplace, would be the test of his abilities.

He was "the Canadian-born Mr. Day," the man from rustic Nova Scotia, but gradually they dropped the Canadian bit. He remembers his public relations aide during the Rover days saying to him, "Oh, Graham, you'd be interested to know, you don't seem to be Canadian anymore." He became a part of the British scene, like Cunard and Beaverbrook, Maritimers who fit in. But Beaverbrook was wilful and untrustworthy, changing his political affections as promiscuously as he discarded mistresses. Day built his reputation on trust—particularly trust to two women: his wife and a political mistress.

The anglicization of Graham Day was a natural outcome of his ubiquity. For a decade, the distinctive bearded man from Canada was constantly in the newspapers or on TV. Day attributes a lot of his good press to John Pullen, his loyal public relations aide. Pullen would say, "Graham, you can't run and hide, that's not an option. You can try and avoid it, but I don't recommend that." He said, "It's part of your job. You're going to have to be available and do it with a smile." Day appreciated the advice, because he knew he had to get certain messages out there. The audience was the public, the politicians, the investors, and, perhaps most important, the employees, who read newspapers and understood best what he was talking about.

He generally got along very well with journalists, and the press clippings from the era reflect his ease and eloquence. "I was only interested in how they reported the facts. And I never ever, ever lied," he says, repeating a familiar Day canon.

He remembers an auto reporter from the *Daily Telegraph* who questioned him: "You're not telling me the whole story." And Day agreed: "I'm in a competitive business, so I can't tell you the whole story, but everything I tell you is true." And so, "by and large, I figure that the British press treated me fairly, reported honestly, and I could live with the hyperbole about how they chose to describe me. That didn't matter." In fact, one article referred to Day as a whiz kid. It is hard to think of a fifty-year-old man as a whiz kid, but he no doubt seemed young compared to the dinosaurs who had been lumbering across the British industrial landscape. He laughs that "they always struggled to try and get a descriptor."

He and his public relations team were good at media management. If the company had some bad news about to break, his people would approach journalists they liked. Rover was a willing participant in the "Friday night drop," whereby business journalists would be fed information on Friday night to write stories for the thick, hernia-inducing Sunday papers. It was typical on a Friday evening to spend time with one or more Sunday journalists, principally those from the *Sunday Times* and the *Sunday Telegraph*. He was always wary of the *Guardian*, which had a political edge. The *Financial Times*, which was generally sympathetic to business, didn't do the Friday night drop, but its reporters were aggressive in going after the facts.

The newspaper coverage of that era shows the efforts to soften the image of this allegedly hard man. One interview with Ann was designed to reveal the kinder, gentler Graham Day. Shortly after the Night of the Long Knives, the *Daily Express* profiled Ann under the headline "He brings me pearls, cashmere, and silk." The condescending piece somewhat illuminated their lives in London. It started with the public image of Graham Day as "the ruthless hatchet man of the Rover Group cutting a swathe through nervous executives to offset a dive in the car giant's fortunes." But, at home, the newspaper reported, "'he is a pussycat,' insists his loyal wife Ann." "Ruthless he ain't," she was quoted as saying. "The kids say he's marshmallow inside. He's very soft in the best kind of way, very considerate of people's feelings. When he's had to cut jobs and get rid of people, there's personal conflict. I've seen sleepless nights over these people's problems."

The story explained that Ann "refuses to put 'housewife' in her passport." Her explanation was, "I do much more than that." She said she organized their three homes: a family house in Nova Scotia, a lakeside holiday cottage, and a London flat. "She has masterminded 14 house moves with only two breakages. She copes with the household bills and chores." Ann said in the article, "He could not operate without a support system. I try to set aside two hours a day organizing and writing letters. I am the general dogsbody, but pretty methodical."

Over years of press coverage, Day had got fairly used to the celebrity status. During their second term in England, the Days were much more relaxed about their lifestyles. The kids were not part of it—they were back in Canada. The couple lived in stylish South Kensington and, left to herself during the weekdays, Ann could walk anywhere anonymously. When Graham was with her, it was different. He was recognized. "Celebrity was hard because we are corduroy and desert-boot people," Ann says. On weekends, they could escape to their little two-storey place in Tunbridge Wells, Kent. "It was one down, two up, you could just slam the door and leave," Ann recalls. "There were no treasures to worry about and people were lovely." And Graham could tool around the English lanes in his latest Beetle, continuing the loving relationship with the car of his courtship. (It would still be going strong in his eighties, when he was having a circa-1960s Beetle rebuilt.)

Was Ann lonely? She did have the flexibility to fly home when she had to, and there were still aging parents and children just starting their work lives. "I was too busy to be lonely, and lonely is an inner thing. You have to be able to live with yourself."

The children were getting on with life. Deborah was launched on an academic career as she gained advanced degrees in education, including a PhD in measurement and evaluation. Donna would get a business degree and gain accreditation as an insurance underwriter—and as an embroiderer, trained in the traditional craft by London's City & Guilds art school.

Michael provided some surprises. As the Days prepared for their second round of British duty in 1983, they got a call from their son, then a student at the University of Saskatchewan. Michael, a track athlete, had suffered another in a series of dispiriting injuries. He was frustrated with university life as he drifted through a series of major subjects. As a lover of the outdoors, he couldn't see being chained to a desk for the next thirty years. So he decided to drop out of school and join the military while he sorted out his life. He called his parents with the news that he would be heading to the Canadian Forces base at Gagetown, New Brunswick, for the selection course.

Graham gave one of his familiar profane responses. Then, stunned silence. But it was out of surprise, not horror. "They had miscalculated my academic ambition and ability at the time," Michael says. Yet, from the first, his parents were supportive.

Michael Day would not leave the military for another thirty-two years. He emerged as one of the Canadian Forces' leaders of his generation, rising in the counterterrorism and special forces community and serving as chief of Canada's special forces. He would rise to a lieutenant-general of Canada's armed forces, with postings to dangerous places such as Afghanistan and Bosnia. He was touted in the press as a potential chief of Canada's defence staff before retiring from the service in 2015. Eventually, he did go back to university as a young officer, and he excelled, receiving a bachelor's degree in politics and a master's in war studies. As with his father, Michael was a late bloomer who needed to figure life out. In a sense, he had the career that Graham might have had if he had been allowed to sign up for the Korean War.

Beyond the lives of their children, the Days kept in touch with home. Old friends would visit from Nova Scotia, and they would be amazed at the Days' life in London. Graham would come to their hotel to pick them up, usually with a driver, often in a Rover, and he had that constant security attention. They would end up at a favourite Italian restaurant where everyone knew his name and the other diners would gawk.

The celebrity status was underlined on vacation to the Mediterranean island of Crete. The Days loved Greece and the islands, and he and Ann had found a charming taverna, which they began to frequent nightly. One evening a British tourist bustled over and said, "Excuse me, but are you Graham Day?" It was unthreatening—he just wanted to know. Day was getting a lot of that. "I've tried to figure out why the hell they would be interested." The Days never went back to the little taverna. The concern was not merely a result of shyness. With fame came worries about security—for himself, his family, and the businesses he served. When he moved to Britain in 1971 to head Cammell Laird, Day had to be processed for a security clearance—after all, Cammell Laird was a warship builder. He was cleared, and, for the first of several occasions, signed the *Official Secrets Act*.

It was a time when sectarian strife in Northern Ireland was bleeding across the Irish Sea. The security services were alert to the large numbers of "Liverpool Irish" in the Mersey area. Many were employed in the shipyard. Incidents in the yard caused shutdowns, curtailed work, and enhanced the need for surveillance. Security officers were always in the yard. When outsiders were present—for example, at ship launchings—the company would host members of the Special Branch and MI5. In the 1970s in Birkenhead, the Day children found themselves collected from school at times of high risk. The concern escalated in 1976, when Day led the organizing committee for British Shipbuilders, whose membership included other makers of warships.

When he left the committee, he was given an exit interview by the security services. He was cautioned that he continued to be bound by the *Official Secrets Act*. In a time of national emergency, if the United Kingdom needed his services, it was expected that he would return. Of course, return he did, quite willingly, at the request of the Thatcher government. By March 1983, the danger from terrorism, both in Northern Ireland and in Europe, was even more grave. When the Days relocated to London, they were required to have attack alarms in areas of their London flat, and they were instructed on appropriate behaviours. When Ann left the apartment, she would lower the floor-to-ceiling shutters with their bars and activate the alarms.

About six months into his job at Shipbuilders, Day was given the services of a new driver/security person, Jeff Stubbings, a former member of the Parachute Regiment and the French Foreign Legion. They were together for the next nine and half years, and Stubbings was a constant, forceful presence. In the mornings, if there was the sense of danger, he would knock on the door of the Days' London home to inform Graham that his car was parked around the corner. The two men would joke that, while Stubbings slept, Day worked, and then the reverse.

They agreed they probably spent more time together than with their own wives.

The high alert only intensified in October 1984 when an IRA bomb exploded at the Grand Hotel in Brighton, where the Conservative leadership had assembled for the party conference. Thatcher barely escaped with her life, but five people were killed and many injured, including cabinet ministers Norman Tebbit and John Wakeham. Tebbit's wife was confined to a wheelchair for life.

When Day moved from Shipbuilders to Rover, the security remained intense. Rover was a manufacturer of military transport vehicles. Now there was a new dimension to the threat in the emergence of terror groups on the continent: Action Direct in France, Baader-Meinhof in West Germany, and Brigado Rosso in Italy. The French group shot and killed the CEO of carmaker Renault outside his flat in Paris. Most chief executives of leading European vehicle businesses lived in "secure" structures. The Days did not. There were constant reminders of a dangerous world. On trips to certain European cities, such as Frankfurt, Day would be joined by a couple of ex–secret service operators. The watchfulness increased when Rover was acquired by British Aerospace, one of the world's major weapons systems suppliers, and thus a key player in the First Gulf War. Day was chairman of BAe when, just around the corner from his London offices, the IRA lobbed a bomb into the grounds of 10 Downing Street. When he led the electricity company PowerGen, its windows were blown in when the NatWest Tower was bombed. He was not in the office at the time.

In all these security challenges, it was not Graham Day, the person, who was the target—it was the holder of the job. Anyone in these kinds of jobs was at risk. Day has little patience with those who think that such risk confers special status or importance. The challenge for the Days was to go about their lives as normally as possible, which was hard as long as the media hovered. “I became too recognizable,” Graham says.

Nova Scotia began to look better all the time.

CHAPTER 14

The Chocolate Chairman

They met for dinner, three middle-aged men in the dining room of the Cadbury Schweppes offices in central London. The hosts were Sir Adrian Cadbury, chairman of the one-hundred-and-fifty-year-old candy and beverage company founded by his Quaker family; and Dominic, his younger brother and the company's CEO. The third man was Graham Day, the leading candidate to join the Cadbury board and ultimately to succeed Sir Adrian, who planned to retire as chairman in a year or so. In late 1988, the two Cadbury brothers were hunting for a director who could prove to the outside world that the company's leadership was not as sweet as its products. It was a tough-minded, professionally managed company that intended to grow and thrive independently.

The brothers found Day to be direct, straightforward, with no agenda other than to serve the company and its shareholders. He had a global perspective and, what's more, he understood North America, where Cadbury Schweppes had significant interests. He did not know much about Cadbury's iconic Creme

Eggs or Schweppes ginger ale, but he knew marketing—he had repositioned the Rover auto brands. He had proved to be agile and decisive in the corporate wars. After several hours of far-ranging conversation, Day left. Sir Adrian commented to his brother: "Well, that's a pretty easy choice."

It was the beginning of a new vista for Day's wandering curiosity and focus. Up to then, he had managed crisis situations, but Cadbury Schweppes was a profitable, well-run publicly traded business with a long and revered history. Yet there was a problem. The Cadbury family was still influential in the company, but did not control it; in fact, it owned less than 10 percent. The family charitable foundations that had once held controlling stakes had seen their interests diluted in a quest for diversification beyond the company shares. Cadbury was in danger of becoming "in play," the stock market's terminology for a company vulnerable to a takeover. A US company, General Cinema, was acquiring shares, and had built its holdings up to 18 percent. Cadbury was searching for a director and prospective chair who could deal with this interloper, while maintaining the family reputation for probity and quality. "We wanted someone who was not afraid to take on a fairly difficult situation," says Dominic Cadbury, speaking twenty-five years later. "We were threatened and under a microscope. We were looking for someone who was not intimidated."

They wanted a chocolate chairman, but one with a hard centre—and that would be Graham Day. He would become a non-executive chairman, with no operating role. In his two earlier big-company assignments, Day had combined the chairman's role with the chief executive's. But those were special situations in which he was driving the company towards privatization and he needed to concentrate both roles to get it done expeditiously. Today, combining those two offices would be considered poor corporate governance, but in the 1980s, especially where a business was in considerable difficulty and privatization was mandated, having one boss was considered vital. "For me, it would have been impossible to tackle Shipbuilders or Rover had I been required to thread the needle of corporate niceties," Day argues.

Of course, at both Shipbuilders and Rover—which had a very small public float—there was a single shareholder, the UK government. Had he failed to deliver, the government would simply have sacked him. "For this shareholder in these situations, corporate governance was largely irrelevant." After the Rover Group was privatized, Day was never again employed as a CEO. Yet in some situations he could use his role as chairman to encourage certain actions. That was the situation at Cadbury Schweppes. In Day's case, he brought an extra gift to any board he served: the reputation for being tough and street-smart.

Cadbury Schweppes had already separated the jobs of chair and CEO. Furthermore, one of the champions of good governance was Sir Adrian Cadbury, who would write an influential report that helped shape the debate worldwide. Graham Day's time at Cadbury became crucial training for his later assignments as a lead director and chair of Canadian companies.

It is not an easy transition from an executive to non-executive chair, Day notes. He sees it in terms of a classic Canadian analogy: the snowball fight. As a CEO, even when subject to a board of directors, Day both made and threw snowballs. As a non-executive chair, he might give advice from time to time on the making and throwing of snowballs. But his major responsibility was to ensure that the CEO and management team threw snowballs in a way the board (and shareholders) expected. "It's hard, maybe impossible, for me to judge my own success in such a transition," he says. What he does know is that, as a chair, he performed better when the company had significant challenges than when the situation called for business as usual. He was, in temperament and training, a crisis manager.

When Day joined Cadbury, he was fifty-five and at the height of his reputation. His two biggest jobs were largely behind him, although he was still chair of the Rover unit inside British Aerospace, as well as a board member at BAe. He had time to take on extra roles, especially of a non-executive kind. The danger was that, although each of these invitations on its own was manageable, the cumulative effects would be overwhelming.

At the meeting with the two Cadbury brothers, the message Day gleaned was that they needed someone who wouldn't have to worry about running the business. His job was to be the unintimidated face of the company if things got dodgy with General Cinema. The message: once you have a reputation for toughness, it might not be necessary to act tough; you just have to be there. But Day turned out to be much more than a figurehead.

Valerie Grove, the profile writer for the *Sunday Times*, summed up the Day persona: "He could be the nicest man who ever axed an entire workforce or fired a senior director on the spot. Look what he managed to do with ailing Rover. What might he not do with the fizzy drink and the creme egg?" In fact, he never fired an entire workforce—never came close—but the image of the charming executioner had seized the public imagination. Nonetheless, this time, Grove wrote, "he finds nobody to sack, no bleeding to staunch: a profitable company in a competitive expanding market, our national consumption of chocolate and fizz being obsessive. (We bought three hundred million gooey Creme Eggs last year.) But the choice of Day as chairman is plainly a strategic move by a company determined to see off foreign predators."

The most visible predator was General Cinema's boss, Richard Smith, a US financier who had inherited a string of drive-in theatres from his father in 1961 and parlayed it into an impressive investment portfolio. The actual business of theatres did not do well, but Smith made big money by buying stakes in undervalued public companies and profiting as more strategic investors jumped in, allowing him to sell out at a profit. Cadbury's undervalued stock fit the profile of an investment target.

But Cadbury was more than a company; it embodied a holistic philosophy of business. The Cadburys were Quakers, a sect that practises strict moral values and a lack of ostentation. In founding its chocolate company in Victorian Britain, the family blended hard work, discipline, and abhorrence of debt with a social mission based on pacifism, philanthropy, and workers' well-being. Nancy Cadbury, in her 2010 history of the chocolate business, says "straight dealing, fair play, honesty, accuracy and truth form the basis of Quaker capitalism." The Cadburys were one of a collection of Quaker businesses that were in the vanguard of Britain's Industrial Revolution. Chocolate was a natural calling because it was seen as a flavourful, non-alcoholic alternative to liquor and beer, sources of the rampant drunkenness of the time. It is no accident that Britain's three great chocolate enterprises—Birmingham's Cadbury, Bristol's Fry, and York's Rowntree—can claim Quaker origins.

In the 1860s, two brothers, Richard and George Cadbury, third-generation Birmingham tradesmen, inherited their father's struggling chocolate factory and turned it into an international success. In 1878, they bought open land just outside Birmingham for a model industrial enterprise known as the Bournville Works, and it began to take shape. "The factory in the field was a revelation: a temple to space and light and order," Nancy Cadbury writes. Outside was a bucolic atmosphere of cricket pitches and gardens, and cottages for key staff, along with train connections to the centre of Birmingham. It was a Utopian conception, based on the view that healthy, contented people were more industrious, productive workers.

One hundred and ten years after the founding of Bournville, the Cadbury family had changed a bit. Many family members had shed their pacifism and fought, often heroically, in two world wars. Their devotion to the Society of Friends had wavered, but the sixth generation running the company still believed in the advancement of moral and social good through business.

Cadbury was now an international company, trading in forty countries and competing against behemoths such as the Swiss conglomerate Nestlé and US confectionery giants Mars and Hershey. A wave of consolidation washed through the confectionery business as diversified food companies eyed lucrative candy markets. Cadbury was a survivor among the old British chocolate companies, but it had merged with Schweppes, the fizzy drinks maker. The share dilution and public listing meant it was no longer a family controlled company.

Global food giants hovered, eager to add the Cadbury brand to their portfolios. General Cinema made its move to acquire shares, sensing a bigger deal in the cards. Cadbury Schweppes was now led by Dominic, a marketing virtuoso with a Stanford MBA, supported by the chairman, Sir Adrian, his elder brother by eleven years and now a widely admired business statesman. Their response was a strategy of expansion that would make the company more valuable to investors and more difficult to take over. Day became a key part of supporting that strategy.

In many countries, the Cadbury executives faced competition rules that made it hard to expand in their core businesses of chocolate and beverages. But they also had a stake in sugar confectionery—non-chocolate candies—which was a widely fragmented business. They saw an opportunity to become a consolidator and to use this as a source of growth. Cadbury started accumulating smaller businesses such as Lion Confectionery, Bassett, and Trebor Group, with its popular mints.

All the while, Day rebuffed the demands of General Cinema for representation on the board. Smith claimed that he wanted "investment with involvement." He was told that he could acquire such shares as would be available to him on the market, but not to expect a board seat. Day made it clear he would receive only such information as was available to all shareholders.

Cadbury's candy purchases were successful in their two purposes. They were profitable and accretive for the firm's shareholders and, as Cadbury Schweppes grew, it became very expensive for General Cinema and any other raider to buy. As the brothers had hoped, in the end Smith just went away, although he did very well on his investment. Cadbury Schweppes even helped him dispose of his shares through the stock market. But Day and the brothers had held firm and preserved the company and its Quaker culture as an independent entity.

With General Cinema sent packing, Day enjoyed working with the Cadbury brothers. He would often travel with Sir Adrian, a role model of statesmanlike wisdom. The elder Cadbury brother liked doing the yearly milk run of recruiting trips to British universities, where he gained insight into the kind of young people the company needed to attract. The conversation often came around to the proper conduct of the individual in business. In one question-and-answer session, a young woman stood up and asked Sir Adrian, as a businessman, how he decided on a particular course of action in a tricky ethical situation. She said: "You have to ask yourself: do I do this or do I not? How do you resolve that?" And Sir Adrian said, "If you have to ask the question, the answer is always no."

The Cadbury brothers did face criticism of their moral stance on one issue: South Africa. During the 1980s, the racially riven country, mired in repugnant, white-imposed apartheid, had become the centre of a global political firestorm. Civil rights groups pushed hard for economic sanctions and for corporate disinvestment. Cadbury Schweppes had a long history in the country and, echoing its Quaker ethics, was considered a good employer, with extensive housing, education, and social support of its overwhelmingly black workforce. But it was under great pressure in the United Kingdom and elsewhere to step back from its investment. Canadian prime minister Brian Mulroney was a leader in advocating government sanctions against the pariah regime.

Cadbury financially supported anti-apartheid organizations, but it would not surrender its presence in the country. It felt a moral responsibility to its African employees and to its shareholders worldwide. So the company came up with a simple construction: it would build a ring-fence around its South African operations. Within that fence, it would not invest any new money from the parent company, and it would not declare any dividends back to the parent company. It would remain in South Africa, but it would isolate the business financially.

Dominic, who had worked extensively in South Africa, says: "We always took the view that we actually were a force for good in the South African economy, and we didn't think that pulling out of South Africa and simply dumping the thing was going to help the races in South Africa. We employed a lot of people, and the conditions under which they were employed were good. So we never subscribed to the idea that it would be beneficial to the average South Africans if we disinvested." Margaret Thatcher was kept informed, and she approved of Cadbury's stance. That remained the company's approach as South Africa began to make the transition, still difficult, from an apartheid state to a functioning democracy in the twenty-first century.

Day had assumed that, in his role as Cadbury Schweppes chair, there would be fewer security concerns than in state-owned companies. But one morning he received a visit from national security officers who informed him that the Irish police had found his name, with others, on an IRA list. Cadbury Schweppes was a significant employer in Ireland, and this added a further dimension to his personal security issues. On the few occasions he visited the republic, he travelled under an assumed name, was met by the police, and never registered or checked out of his hotel.

The security threat was exacerbated by Day's high profile, as his name kept popping up as someone who would take on hard jobs: he was still seen as safe hands by politicians, the media, and markets. The calls for help invariably originated in the prime minister's office, and one came in November 1990. The government had announced its intention to privatize the Central Electricity Generating Board, which provided electricity to England and Wales and controlled the two state-owned Scottish power companies. The plan was to separate generation from transmission and distribution. The generation part was to be divided into three companies, two "conventional" and one nuclear.

Privatization of the nuclear business was postponed, but the two conventional companies, PowerGen and National Power, were formed. Because of his privatization experience, Day was asked to join the PowerGen board. Planning was under way to sell both generator companies through 100 percent share offerings on the London Stock Exchange. By now, Day could write the textbook on privatization: strengthen the board by bringing on people who are credible to the markets; get the best management you can, and ensure they are competitively paid and not liable to poaching; make sure the accounting is accurate (often a big challenge because incumbent accounting firms are wedded to their valuations); try to get the unions onside, and give workers participation through shares.

But, at PowerGen, they had trouble following that script. About two months before the offering, Day got a request to see John Wakeham, secretary of state for energy. Wakeham's message: the investment bank advising the government on the flotation felt PowerGen's chairman elect, Robert Malpas, was not "suitable" to lead the share issue. The bankers and the government wanted Day to take the job. Again, he had that presence.

Day had two concerns: Ann had to agree, particularly since they had started to enjoy more time together. And he would have to get the okay from the Cadbury Schweppes board. He told Wakeham it was not a job he wanted. The minister replied that Day could say no to him, but he should understand that "*she* will wish to speak with you." Day said, "John, why me?" Wakeham replied, "She trusts you."

Ann consented, and so did Cadbury Schweppes, which agreed that a non-executive chair's job would not distract him too much, and there was this obligation of public service. The next day, he told Wakeham: "John, if I'm going to cave in, I'd just as soon do it to you and not the PM."

Meanwhile, the media were intrigued by Day's frenzied ubiquity, landing in one difficult job after another. The day after he took on the PowerGen chair's role, Charles Leadbeater, industrial editor at the *Financial Times*, commented: "One of the most intriguing questions posed by yesterday's upheavals at PowerGen, the electricity generator, is how many days does Sir Graham Day have in his week? Over the past eight years Sir

Graham has developed an increasingly bewildering juggling act of top jobs in British industry." Leadbeater proceeded to list Day's array of roles: chairman of Rover and Cadbury Schweppes, deputy chairman of MAI, the media and insurance broking group, as well as a non-executive director at British Aerospace and at Thorn EMI, the media and entertainment company. "At first sight, running a confectionery and soft-drinks company or restructuring ailing British manufacturing companies...would not seem to be ideal qualifications for the top job at the nation's second-largest electricity generator," Leadbeater noted. "Yet for most of his career Sir Graham has worked in the grey zone between politics and business. His experience in dealing with privatisation will be one of the greatest assets he will bring to PowerGen."

In the end, the share offering was an unqualified success. In Day's view, PowerGen, now free of state ownership, became much more efficient. The chairman's job became straightforward, as Day worked with a CEO who understood operations but lacked corporate experience. Day and the board filled in the gaps. It meant, however, that Day would cross swords with Michael Heseltine, the fiery politician who had seized the mace during the Shipbuilders vote and was now environment minister. The two men clashed over the role of coal in PowerGen's mix of energy sources. "I kept the management away from this and dealt with him," Day recalls. In his dealings with Heseltine, Day says he found the cabinet minister to be arrogant, aggressive, and often lacking command of the facts.

The diversions into Britain's corporate world would only intensify. Day was home in Nova Scotia for Christmas in 1989 when he got a phone call from fellow directors at British Aerospace. Was he aware of secret discussions that chairman Roland Smith was conducting about merging BAe with another

British company? Day said he was not. The upshot was that the board wanted Smith out. The government still had an interest in the future of BAe, and agreed with the directors: Day would succeed Smith as chair.

Day knew Smith well. The two men had been instrumental in joining Rover Group with British Aerospace. Smith was a prime mover in the diversification of BAe, but he was a lone wolf who did not appreciate the nuances of corporate governance. The company was reeling from a badly botched public rights issue, and then the board had discovered that Smith was having secret talks without keeping it informed. With the approval of Cadbury, Day agreed to serve through the inevitable crisis that would hit BAe shares and until a "permanent" chairman suitable to the board could be recruited.

The company faced a brace of challenges arising from the Gulf War of 1990–91 and from its shareholding in Airbus Industries and the complexities of being a significant arms manufacturer. Smith's dismissal put pressure on the share price because the company was constrained in what it could say about his departure. Also, the British conglomerate General Electric Co. (GEC, not to be confused with US-based General Electric) was sniffing around, and the government was concerned about BAe's financial exposure.

Day visited major institutional shareholders, explaining what had happened, without implicating personalities, and stressing that the company operationally was sound. Once again, his mere reputation was a factor in cooling rumours and easing pressure on the shares. GEC did not move against the company, although it would have been easy to do so. Day had several conversations with the GEC chairman, the wily empire builder Lord Weinstock. In time, the BAe share price recovered, a successor chairman was found, and Day was able to resign as chairman and as a director.

It was all very satisfying because these assignments had real value, but any hope of a more relaxed lifestyle went out the window. For about two years, as the jobs piled up, Day worked harder than ever. He had three London offices—Cadbury, near Marble Arch, British Aerospace on the Strand, and PowerGen in the City—but he did most of his work in his car, moving from one place to another, sharing the vehicle with a secretary and Jeff Stubbings. For several months, he never had more than five hours of sleep a night.

Ann Day was worried. She knew her husband needed sleep or he got twitchy and unhappy. That was his state for nine or ten months. She kept wondering when it was going to end. If Graham got to sleep at night, he was usually fine for a good night, but getting to that point was a challenge.

In time, Day concluded that Dominic Cadbury should succeed him as chairman of the chocolate and beverage company. He handed over the reins in 1993, a year earlier than originally agreed. There was no value in continuing. Dominic was ready, and he had successors from which the board could choose to replace him as CEO. "Too often, I have observed senior people outstaying their time and role. I was determined never to be one of those and I never have," Day says. "I have no patience with people who have to have their fingers pried off the desk. Ian Sinclair should have gone at least five, maybe ten years before he did."

During Day's period as chairman, Dominic Cadbury says, "we prospered as a public company, and that five years was a very critical time. That was the time when, from my perspective, we were most vulnerable. By the time he left, we were in pretty calm waters. The performance had been sustained, we had got rid of General Cinema, our results were good."

Day is proud of his work with Cadbury, particularly in keeping a great company from falling into raiders' hands. But the family shareholding continued to slide. The shareholder group became dominated by investors with no personal links to the company. "The Quaker voice no longer held sway in the boardroom," Nancy Cadbury writes. That became evident as Dominic himself left the board in 2000, and pressure mounted from activist investors to enhance shareholder value. In 2007, the company split off Schweppes into a separate entity. That left the core chocolate company vulnerable. In August 2009, the US food conglomerate Kraft launched a takeover bid and, after some back-and-forth, the Cadbury board surrendered to an improved offer. It was the end of the independent company.

The Cadburys, now gone from direct involvement, were horrified as Kraft and its spin-off successor Mondelez were widely seen as cheapening age-old processes. In March 2016, I interviewed Dominic in his London townhome, the day after he had, with sadness, watched a TV documentary outlining the dispiriting litany of offences: changing the formula for the Creme Eggs, closing a British plant and outsourcing its production to Poland, ditching the company's beloved chocolate coins. The company had even ended the tradition of the gift of chocolates at Christmas to long-term company pensioners.

For Day, there was a particular sadness in all this. In his opinion, the surrender to Kraft was a case of excessive timidity. "I believe the board didn't have the guts to find another way. Not everybody is prepared to fight, or have a plan to be bloody mindedly determined."

Not like Graham Day.

CHAPTER 15

Homecoming

On November 28, 1990, Graham Day was a passenger in a car heading north on the M1, the spine of expressway that extends up the middle of England. His driver and security person Jeff Stubbings was at the wheel, and they were en route to a private girls' school in the West Midlands, where he was to give a talk.

A call came in from his executive assistant in London. "Do you have the radio on?"

"No," he said.

"She's gone."

No one had died, but an era had: Margaret Thatcher had been turfed out by the Conservative MPs she had led to power eleven years earlier, changing the face of the country by rolling back the powers of the state.

Having digested that information, Day arrived at the school and was greeted by the scene of many of the adults—school mothers and grandmothers—openly crying. As he spoke to the students, he discarded his planned script. He talked to them about Thatcher and what she meant as a role model for young women, and he too was caught in the emotion.

There were many actors in the overthrow of Margaret Thatcher. The leadership vote was driven by her long-time nemesis, Michael Heseltine, he of mace-wielding theatrics during the Shipbuilders nationalization. Heseltine's decision to oppose her in the caucus vote set off a full rebellion that ultimately made John Major her successor. But the turning point had been a devastating speech by Geoffrey Howe, the beaten-up former Thatcher ally who had resigned in sadness and anger at her uncompromising stance against a British role in monetary alignment in Europe—in retrospect, probably a wise position.

Below the surface, the underlying factor was Thatcher's harsh treatment of the people around her. After fifteen years of her leadership, many were just tired of her. And she had broken one of Graham Day's rules: let go of power before it lets go of you. Day felt that Thatcher didn't go out of her way to be hurtful, but she wasn't necessarily sensitive to her senior people's feelings. She could be very attentive to the woman who brought her tea; yet, if you were in her inner circle, she felt you were a big boy or girl and could handle a bit of handbagging. Day had felt the sting of her questioning but he learned how to respond. She did not appreciate people who just rolled over.

Her departure was the beginning of the end of Day's time in Britain. He had taken on jobs because she wanted him to. He had become much more than a corporate fixer. He had sat on the National Health Service policy board, and helped introduce non-medical business procedures to the service. Later, Thatcher's successor, John Major, would appoint him as the first chair of the new School Teachers' Review Body, which makes recommendations on the pay for almost half a million teachers in England and Wales.

Day learned there had been a history of labour difficulty in education. Under the then-existing agreements, teachers knew what they were paid, but they seldom knew how that pay was determined, except in a teacher's early years, when pay raises were automatic. Moreover, there were no performance incentives. In his three years on the committee, there was labour peace, the pay metrics were reformed and made known, and pay points for excellence in teaching were awarded. Some say the teachers' incentive system has been one of Day's most lasting legacies.

However, his sense of duty became less pressing. He was basically finishing up matters. With the exception of the Cadbury chairmanship, his important jobs in Britain had flowed from Thatcher's support and his loyalty to her, and now she was gone.

One board that did lure him was Thorn EMI, a powerhouse of musical recording under a number of labels, with artists ranging from the Beatles to the Sex Pistols. In the 1990s, it was trying to come to grips with the future delivery of recorded music. Management believed there would be a new development to continue the sequence of 78, 45, and 33 rpm discs, but it did not expect fundamental change. Day was one of two directors who felt there would be disruptive change, and it would be more than hardware tweaks. This continuing difference of opinion helped persuade him in 1998, after nine years, that it was time to resign. Clearly, the company did not anticipate the era of Spotify and iTunes.

Day's last remaining British directorship was close to his heart. He had been invited by his friend John Gardiner to join the board of the Laird Group, just as Gardiner had come onto boards where Day was chair. He owed Gardiner a lot, and he continued his involvement for several years after he returned to Canada before concluding it was too much.

He was paving the way for that eventuality as early as 1989, after he received a phone call from the Bank of Nova Scotia's City of London office asking if he would be free to meet Cedric "Ced" Ritchie, the bank's chairman. Day had known Ritchie for many years as a fellow member of the so-called Maritime Mafia, the network of East Coasters who formed one of the most durable business elites in the country. Ritchie's was a remarkable story. As a teenager in a poor family with a widowed mother, he had applied as a teller at the Bank of Nova Scotia in Bath, New Brunswick, and had risen to the summit of the bank. He dominated it for two decades, outlasting would-be successors and building the bank's international presence, particularly in the southern hemisphere.

Ritchie asked if Day would be interested in becoming a director. "Saying 'yes' was the easiest career decision I ever took," Day recalls. Ritchie saw Day as a double threat: a director with considerable international experience and with ties to Atlantic Canada. Ritchie made it clear the job would involve flying regularly to Canada or elsewhere for meetings. Day responded that he would likely return to Nova Scotia in a few years and that he had retained a home (and a Scotiabank account) in Hantsport. Indeed, his father had opened an account with the bank on his arrival in Canada in the early 1920s. (In those days, customers had to write their account numbers on cheques, and he remembers his dad's number was 333.)

It was a stage in the circularity of Day's life, from Nova Scotia boyhood to big central Canadian job to British corporate stardom, and now he was planning to return to Nova Scotia. Day joined the bank's board, which would be one of his re-entry points to the Canadian business world.

In his final years in Britain, Day was constantly going home to Canada—particularly to Nova Scotia—to give speeches. One was attended by Allan Shaw, who headed the Shaw Group, a 125-year-old business heavily involved in the construction materials industry in Nova Scotia. Well known for its brick-making roots and formerly a family business, it was now owned by senior managers. Allan Shaw, the remaining link to the family ownership, knew of Day but had never met him. As he listened to the speech, Shaw thought, "I want this guy to be a director of our company." Shaw introduced himself, and noted that Day was about to return to Nova Scotia. Would he join the Shaw Group as a director? Day certainly knew of the company. It had been very active in the Annapolis Valley: Shaw Brick had been on hand when, in 1897, the town of Windsor burned to the ground; the Shaw family had bought its first brick-making machine to supply hundreds of thousands of bricks to rebuild the town, and later turned its hand to helping reconstruct Halifax after the devastating 1917 explosion.

Day agreed to join, and Allan Shaw would be a collaborator in some of his most important roles: on the boards of the Bank of Nova Scotia and Dalhousie University. Meanwhile, the word was getting around that here was a proven director with global stature, and he would soon be returning to Canada. He was experienced, battle proven, and he was one of them.

Donald Sobey, one of the siblings who ran a successful Nova Scotia retail business, had met Day on a trip to London. They had dined with mutual friends at a nice Italian restaurant where the waiters knew Day and would stop and sing opera once in a while during the meal. On a later trip, Donald had a more serious purpose. The Sobeys owned an insurance company in London that provided reinsurance through British and US underwriting companies. It was not performing well, and Day was asked to be a director. When the British-American partners were told that Sir Graham Day was joining the board, they were impressed.

They couldn't believe they could land a knight as a director. It also paved the way for a reunion of two Dalhousie alumni. In the Sobey family, Donald was the consummate investor while his brother David was the one who liked to roll up his sleeves in the stores. David had known Day slightly as a student at Dalhousie, and was amazed to learn of his career path.

Even with Day on the board, the Sobeys' British insurance business was not improving, so the directors gathered to decide what to do. As they prepared to close it down, Day could see one positive side: "Well, we'll be the ones who turn out the lights." Day's being pulled into the Sobeys' orbit opened up possibilities, as the family expanded the breadth of its businesses and prepared to strengthen its Canadian boards, including that of Empire, the family's holding company for its supermarket, pharmacy, and other interests. In 1992, Day joined that board as well.

That same year, as Day was preparing to go home to Nova Scotia, he heard from the province's premier, Donald Cameron, who had an urgent problem. The province was in the process of privatizing its electricity company, Nova Scotia Power, and it was at most three months away from a massive initial public offering of shares. The province's investment advisor had informed the cabinet that it could not go to the market with the current board, a group of largely political appointees reflecting the company's history as a Crown corporation. The premier had to assemble very quickly a business-oriented board that would be acceptable to the market. Day was on his list.

Day agreed to do it, and derived some perverse satisfaction that among the retiring directors of the former board was his father-in-law, Jake Creighton. The deal got done—a record Canadian initial public offering (IPO) at the time, at over a billion dollars. He would stay on the board through the privatization plus a couple of years. Meanwhile, he made lasting friendships, one with Derek Oland, scion of the Maritimes brewery dynasty, and another with Louis Comeau, the gregarious CEO who led the power company. Comeau, who once had been a Conservative MP and had run the power utility for thirteen years, provided an entry into the world of Acadian society and business. Day became a champion of Acadian institutions.

As he was facing the end of his time in Britain, Day was mindful of his obligation to Ann, who had dealt with all the moves, the absences, the times alone with the kids. Mind you, she got great enjoyment out of the life they led, and savoured the insight into the British governing classes. But before he took the Rover job, the two had drawn a line in the sand. They would leave when he turned sixty, which would be in May 1993. And 1993 was fast approaching.

At one point, Ann told him that she would go back to Nova Scotia in mid-1993, and he could choose to join her or not. "I need to be settled in a place, to have my garden, and know I have a base," Ann told him. Ann, even more than Graham, saw herself as a Nova Scotian. Her British life had been a magnificent adventure, but it was not really her. "I am just a little girl from Dartmouth, and when I was growing up Dartmouth was six thousand people and you knew everybody. Nobody thought twice about little Ann Creighton walking down the road to the ferry with her friends, and knowing every shopkeeper along the way." In a sense, she was returning to that freedom—her friends, her bridge games, her garden, with nary a security guard trailing behind. Nova Scotia is where she is at peace, says her son Michael. "Whereas Mum can go anywhere in Windsor or Hantsport or Halifax and she feels this is her community, I'm not sure she ever felt that in London. She had to be the wife of Sir Graham, one of the leading half-dozen industrialists in Great Britain. In Hantsport, she's Ann. She likes being Ann. She's always liked just being Ann."

Graham was more conflicted. He felt he belonged in Britain because he was part of the business community, even though, as Michael suggests, he inevitably would encounter the implied sneers that he was "NQ"—"not quite one of us, old boy." He had amassed seven honorary degrees from British institutions, membership in a couple of London's venerable livery companies, including the Worshipful Company of Shipwrights, and inclusion in the elite Whitehall Dining Club, whose dinners and discussions drew the top business and government leaders. "It was something which I think the Brits are very good at: providing lubrication between the upper reaches of the civil service and the upper reaches of business and industry," Day says. That is harder to do in a geographically sprawling nation such as Canada.

But Ann felt her husband badly needed to pull back. Certainly, he was apprehensive about returning—he had been so busy in Britain—but he was also very tired. There were opportunities in Britain, but he had to say no. He was both blessed and cursed with the reputation as a crisis manager. The UK government's thinking was: Something bad is happening! Who have we got? Oh, right. Graham.

In Britain, there is speculation to this day as to why he left. Ill health? Family crisis? Troubled marriage? Didn't he miss being a player in the big leagues? Deborah Jones, writing in *Financial Post Magazine* in 1994, said, "The choice to leave was his, and Brits do not quite believe that their adopted dragon slayer has really gone to Canada, of all places." Many did not understand the move. "If you've been a man as powerful as Graham has been in his career, and as high-profile, it must be very, very difficult just to switch out the lights and go back to whatever Nova Scotia is like," commented George Simpson, Day's successor as chairman of Rover Group.

Right to the end, other jobs had presented themselves. He got a feeler about becoming a "working peer," a government appointee to the House of Lords, someone with specialist knowledge or experience who would become a junior minister. He had no knowledge as to the authority of the person inquiring, but he said no right away. He was committed to going home. Besides, he would never have been happy in a junior minister's role. "I consider myself to be very fortunate that I missed being seduced by politics," he says. "I realized early enough that I would not have been either an effective or a happy politician."

Day certainly looked forward to some privacy. The loss of personal space was the hardest part of the Decade of Graham Day in Britain. And yet, in 2016, more than twenty years after leaving Britain, he admitted that "I miss the game, absolutely." During the last seven years in Britain, "I performed as well as I ever had or could. It didn't mean I was performing flawlessly, but within the limitations which we all have, I could not have performed better. I was absolutely at the best of my game."

What was the Graham Day legacy in Britain? He was part of a revolution. In the 1970s, when he left Britain the first time, state-owned industries accounted for 10 percent of gross domestic product. When he left again in 1993, the percentage was down to 3 percent, and he had played a big part in getting there. The Thatcher government had privatized about fifty companies, valued at about US$20 billion, and Day had had a hand in a number of them. He helped unleash the new enterprise culture in Britain, and became one of the heroes of the neo-conservative movement worldwide, although he would hate being labelled in that way. A lot of the stereotypes of radical neo-conservatism did not apply to him.

For a man who could talk tough with unions, he was regarded with grudging respect by many labour people. "He came with a Canadian reputation as a tough, clear-minded manager," says Lord Monks, a Labour peer who, as John Monks, had been a moderate official in the union movement in the 1980s. And, Monks says, he retained that reputation even through difficult assignments. "He was respected as a manager. He did not have a huge personality or a great leadership aura about him, but he was calm, and he knew what he was supposed to do, which was get costs down and get these things efficient in a way they weren't."

Monks, like many labour leaders, saw Day as essentially a technocrat who did Thatcher's bidding, but who was fair in his approach and generally not ideological. His most damning indictment was that Day left little lasting imprint on British life, when all was said and done. He just moved assets around. He was viewed as better than most of the rest of Thatcher's people. Coming from a unionist, it was probably high praise.

Yet it contrasts with the perspective inside the companies Day ran, among the management teams who worked with him. There, the image is more of a leader who was honest, warm, strategic—and inspirational—in how he approached his job. Day's most effective management tools—humour, persuasion, the human touch—worked best at close quarters. His supporters say his legacy was keeping companies whole and giving them a chance to survive and succeed. And, above all, he could recognize great people and bring them along.

For Roger Vaughan, his old shipyard colleague, Day was the best mentor he ever had, with good values and a dry sense of humour. "In Lancashire, we would say there is no 'side' to him. During my career, there was a little voice at the back of my head: 'Would Graham have done it that way?'" Just as Day himself had said about Les Smith. From the outside, it might be hard to see Day's impact. "He didn't seek a great public presence," says Vaughan, who would help lead a management buyout of one of the privatized shipyards and was later instrumental in developing the business school at the University of Newcastle. "He was charismatic, but he did not put himself out there—he just got on with the job."

Which is very Canadian.

John Gardiner credits Day, in many of his jobs, with being very good at managing industrial decline—at being realistic about goals, saving what was salvageable, and discarding what had no future. That is not a flashy description, but it is a rare talent, Gardiner says. Day was also skilled in navigating the vagaries of government policy and bureaucracy, which Gardiner likens to scaling the most treacherous Alpine peak: "He was the man who could climb the Eiger in the winter with ice on its face."

So the Days returned to their Cape Cod home on the Avon River in Hantsport, which they had built in the 1970s. That was the pact, after all, they had made a decade earlier. Deborah Jones, in her *Financial Post Magazine* article, said Day became a Canadian taxpayer on July 27, 1993—"at 3:10 in the afternoon," he noted, unhappy that he now had to pay income tax at a 55 percent rate, up from Britain's 40 percent. He marvelled that, in Hantsport, "he recently stayed put for three whole days, never once put on a shirt and tie, and dined on a bean supper at the local fire hall."

But he did not, as George Simpson remarked, just switch off the lights. He re-enlisted in that coterie of company founders, entrepreneurs, and professionals that form the so-called Maritime Mafia. There are many ways in which the Maritimes are disadvantaged in the global marketplace: a small and dramatically aging population, a declining resource base in fisheries and forestry, a meagre immigrant inflow. But collectively, the three provinces have a major competitive advantage: a business elite that is tight, collegial, and with a shared sense of a duty to serve the region. In 1993, the elite was led by a group of powerful directors and executives, including Toronto superdirector Purdy Crawford (now deceased), members of the Sobey family, New Brunswick premier Frank McKenna, blueberry and broadband supplier John Bragg, entrepreneur-investor John Risley, and the french fry–making McCain family. Graham Day settled into that milieu.

In this environment, the director jobs found him, and he could pick and choose—everything from Jacques Whitford, a Halifax-based environmental engineering firm, to a couple of Norwegian shipping companies. He enjoyed the work. He also found pockets of enterprise that he would support and encourage, and where his sense of justice would come into play. After the Nova Scotia Power offering, Day felt that CEO Louis Comeau was never paid adequately and that his contributions were undervalued by the board. It angered Day, who respected Comeau as a capable, underrated manager. When it was clear that Comeau would be leaving, Day said he would leave the board the same day.

Day and Comeau remained friends. Day soon got a call from headhunters charged with finding directors for NAV Canada, the company than runs Canada's air traffic control system. He said Comeau would be their guy: he understood regulation, he was bilingual, and he had been an MP. He got along well with everyone, including unions. Comeau went on the NAV Canada board and ultimately became chair. In turn, Comeau was helping put together an advisory board for a company called Acadian Seaplants, owned by the Deveau family of Halifax. The company was a leader in the science and processing of seaweed for all kinds of purposes, from human to animal food, fertilizer, and pharmaceuticals. It was international in scope, and Day agreed to join the board.

He also plugged into a thriving subsection of the Maritime Mafia, the Acadian connection. Friends saw how enthusiastically he supported a group of people who had survived conquest, expulsion, and treatment as second-class citizens, only to emerge with a resilient culture and a vibrant entrepreneurial spirit. Aldéa Landry, a high-profile New Brunswick Acadian—and former deputy premier in McKenna's Liberal government—found herself sitting on boards with this very impressive guy from London. She was intimidated by his CV, but he disarmed her with his down-to-earth ease, and they became fast friends. Asked to explain Day's connection with Acadian institutions, Landry says, "I think it is his sense of fairness."

Day himself says it is impossible to live in the Annapolis Valley without being reminded of the cruel expulsion of the Acadians by the British in the 1700s. So he has stepped up with support. Aldéa Landry has served as chancellor of Université Sainte-Anne, a francophone institution on the northwest shore of Nova Scotia, and Ann and Graham Day have backed a scholarship for young women in her name at the university. When Day, in his seventies, was diagnosed with prostate cancer, he received very skilled treatment at an Acadian hospital in Moncton, the Dr. Georges-L.-Dumont University Hospital Centre. It cemented his sense of connection with the Acadian population of the Maritimes.

At first, Ann felt guilty she had dragged him away from the bright lights of London, but when he got home, he was so busy it didn't matter. "He said the timing was right. He wasn't really sure at the time, but it turned out he was right," Ann says. As Graham would tell a reporter, in the years ahead, "I was determined to wear out rather than rust out."

It meant reuniting with families he had known or had heard of as a young man. In the Acadian connection and other projects he took on he also found a new mission: preparing the next generation of Canadian leaders.

CHAPTER 16

The Bank Job

Over most of Canadian business history, directors of major public companies were like celibates at an orgy. Interesting things were happening all around them, but they could not participate. They might nod and agree to what was taking place, but play no significant part in influencing the action. It was a position with theoretical power—after all, the board represents the actual owners—but hollow in its impotence.

Graham Day would never be that kind of director. He was never the passive kind who was just there for the fancy title or the canapés. What's more, he joined the Bank of Nova Scotia board during the transition to meaningful corporate governance. This is no coincidence. The governance of Canadian companies is not perfect now, but it is markedly better, and Day played his part.

The bank that he joined as director in 1988 could trace its origins to a meeting of Halifax business people in a coffee house on New Year's Eve 1831. The group was concerned about the monopoly of the private bank that dominated the city's commerce, and sought an alternative option. Three months later, the Bank of Nova Scotia was born. The bank spread geographically, and in the twentieth century its operating centre would move to Toronto. But Maritimers were always well represented among the bank's leadership. These leaders pushed the bank south to the Caribbean, where traditional trading ties led to banking connections. In 1889, the bank opened a branch in Kingston, Jamaica, to allow the trading of sugar, rum, and fish, the underpinnings of the triangular trade with Atlantic Canada and Britain. Scotiabank evolved into the Canadian bank—indeed, the Canadian company—most engaged in Latin America. Successive leaders would cement and extend those ties. Despite this broad hemispheric vision, Scotiabank also became the most conservative of the Big Five Canadian banks in its management and public profile.

It is hard to change a large Canadian bank. These are huge ships that cannot be turned by a single director, especially in the era of the rubber-stamp board presided over by an all-dominant chairman-CEO. But Graham Day would be part of the group that guided Scotiabank through expanded internationalization, a stronger consumer loan offering, and a new governance relationship between the board and the management team. And he worked with people to make them better.

His primary contact at the beginning was chairman and CEO Cedric Ritchie. Ritchie, whose low-key style belied his absolute mastery of the bank's politics and machinery, didn't need mentoring—he, in fact, taught Day a lot about banking and leadership. Ritchie was an old-style banker who became a rural branch teller in 1945 and stayed with the bank for fifty years. When he reached the top, he combined the jobs of CEO and chairman, as was typical. He was the personification of the prudent, hard-working banker; the institution reflected the man at the top.

"Cedric was very capable and steadfast, not an outward guy, not great in speech-making," says Rick Waugh, a Winnipeg boy whom Ritchie helped promote in the bank. Ritchie had a high school education, and came up through the bank as an internal auditor, travelling the country examining the branches' books. He got to know his craft better than the slick communicators. As a twenty-something analyst working for the department handling the bank pension fund, Waugh came before the senior bankers, including Ritchie, to discuss a potential investment. He explained that companies such as the one being discussed were valued according to cash flow, including one variation: earnings before interest, taxes, depreciation, and amortization, or EBITDA. Today, any punter on the street can talk about EBITDA, but this was the early 1970s. Ritchie, then general manager, asked: "What is EBITDA?" Waugh was dumbstruck, not by Ritchie's gap in learning, but by the courage to ask the question. That was his great talent. Waugh observes that "the banks were very hierarchical, very vertical, and very centralized. The position [of chairman and CEO] had a lot of power, and Ritchie had that position a long time."

Faced with an imperial CEO—even one with a non-imperial manner—the bank's board was relatively toothless. It sported as many as forty directors, representing provinces and territories, which made it unwieldy for effective decision making. The role was further diminished by the volumes of data dumped on directors at the beginning of meetings. The most meaningful discussion was held by the handful of powerful directors, including the chairman-CEO, who constituted the executive committee. Long-time Scotiabank director Allan Shaw remembers that, as they entered board meetings, directors would be handed a thick book of "credits" or bank loans. They were expected to wade through all the information, comment, and ask questions—and all within a couple of hours. It was impossible. It was a similar story with the audit committee: Shaw and his colleagues found there was simply too much to get through to make informed decisions. Shaw approached Ritchie with trepidation, asking that the directors be given packages of information in advance. The compromise solution was a "lockup" for an hour or two before the meeting. Similarly, smaller credits were dealt with elsewhere by staff, leaving the big loans for board members to peruse. It doesn't sound revolutionary, but it was a start.

The Maritime provinces were well represented on the Scotiabank board. Annapolis valley industrialist Roy Jodrey was a director for years, and then his son John. Also prominent were Shaw, of the eponymous Halifax construction materials concern, and frozen-food titan Harrison McCain. Then along came Graham Day, who, in the late 1980s, was still in England and preparing to re-enter the Maritime universe. He was a new breed: a professional corporate director with broad governance experience, but almost exclusively in Britain.

Day joined the bank's board knowing there were two kinds of directors: the ones who took up space and were wise to keep quiet, and the ones who "busted their asses to know the business." He would be the latter, but he had to relearn the Canadian way of business. The accounting terminology, processes, regulation, approvals processes, and risk factors were all new. His first committee appointment was as a member of the audit committee, because Ritchie—a master of audit—had told him this was the quickest way to learn about the bank. Day found he was right.

Day flew several times with Ritchie between Canada and Britain. "Each of these trips was a learning experience, as Ced did not sleep and offered me a monologue on a particular current issue. I remember particularly the one on liquidity." Day felt he contributed little of value in his first couple of years, but he worked hard and began to join more committees. He became the first chair of the bank's corporate governance committee. Even the existence of that committee meant a more serious commitment to governance issues. Allan Shaw says Day opened the way for a more questioning and effective board. He could go "toe-to-toe with those guys"—the senior managers—"and lots of people couldn't." Shaw says he and Day were there during a transition. "When I went on that board, nobody said anything unless they were asked." That would change.

The senior ranks of Canadian chartered banks resemble the Renaissance courts of Medici and Borgia for their palace intrigues, factions, and succession struggles. Scotiabank was no different. Ritchie would stay on top for two decades, as would-be rivals and successors came and went, frustrated that there was no movement at the top. Then Peter Godsoe emerged from the ranks, and he was a key transitional figure. He was born in Toronto, but he had impeccable Maritime credentials. His parents were from Nova Scotia and his brother Gerald was a prominent lawyer at Stewart McKelvey in Halifax. As a boy he had returned every summer, often visiting bucolic Chester, ocean playground for the Nova Scotia elite.

Peter Godsoe had also earned an MBA from Harvard, a sharp departure from the branch-to-boardroom background of Ced Ritchie. He embodied the shift in bank leadership from the employee who learned the trade on the job to someone who came out of university with a strong grounding, not yet applied, in management and risk. The emergence of the MBA as a management credential in Canada had started in the late 1950s with Richard Thomson, a smart MBA out of Harvard who joined the Toronto-Dominion Bank. Thomson had risen to the CEO post and surrounded himself with other MBAs, including Robert Korthals, Charles Baillie, and a group of up-and-comers from the business school at the University of Western Ontario. More than any institution, the TD Bank established in Canada the idea of the MBA as the must-have degree for the rising business person. By the 1990s, the concept had invaded all the banks; even bankers who started in the lowly branches were expected to add gravitas through a Harvard executive program.

Godsoe learned the ropes and emerged as vice-chairman with a clear shot at the top when, if ever, Ritchie left. "It was probably a flip of the coin whether I'd ever get the job or not, but they sort of ran out of people," Godsoe says, with his classic self-deprecation. He remembers going to London for business and having dinner with director Graham Day. Day picked him up at the hotel on a day when his picture had been splashed across the business pages of the newspapers. When they entered the restaurant, people turned to catch a glimpse of him. Day had a face that was known. "I had a lovely dinner, and I was with this rock star," Godsoe recalls. "He's very good company. He's sort of a bit of a Renaissance man, he reads broadly, and he does all these other things [besides business]." And, Godsoe adds, "he had that military bearing. He sort of stands that way. You'd think he's right out of the Guards."

It was the beginning of a strong personal bond. In 1995, when Ritchie finally stepped aside as CEO and chairman, Godsoe was appointed his successor. Day would be a rock of support as Godsoe sought to put his stamp on the bank after the long reign of Cedric Ritchie. (In retirement, Ritchie kept coming to the office most days, even after he lost his sight and almost to the day he died in March 2016 at age eighty-eight.) By that time, a working relationship had developed. "Graham was the role model of a director for my generation." Godsoe says. "He's as good as I've come across." In Godsoe's view, "[Day] doesn't waste a lot of time, it's just not his way. He has no real issue other than to give you his view of what was going on there, what you were doing, how you were doing it. There would be no looking for some return. He's not looking for power—he doesn't care about those things. He cares about it working, and he cares about people." Godsoe received an education in the directorial art, which he put to his own use as a chairman and a lead director in other companies. "I was watching a very honest man, a very smart man who really only has two things that he wants done: to make that board and the company work well, and you as the CEO to work well."

Day realized he was not dealing with a normal succession. It was a sea change. Ritchie had an innate judgment of what made sense for the bank and its customers, honed by years of experience. Godsoe had a quicksilver mind, a grasp of the possible, and a highly developed sense of risk. As a member of the HR committee, Day applauded Godsoe's initiative in opening up prospects for women to join the senior ranks. "Fairness aside, the talent pool was dramatically improved."

It was a tumultuous period, dominated by merger talk among the Big Five banks. Royal Bank of Canada and the Bank of Montreal announced plans to merge in 1998, and then the Toronto-Dominion Bank and the Canadian Imperial Bank of Commerce stepped forward to say they would join, too. These deals would have dramatically reshaped Canadian business and society, but the federal government moved to squelch them. The Bank of Nova Scotia initially had been the odd man out, but three years later Godsoe led the bank into talks with the Bank of Montreal. This transaction, too, was shot down. After all the jockeying, the Big Five rolled on as before. But within the goup, there was movement. The period of Godsoe's leadership was a heady time for Scotiabank as it moved up in the standings from a perennial fourth or fifth to the number two bank in size.

Rick Waugh was also part of that growth story as he rose to become a contender for the top job post-Godsoe. He had started off in a Winnipeg branch, and was transferred to Toronto, where, in his late twenties, he managed the main branch on King Street. He acquired an MBA from York University, and had mentors who pushed him into the all-important credit side of the bank. As an executive in corporate lending, Waugh would go to the board for major loan approvals. Graham Day did not have a lot of questions—it was not the nature of boards in those days—but he had his favourites. Waugh knew that, if the deal involved shipping, Day would be very alert to the risks. He was sure to ask his classic question: where was the ship built? If the answer was South Korea, which it often was, "we would have a real battle to get it done," Waugh recalls. Day would counsel the bank to be careful about the quality of construction. "It was a good question," Waugh says, "and he had the expertise. So I would say to the others, 'Okay, get ready for this one.'"

Day would also focus on what changes to bank policy or practice would mean for employees and customers. As a result, Hantsport, Nova Scotia, became perhaps the most closely watched branch in the country. When an issue came up, he wanted to know how it would affect the people on the front line, and Hantsport was where he could do his due diligence. "You had to be ready for that customer-service, employee-satisfaction kind of question," Waugh says.

As Cedric Ritchie built Canada's most international bank, he tapped the views of Day and McCain, who were those rare directors with direct international experience: Day as a globe-trotting executive and McCain as an entrepreneur building a worldwide food company. And both sat on the board's powerful executive committee. International banking was volatile, and the Latin American economies went through periodic crises. But Ritchie had a long-term view, and stayed the course. Waugh notes that "originally, he was the guy from Bath, New Brunswick. And then he started really pushing [the international side]. Those two directors would have been very important."

In time, Day would emerge as a pivotal player in the broader push to make corporate boards better informed, better prepared, and more meaningful. For many shareholder activists, a key change would be to separate the roles of chair of the board and chief executive officer. *Globe and Mail* columnist Eric Reguly saw that change as a watershed in corporate governance: "A separate chairman reinforces the principle, conveniently forgotten in some companies, that management in general and the CEO in particular are accountable to the board, and the board to shareholders. As many institutional investors have pointed out, the board cannot effectively monitor management if the lead manager runs the board. It's called a conflict of interest."

Governance advocates focused most intently on the banks, the companies with the widest reach, the most shareholders, and the highest profile. The banks fought back, claiming their history of combining the two roles had not harmed performance or decision making. Also, they argued that chief executives needed the added authority, especially since there was little movement in the United States in this direction. In Canada, the issue constantly arose at annual general meetings. The turning point came when the activists' campaign was joined by two major pension funds, the massive Caisse de dépôt et placement du Québec and the Ontario Teachers' Pension Plan. In early 2001, the Royal Bank, as it prepared to pass the baton to new CEO Gord Nixon, became the first to separate the jobs of chair and CEO; the rest of the banks followed.

The Bank of Nova Scotia, however, did not want to make the change in the midst of Godsoe's tenure. "It was a magic time to be in the bank because you made money whether you were good, bad, or indifferent," Godsoe recalls. "And we were doing very well. They couldn't make a good argument for changing at that time." So the board settled on an interim plan: Peter Godsoe would be the last officer to hold the combined offices of chairman and CEO. Until his successor as CEO and a non-executive chairman were appointed, Graham Day would be the lead director and would chair the executive committee. The lead director is the senior independent director, but, in the evolution of governance, the role was similar to a non-executive chairman. Essentially, Day and Godsoe became co-chairs.

Helen Parker served on the Scotiabank board for twenty-six years, often commuting from the Northwest Territories, where her husband had a stint as commissioner. She says of Day, "As lead director, he was very effective. He grasped issues so quickly himself, but had great patience with others not doing it as quickly. He has a sense of humour he could use effectively." In her long term as a director, Parker saw the rising importance of board committees and the work they did, and the shift to a much more democratic process. The board became a more effective forum as it shrank in numbers from forty-one to twenty-nine and now to seventeen. But, as a result, being a board member today is a much more demanding role. "Graham was a significant instrument of change, in a very quiet way and not by pushing," she says, attributing his style to his Maritime roots.

As for Day, he supported the separation of the chair and CEO jobs, but his thinking had a strong pragmatic side. "I was absolutely convinced that this wasn't a ditch we should die in," he says now. The board was well aware at annual meetings that the question was top of mind for many shareholders. People were very polite in saying that this was not personal—Godsoe was well liked—but Day could see the inevitable. If so, sooner was better than later, although he could not say that he felt the bank would be better governed.

As lead director, he had chaired the executive committee, and he felt that his relationship with Godsoe had been frank and open. "I also believed that the executive committee functioned well, and that we very adequately kept the board advised. So, in a pure governance point of view, I didn't think a lot would change. And I don't think it has." But, at the time, Day's other reason to advocate splitting the jobs was to support the new CEO. "I thought that to have a pretty solid chairman might be helpful to Rick Waugh even if he didn't want the help—because he wasn't Peter Godsoe."

Indeed, the bank had appointed Waugh as president, thus signalling he was the favourite to succeed Godsoe. Just as Ritchie and Godsoe were different, Godsoe and Waugh were like night and day. Godsoe was cerebral and soft-spoken; Waugh was outgoing and ebullient, with a tendency to speak before he thought. Waugh had developed his reputation as an unconventional populist banker. He would often show up at board events in a sports jacket, not a suit. Harrison McCain would lead the jokes, pointing out the casual style of this westerner. Among the eastern-flavoured board, Waugh would call his sports jacket "my Winnipeg suit." Both Godsoe and Waugh were able executives, but on the board there were some concerns about Waugh and whether the bank should skip a generation in choosing a CEO. And once the choice was made, Day says, "Rick had to understand that, if he wanted to be the chief executive, that's what he was going to be. He was not going to be the chairman."

As the bank and other companies absorbed these changes, Day grasped the broader evolution in the corporate world. A *Globe and Mail* article in February 1996 reported on Day's testimony to the Senate banking committee, where he strongly urged a standard training course for directors. "A first-time parent and a first appointment to a public company board are two very responsible roles for which, in our culture, we demand little if any preparation," he said. Most directors learned on the job, he observed. Instead, he said first-time directors should have basic knowledge before joining a public company. He proposed that an unspecified organization set up a training program that would be offered in a variety of locations across Canada, probably within universities. Thus the early thinking behind programs such as the Institute of Corporate Directors and the Directors College, now accepted foundations for a directorial career.

Day's time on the board was coming to an end. He and Peter Godsoe both retired from the bank at its annual meeting in 2004. Rick Waugh assumed the role of CEO; Toronto corporate lawyer Arthur Scace would be the first non-executive chairman. Waugh insists he did not take the separation of powers personally. He had plenty of experience taking deals to the board for approval, so he could work well within the new framework. The title did not matter in terms of his ability to function internally. But outside the bank, his peers in the United States would ask how he could do his job without the authority of the two titles. When he travelled in international banking circles, he was concerned about the tendency to write him off. "You have to wonder if they thought they were wasting their time talking to you," Waugh says, as if he was not quite equal as, say, Jamie Dimon, the powerful chair and CEO of JP Morgan Chase.

Day insists that, in the end, it didn't matter much. As the other Canadian banks conformed, it ceased to be an issue. "No one doubted who the leader was in the public eye. You know, no financial journalist wrote about the chairman of the Bank of Nova Scotia." Today, it is hard to think the public even knows who the bank's chairman is. Titles matter, Waugh agrees, and in the final analysis, the word "chief," as in chief executive officer, is the one that confers authority. "To have a *c* in your title is what you want; it tells the people at the other end of the table that you are the boss."

After all the anguish about succession, Rick Waugh had an impressive run as CEO. Through the shock of the financial crisis of 2008–09, the bank stood tall, and was one of the few major banks worldwide that did not have to issue shares to boost its capital. Canadian banks all did well, comparatively, and Waugh now believes one factor was the independence of their boards. "There are very many times you can use your board as a defence," he says, often by saying, "I have to talk to my board." If you are chair as well as CEO, that is a harder thing to say. "Many times I would do that," Waugh says. Looking back, Day is proud of his time at the bank. It was work that was important for Canada. He had the intuitive feeling that, of all the commercial activities in Canada, the single most important is the work of Canada's banks.

As a pioneer in corporate governance, however, he worries that the debate has gone too far: that "the governance tail wags the business dog." He was an early supporter of directors' courses, and was honoured as a Fellow of the Institute of Corporate Directors. But he now worries about the attitude that "look, I've got this designation from the director's school. Therefore I must be a skilled director." No, he warns, that is not true. You might have this suite of courses, and you might understand the form of good governance, but you cannot be prepared fully for a corporate directorship until you have commercial experience and understand the language and processes of business. It's a matter of form *and* substance, he maintains.

Looking back, the job of a director has become more demanding because of the volume of work, including the massive task of complying with new governance rules. Day wonders if CEOs might welcome the added burden on directors. If you believe in conspiracy theories, he says, you might consider whether chief executive officers are quite happy to have boards focus on governance because they have less time to critique the business. "I find that very worrying."

His concerns are a reminder that movements come and go, governance trends rise and fall, but, in the end, it is all about people and power.

The Borgias would have understood.

CHAPTER 17

Payback Time

Mark MacDonald was in a dark place. One day in December 2009, he stood before a throng of workers in the port town of Yarmouth, on the far western edge of Nova Scotia, and told them they would lose their jobs. Then MacDonald dealt with a flurry of media questions about his decision to close down the ferry service that ran between Yarmouth and Maine, putting more than a hundred people out of work.

It was a harsh blow for the workers and an emotional hit for MacDonald. Six years earlier, he had made the transition from a lawyer at Stewart McKelvey with a specialization in marine law to a new life as a ferry company chief executive and, later, owner. He joined the company that operated Bay Ferries, a key link in Atlantic Canada's transportation network. Bay Ferries had been running ships between Nova Scotia and Maine for years, including the Yarmouth-Portland-Bar Harbor service. But the provincial government, caught up in an austerity drive, had withdrawn its subsidy. In the face of an already weak economy, buffeted by the high Canadian dollar, Bay Ferries could not continue the service, and the cost would be jobs and loss of tourism revenue.

After delivering the crushing news that morning, it was time for MacDonald to head back to Halifax, and he had a couple of options. He could take the route up the South Shore, the way he had come. He decided instead on the other way around, skirting the northwest coast and passing through the Annapolis Valley on his way to the little town of Hantsport.

"I placed a call to Graham and asked if he was available," MacDonald says. "Graham" was Graham Day, who gave one of his familiar replies: "Yes, I am, young man." (To Day, you were a young man even if you had bade farewell to youth long ago.) So Mark MacDonald ended up at the Day house for what he calls "a couple of hours of advice and psychotherapy."

Day was always there for MacDonald, just as he was for many people, including not a few young lawyers, past and present, at Stewart McKelvey. MacDonald didn't go to Hantsport for any miracle cure. It was just to talk to someone who had been through all kinds of change. "He can talk with authority that, yes, the sun is going to come up tomorrow and probably it will shine. That was the way it was."

Ever since MacDonald met Day two decades earlier, the older man had been part of his decision making whenever he reached an important professional crossroads. So, when MacDonald left the law practice to become a ferryboat service operator, Day was there for him. When he took on full ownership of the company, Day was there again—as he was on the day of the ferry closing.

Day does not practise mentorship so much as sponsorship. He becomes fully engaged in the lives of the people he backs. It is not just periodic advice, but a kind of pact. His interest does not stop at the going-away party. If his protegés leave the place where Day first found them, his support goes with them and continues through the phases of their lives. He is there for the good times and the bad.

Mark MacDonald got through his day from hell, and in 2016 the provincial government invited him back to run the service between Yarmouth and Portland. The day we talked, MacDonald described how he had been messaging back and forth with Graham Day as they discussed the design of the new catamaran ferry the company was leasing from the US Navy.

For Day, a giant on the international scene, coming home to Canada provided opportunities to thank the institutions and people that had contributed to his successful career. What better way to do that than to help develop new generations of leaders? He could provide the kind of guidance that had helped him escape a frustrated teenage existence and outgrow a humdrum law practice. He could offer his experience to places such as Dalhousie University, where he first learned the law; the Canadian military, where he learned the value of service; and the law firm that never employed him, but whose managing partner was so important in kick-starting his business career.

Gordon Cowan, distinguished teacher, jurist, and one-time Liberal candidate, was heading a predecessor firm to Stewart McKelvey when he concluded that Day would never be content with small-town law, and pulled strings to get him into Canadian Pacific. It reflected a time-honoured tradition in those days, when senior Nova Scotia lawyers lent a hand to junior solicitors. It came out of a sense of obligation to the profession that went beyond making money. But this practice faded as the law became a much more blatantly commercial enterprise and there was less time for personal mentoring. Day, however, believed there was value in keeping the tradition alive. That became his mission, and it drove his support of young lawyers such as Mark

MacDonald, Lydia Bugden, Jim Dickson, and a host of others.

It was, in fact, Mark MacDonald who reconnected Graham Day with Gordon Cowan's firm. As a young lawyer in the late 1980s, he happened to read that a Nova Scotian named Graham Day had been knighted by the queen. MacDonald was on the management committee of Stewart McKelvey, and proposed that its members explore whether Day might consider a working relationship with the firm.

By this time, Cowan's old Halifax practice had mushroomed into a regional superfirm: along with McInnes Cooper, one of Atlantic Canada's Big Two. McInnes Cooper had a long history—it had acted for the White Star Line, whose new ship, the *Titanic*, sank in the North Atlantic in 1912—and it had employed George Robertson, another of Graham Day's mentors. Stewart McKelvey's predecessor firms had employed towering figures in Nova Scotia law—not just Cowan, but also his powerful rival for pre-eminence, Frank Covert, whose last name captures the spirit of his confidential services to empire builders such as Frank Sobey and Roy Jodrey.

Day accepted the offer from Stewart McKelvey, and in January 1990 became the firm's counsel, thus gaining a home base for his reimmersion into Canadian business life. As counsel, it would have been easy for Day to coast on his contacts and laurels as a rainmaker. But he dove more deeply into Stewart McKelvey's DNA, taking a direct hand in influencing its culture and its continuity. His circle of contacts rippled wider as new lawyers entered the firm. In one instance, MacDonald recruited a young woman, Lydia Bugden, to the firm. After an interval, MacDonald knew he might be leaving Stewart McKelvey, and he felt it was imperative that she meet Day. "My reaction was: why would Sir Graham want to meet with me?" Bugden recalls. But she and MacDonald did the pilgrimage to Hantsport to lunch with the firm's counsel at one of his favourite spots: the Grand Pré winery, on the edge of nearby Wolfville. From that time, Day became the invisible hand in helping her career along. "Graham works in mysterious ways," Bugden says. "He has a plan, and the end result is more than you could possibly expect. And he has a keen interest in the advancement of women and women around boardroom tables."

The Day method is to have a talk with a young lawyer, perhaps at one of his famous lunches, and get a sense of what he or she is all about. Not long afterward, a call comes in with the offer of an assignment, a directorship, a new client. There is no immediate information on how the connection was made, but there is always the suspicion of Day's invisible hand. Bugden had been with Stewart McKelvey for about seven years and had made partner, when she started to work on the files of the Jodrey family in the Annapolis Valley. Later, she was pulled into the massively complex and rewarding legal megaproject to reorganize the Jodrey holdings. In 2015, her skills were rewarded, as she became the CEO of Stewart McKelvey. "[Day] is such a visionary in how he approaches things," Bugden says. "He always has an interest in what he calls 'the great firm.' We know client relationships are maintained and work comes our way because of Graham."

That work reflects a passionate interest in the progress of Atlantic companies big and small. Day is known to guide a small business new to the legal system by making an introduction to a lawyer. When an expanding Atlantic business wants to go global, it might assume it has outgrown the local law firm. There is a tendency to think it needs the expertise of a bigger law firm based in Toronto, New York, or London. Day has convinced companies that the required expertise resides within Halifax and the law firm he represents.

The advice is not limited to law. Day's acolytes find they can talk to him on just about any subject. They know their mentor has broad expertise not just in ships, but in cars, trains, chocolate eggs, and power stations. He knows the places to find great sushi, the operas of Puccini, and the on-base percentage of José Bautista—all fodder for the man's restless curiosity. "You know the beer commercial, the one about the most interesting man in the world?" Mark MacDonald asks. "It's that sort of thing. Without trivializing it, that is what it is all about." MacDonald adds that Day's authority emanates from the fact that "I don't think there is anyone in the world with his experience."

Day's return to Halifax also meant a reunion with another institution so influential in his life. Allan Shaw, his cohort on the Scotiabank board, was then also chair of the board of governors at Dalhousie University. Shortly after Day relocated to Hantsport, Shaw approached him to become the university's chancellor. As a young man, Day had had rocky relations with the university hierarchy, but the place had been pivotal in his development as a lawyer and a leader, and now he appreciated the university's positive influence on Maritime, and Canadian, society. He accepted Shaw's proposal, becoming the university's fourth chancellor in 1994.

At the time, Dalhousie's president, Howard Clark, was facing significant financial challenges and a difficult labour situation. In Day's view, much is owed to Clark for establishing a solid financial basis on which Dalhousie could build. He credits Allan Shaw for leading structural reforms that, while maintaining a balance of interests, reduced the numbers on the board of governors and the senate, making them more effective bodies.

Shaw and Day were both occupying their roles of chair and chancellor when Winnipeg-born historian Tom Traves became president. Day believes his most effective time as chancellor was in the first two years of Traves's appointment, when he and Shaw were able to advise him on crucial governance issues. Those who know him say Day loved being chancellor, even though his old antipathy towards campus politics resurfaced at times. Eventually, he felt his role had become largely ceremonial. Day understands the importance of ceremony in an institution such as Dalhousie, but in 2001 he felt it was the right time to leave.

The ties to Dalhousie remain strong, cemented by personal relationships and the fact that there is a scholarship fund in Day's name in the school of management. It was the initiative of entrepreneur John Bragg, who encouraged many of Day's business friends to contribute. Day himself has been adding funds and preparing for future provisions. The scholarships—up to $50,000—are available to students from Atlantic Canada who meet academic conditions and who might have an economic need. He also supports the law school's annual Sir Graham Day Ethics, Morality, and the Law Lecture, a rich contribution to the intellectual life of the university. The funding enables top-flight international speakers to come to Dalhousie to deliver thought-provoking talks. A partnership with the CBC Radio program *Ideas* gives the lecture a national profile. Lydia Bugden marvels that, on a Friday night in Halifax, a town of lively pubs and restaurants, the lecture can draw a full house of mostly university students.

Day's payback obligations extend to his military experience. He never went to war. He never faced enemy fire or the emotional anguish of friends dying around him, but he is a military man in spirit and instinct. He believes in service, and military service is the highest calling he can imagine. He was a child during the Second World War, and as an eighteen-year-old yearned to go to Korea to escape his adolescent funk, but he knew his father would not consent. But he has done his part as a reservist, honorary regimental colonel, mentor to senior military people, and a father to a military leader.

Part of his attachment springs from his respect for history, hierarchy, and tradition. He is not one who likes to use warlike analogies for business, as they trivialize life-and-death danger. Yet he can appreciate the parallels. He likes to formulate and articulate strategy, but he understands that he has to give rein to the people on the spot. Military and business campaigns are won on the ground by the men and women you equip and command.

As a young lawyer in Windsor, Nova Scotia, Day was a member of the army reserves, and had a brief stint in the judge advocate general branch during the Cuban Missile Crisis. When he moved to Montreal in 1964, he transferred to the Victoria Rifles, but after two years, the pressures of his Canadian Pacific job forced him to leave the reserves.

In Britain, he was close to military people and events, as his companies manufactured everything from nuclear and conventional submarines to wheeled vehicles to missiles to small arms. This brought him into regular contact with the Ministry of Defence and senior officers. Through the mid-1980s and early 1990s, Day served on committees that advised the defence establishment on resources and procurement. He would occasionally lecture at staff colleges, and he did finally get to Sandhurst—as a reviewing officer.

His connection with the military became intensely personal on the day in 1983 when son Michael phoned to say he was joining the Canadian Forces. To some extent, Graham has lived the military life through his son's impressive career. Michael feels he was fortunate to have a father who so knowingly understands his life and career choices. And, of course, there have been long telephone conversations about military strategy, for both are students of the discipline. "The Second World War for him looms huge," Michael says, sitting in his home in Ottawa on a dark winter afternoon. "If you went down to my library, he's responsible for about 50 percent of it, because he buys me books." Michael's house contains three thousand books on military history and politics, and Graham's basement library in Hantsport is similarly adorned with military books, along with shelves of mysteries and thrillers, which he devours on airplane trips.

Michael is always quick to add that his father had nothing to do with his decision to enlist—"with the exception that it was always seen to be an honourable profession and that that was a good thing to do." That good thing continued after Graham returned to Canada and renewed his interests and connections. In May 2005, he was asked to become the honorary colonel of the West Nova Scotia Regiment, one of Canada's oldest regiments.

Several years later, the judge advocate general of the Canadian Forces, Major-General Blaise Cathcart, was looking for a new colonel commandant, one who would be not just a ceremonial figure, but a distinguished lawyer who could engage with the JAG mission, strategy, and outreach. He had read a magazine piece on Canada's top lawyers and noticed Graham Day's name. Cathcart and Michael Day knew each other, and Cathcart asked if Michael's father might be interested in joining JAG. He certainly was. He took up the appointment in May 2011 and served for four years.

At that time, Cathcart felt there was a lot of misinformation about military law and the work of the JAG branch, particularly regarding the controversial transfer of prisoners in Afghanistan to the local authorities. He concluded he needed help educating the public. He also could use someone to work internally with legal officers, and help advise Cathcart himself.

In explaining military law, people in uniform often were tuned out by a sceptical public. But Day could talk to civilians, including lawyers, about how the system worked. In JAG, "you are serving two professions, the legal profession and the profession of arms," Cathcart explains. "They come together at times, quite starkly when we are putting men and women in harm's way. Having someone of Graham's experience was invaluable."

A high point for Cathcart and Day was when the queen accepted to become colonel-in-chief of the JAG branch. Cathcart explains that the queen is very selective with the honours she takes. The JAG branch had actually been approached by the royal secretary, who asked if it would agree to the queen's service. It certainly would! In June 2014, the two men were invited to Buckingham Palace for a private audience. Day was just finishing up his tenure with the JAG branch, and it was a special moment. Cathcart remembers Sir Graham's comment to the queen was that she had knighted him in 1989 and here he was again. "You're still working," the queen drily observed. Day had to bite his tongue not to say: "And so are you, Your Majesty."

Day is someone who recognizes the human character in its varied manifestations. He supports and encourages leadership, wherever it appears. His backing of Acadian leaders reflects that open-mindedness; so does his sponsorship of women. He also feels that military leadership is a compelling preparation for leadership in other worlds, such as business.

He is encouraging Michael in his transition to civilian life. Michael, like his father before him, is working with the Bragg family company as a member of the advisory board and, still young in his fifties, no doubt will seek other roles in the business world.

Graham has helped others make such transitions. Vice-Admiral Greg Maddison had one of Canada's most distinguished military careers, rising to the role of senior naval officer before retiring as vice-chief of the defence staff. The highlight was his key role in commanding the operations of Canada's forces worldwide during the war in Afghanistan. But he faced the common dilemma of defence leaders: how to find similar fulfilment in their post-military lives. He remembers getting a call from Graham Day, who was on the board of Canada Steamship Lines (now CSL). How would he like to be a corporate director?

It arose from conversations between Day and his son about the potential for ex-military leaders in corporate roles. Canadian companies do not have a history of looking for leaders among retired officers, unlike those in the United States, Britain, and France, where leadership is leadership, wherever it is found, and the qualities are transferable. Day believes the Canadian attitude is an extension of how shabbily our military people are treated in peacetime.

Graham Day is no longer on the CSL board, but Maddison remains. He feels it is a group with much of the same integrity he encountered in the Canadian Forces. "It was a pretty easy fit," he says, and Day helped ease the transition through advice and mentoring. Day is often credited with helping guide CSL through a period of growth when it moved beyond the Great Lakes to become a global bulk shipping company. CSL once had an old-boys-network board, but as the company expanded and became more complex, its owners, the Martin family, decided to diversify with genuinely independent directors, such as Day. In turn, the new crew helped pull in other strong candidates, such as Maddison. Day had heard from his son that Maddison was very good in assessing talent. At the time, Day was on CSL's human resources committee, which Maddison joined. He became the committee chairman after Day retired.

Day continued to clear a path for the former senior soldier's development. "He takes people through a level of experience and advice for a few years, and then bingo, you've got it," Maddison says. He recalls that, soon after he retired from the forces, he began sitting down with Day to talk through his experiences, some in difficult situations in Afghanistan. Day would listen, then add his observations of Thatcher and other leaders in crisis situations. Maddison could see the parallels, and they would explore what they learned.

Day is a very modern kind of leader in his mentoring, particularly in his support of women and underdogs. But he is also an old-time story spinner in the Maritime tradition, who can hold a room spellbound. Sometimes, he just wants to correct the flawed representation of history. One incident stands out. It concerns a scene in a movie showing an elderly woman in a raincoat entering a little grocery store. She appears to be in a daze as she buys a pint of milk and worries about the price. As the movie *Iron Lady* unfolds, it becomes apparent that this is Margaret Thatcher, once a powerful prime minister, now reduced to an old woman in an advanced stage of dementia, as played by the gifted actor Meryl Streep.

The Stewart McKelvey lawyers were treated to a showing of the movie, with Day offering commentary. He explained that he could never buy this cinematic portrait of the woman he served. For one thing, there was no security officer shown in the scene, he said, and she always had security with her. He could list all the ways the movie did not measure up. But one aspect he liked. Thatcher had this facial thing, a subtle way of clenching her teeth to denote determination. A couple of muscles would tense up. Day saw Streep do this. "It was a powerfully true portrayal in a bad movie."

Another thing bugged him. Thatcher always wore a brooch, and always on the left. In the movie, the brooches moved from one side to the other. It was a small thing, but Day remains unflaggingly true to the memory of the woman who changed his life. Loyalty, to the people and institutions that made him, would be centre stage in all his performances.

CHAPTER 18

Family Man

Bill McEwan remembers his initiation into the supermarket company known as Sobeys and its founding family from northern Nova Scotia. He was sitting in a room in Toronto with a group of board members, who were sizing him up as their potential next CEO.

McEwan was a career grocer in his mid-forties who had grown up in British Columbia, started bagging groceries in a local store at fifteen, and climbed to the top ranks of the A&P grocery chain as head of its US Atlantic division. It was now 2000, and he had been headhunted by the Sobeys to run their dramatically expanding supermarket company.

The Sobeys were just coming off a blockbuster takeover of the Oshawa Group, a national food distributor and retailer more than three times their own size. "The Sobeys had literally swallowed a whale," remembers one of their former senior managers. The takeover meant formidable integration challenges for what, for many years, had been a regional company based in tiny Stellarton, in Nova Scotia's Pictou County. The company's ownership was in the second generation, after builder Frank Sobey had taken over his father's little store in Stellarton. The family was moving from hands-on management to a more detached ownership role, and for the second consecutive time, the next CEO would be a non-family outsider. The job, however, would be much bigger and more challenging than ever before.

It was McEwan's first interview for the job, and here he was, confronting a search committee that included David and Donald Sobey, the two brothers who had expanded their father's company into the number two supermarket chain in Canada; Paul Sobey, David's accountant son and a key architect of the Oshawa Group deal; and some independent directors, including a tall, bearded man with a deep voice and a sparkle in his eye.

McEwan, a quick-witted, irreverent type, was in a good mood, enjoying the interview, when, two-thirds of the way through, David Sobey asked a question. It was an important question, reflecting the tug of war pulling the family between two forces: the company's sacred Nova Scotia roots and its westward business push to central and western Canada. David observed that McEwan must have discussed the job with his wife Donna. So how would she feel about moving to relatively isolated Stellarton, after living in New Jersey, close to where A&P's Atlantic operations were based?

"She says she is going to miss me," was McEwan's deadpan retort. There was a moment of silence as the group processed this answer.

Suddenly the guy with the beard, name of Graham Day, piped up: "Where is Donna from?" "Meaford, Ontario," McEwan volunteered, referring to a town on Georgian Bay in rural Ontario. "Wait a minute," Day said, "if she could live in Meaford, she can live in Stellarton." The whole room relaxed, and there were chuckles. It was the right comment at the right time. "That was my first fond memory of Graham," Bill McEwan remembers sixteen years later. (Day, in fact, knew Meaford, because his daughter-in-law came from there.)

There would be plenty of those moments. McEwan took the job at Sobeys, guiding it through the integration and its expansion as a national retailer until he retired because of poor health in 2012. Yes, both McEwans did move to Stellarton. And Day became someone Bill could rely on for wisdom, humour, and the perfect thought, the ideal epigram, that would lift the younger man out of a funk and guide his forward thinking.

It is typical of Day's role on boards. He had earned a reputation as a shoot-from-the-hip CEO who could make decisions on the fly. He had been a high-profile captain of industry in Britain. But his new role was more subtle and discreet. He could still be shockingly decisive—one of his mottos, remember, is "sometimes wrong, never in doubt." But he got very good at the quiet background conversations that stiffen the spine of a CEO, a board member, or a chair.

Day would gain a lot of experience with private, family-owned companies, largely but not exclusively in Atlantic Canada. Paul Martin's Montreal-based CSL is one prominent example from outside the region. Through all these associations, two challenges were pre-eminent: management succession and oversight—sometimes expressed as governance. Some families handle these things better than others. Says Day, "These issues exist outside family business, but family adds a dynamic which sometimes can be toxic."

He sees family businesses following a classic evolution: First comes the entrepreneur phase, with a founder or founders who chart their own path, often with little outside input. The second stage is the owner-manager phase, when the business is more complex and decisions are reached more collegially. Third is the investor stage, when the family steps back and leaves the management decision making to other people.

The transition from stage one to stage two is often the most seamless—it just happens—but very few family businesses reach the investor stage. "Stage three requires shareholder maturity, the exercise of judgment, and the avoidance of meddling," Day says. Mechanisms such as family councils seek to combine ownership interests and the avoidance of tinkering. But, too often, "hope triumphs over achievement." "There is no silver bullet," he concludes, although families can improve their chances by, for example, preparing younger members through education, on-the-job skills training, and simply tough love.

He speaks as much through sadness as recrimination. One of his early brushes with family companies came through Harrison McCain, when they were both directors at the Bank of Nova Scotia. McCain was half of a remarkable brother team that built a global food company from Florenceville, New Brunswick, a small village in the St. John River valley. Several times, Harrison discussed the possibility of Day's joining McCain Foods, but he could never see it as something he wanted to do. Then, one weekend in 1994, Harrison phoned and said he needed a favour. The relationship between Harrison and his brother Wallace had reached the breaking point as they battled over succession. Wallace had pushed for his son Michael to become the future CEO; Harrison strenuously opposed the idea.

The dispute cut a chasm through the Atlantic Canada business class. People who wanted no part of the family argument, who respected both men, were sometimes forced to choose sides. Toronto lawyer Purdy Crawford had been a university friend of Wallace, so he was automatically in the Wallace camp. Day and Harrison were friends, so Day found himself at Harrison's side.

The dispute escalated to the point where Wallace triggered a provision in the shareholders' agreement that allowed disputes to be addressed through a private trial in New Brunswick under the rules of the province's supreme court. Wallace and his family claimed that they were oppressed minority shareholders. The remedy they sought was the breakup and sale of parts of the McCain business. Harrison asked Graham Day to be a witness. Harrison's counsel advised that not only must Harrison defend the primary allegation, he must also argue against the remedy sought—breaking up the company. Day's role was to be an expert on brands and brand values, drawing on his experience with Cadbury Schweppes. In the end, the testimony was not critical, as the court ruled against Wallace's claim of being an oppressed minority shareholder.

Wallace left the company, along with his two sons, Michael and Scott. The family relocated to Toronto and bought another major food company, Maple Leaf Foods. The rift between the brothers continued for years until they achieved a personal rapprochement before Harrison's death in 2004. Wallace died in 2011.

Day's involvement in the trial had been time-consuming and emotionally distressing. From the beginning, Harrison proposed to pay him for his time and reimburse his expenses. Day reminded him he was acting as a friend and refused all payment, though he was reimbursed for travel, hotel, and meals. "It was a long and grim affair," he says, and "an extreme example of a family's failure to come to grips with the succession issue." There would be others.

The Sobey outcome was more successful. Frank Sobey had been the entrepreneur, the grocer from Stellarton who established the chain. By the 1990s, the business was in the hands of his sons: David, the manager of stores, and Donald, the manager of capital. Day would help the family as it tried to move to stage three, the investor phase. "Collectively, they are almost there. It has not been an easy journey," he says.

There have been tensions among family members, but the Sobeys have managed conflict through their family council and the governance of their companies. The family retained control of the voting shares in the public companies; meanwhile, nonvoting A shares were listed on the Toronto Stock Exchange. Because of the public listings, the companies practised standard corporate governance, and the boards exercised their normal rights and duties. This has been an advantage for the Sobeys: they have had to listen to other voices around the table.

Graham Day brought a worldly international experience that would help a regional company take its first steps out on the wider stage. Day first sat on the board of Empire, the holding company, as the family made its Oshawa Group acquisition. Then he joined the supermarket subsidiary, Sobeys Inc., when it went public to raise money and needed a public-company-quality board. Day understood the challenges of the Oshawa Group purchase. He would tell the Empire board that it was like the proverbial dog chasing the car: "When he catches it, he doesn't know what to do with it." That turned out to be prescient.

David Sobey found that, if he needed to talk to someone, Day was at the top of the list. He felt Day and Nova Scotia blueberry entrepreneur John Bragg were the best board members for this purpose, and they had the advantage of closeness. You could always drop in to see them to talk over the business, and they would find time. It was a reflection of the personal approach that was lacking on Bay Street or Wall Street, but that characterized the Atlantic style: the handshake, the quiet conversation, the nod of recognition, the shared experience. It was David Sobey, after all, who had made the initial call to a friend of a friend of Bill McEwan to sound him out on the job of CEO. And, like David, Bill McEwan came to rely on Graham Day as a sounding board.

McEwan was hired on November 25, 2000. Two days later, the stores' computer systems crashed. Sobeys had just installed an $89 million enterprise software system provided by the German technology provider SAP, and it collapsed under the strain of the combined companies' demands. A 2003 article by Stephen Kimber in *Report on Business Magazine* summed up the crisis: "The system stayed down for five days. That put Sobeys five weeks behind in the middle of a peak period. The system would have to go. That would cost the company plenty, not only in actual dollars but also—and more importantly—in Street credibility." As one former Sobeys director put it, "When the shelves are bare, you know you have a problem."

McEwan was essentially paying for the unpreparedness of previous management. The company took a $49.3 million writeoff on the failed software. For McEwan, it was not a great "welcome to Sobeys" moment. The stock price collapsed, and he had to rebuild the company's image. He crafted a vision of the company based on a concept of "sustainable worth" that would appeal to employees, franchisees, investors, and customers. Sobeys began to work its way back.

When McEwan joined the business, David Sobey remained chairman of Sobeys Inc. for about a year before giving way to Graham Day. McEwan admired David as a savvy retailer, and now Day became his lifeline in trying times. It was lonely being the outsider CEO in a family company. Whom do you talk to? Day became a sounding board. It was a model of the chair-CEO relationships that corporate governance gurus like to talk about.

"He did not dominate, he did not push, but he helped me navigate the waters in a way that was very calm, gentle, and disciplined, with a sense of humour and incredibly precise instincts in difficult situations," McEwan says.

Day agrees he and McEwan were a good team: "He knew the grocery business, I brought the corporate background." In Stellarton, the Sobey business interests occupied two buildings, facing each other across the street. The grocery operating company, Sobeys, sat on one side, the family holding company, Empire, on the other, with a pedway connecting the two. Day explained to McEwan, "Bill, you worry about Sobeys; I will worry about everything across the pedway."

The Sobey supermarkets recovered from the systems crisis, but faced another life-and-death challenge. Walmart, the US retail behemoth, had entered Canada in the mid-1990s and was furiously ramping up operations. It launched an assault on all Canadian retail players, because of the Walmart superstores' broad expanse of product categories, including groceries. The chains would have to go up against Walmart's aggressive everyday low pricing in everything from detergent to food. Loblaw's, the leading Canadian supermarket company, decided to meet Walmart head on by diversifying into a range of clothing and dry goods. As the number two grocer, Sobeys had smaller stores and its expertise was clearly groceries. Its resources were already stretched by the chain's sudden expansion, and it couldn't see making the capital commitments to become an all-things retailer. Under McEwan, it chose to focus on food and the much-promoted promise of freshness.

It was a controversial response, and some investment analysts deemed it inadequate. Not even all board members seemed sold on it. McEwan came to rely on Day more than ever. Day was in Stellarton about twice a week, and the two would sometimes also meet in Toronto, where they found themselves frequently. Day had a favourite Greek restaurant called The Palace, just steps off Toronto's Danforth Avenue, and that is where the two men convened in the depth of McEwan's personal crisis.

The staff was spontaneous in its joy at seeing Day again—he was a frequent customer. Day and McEwan talked about the strategy and its negative reception. "It was rough," the younger man recalls. "I was somewhat down." He expressed his frustration that some board members didn't get it, and complained about the analysts' inability to grasp the merits of the strategy.

Day looked at him and slowed down that sonorous voice of his: "Bill, you can build a solid foundation with the bricks that others throw at you."

It is amazing how a well-timed, well-crafted sentence can make the difference. "All I needed was that one word of encouragement to channel and deal with the criticism," McEwan says. He was already confident his strategy was right, even if some directors didn't support him. McEwan would stand behind that strategy, and if it turned out to be wrong, he would go down with it. "You've got to believe in what you believe. If they determine it is not the right course, they need someone else to navigate the ship." McEwan believes strategies usually don't fail because they are bad but because management lacks the courage to stick with them. "That moment was singularly critical in helping me navigate the next several years," he says.

As a young man, McEwan had come under the guidance of a wise West Coast grocer who taught him the trade. Now, in middle age, he needed a mentor wise in the way of corporate politics. Day's words, over moussaka and baklava, gave him resolve. "I was a different person as a leader from that day forward," says McEwan, speaking in 2016 on the phone from, yes, Meaford, where he and Donna have a home on her family's farm.

The Sobeys survived the Walmart threat, but as this book was being written in 2016, they were dealing with the integration challenges of a massive new acquisition, the Canada Safeway stores, which gave them a big entry into western Canada. The transition was not going well, and yet another CEO was facing a formidable challenge. (Shortly after this interview, Sobeys CEO Marc Poulin would lose his job in the wake of a $2.9 billion writedown.) The tough times seem to roll around in cycles, David Sobey mused one day, adding that "we've got to get down to the quick and the dirty and see what we can do to respond." His brother Donald added, "Your best directors become very important then."

The message: it is a rough business, and it is good to have people like Graham Day in your corner. Through conversations with the Sobeys and other companies on whose boards he has sat, there emerges a profile of Day as a director. As McEwan says, he is a rock of support for management in the tight corners, and he is unflinching in candour and directness—whether he sits on a family advisory board (governance-lite, if you wish) or a public company board with full fiduciary duties. When called on, he is full of ideas, and in some cases, Graham Day can be a real pain in the ass to have on your board.

At the same time, "He is very supportive of management," says John Bragg, who recruited Day to the advisory board of his family company based in Oxford, Nova Scotia. Bragg has amassed a billion-dollar company based on frozen foods and communications—including the large Eastlink cable TV and communications business in Atlantic Canada. He is a firm believer that management needs directors who give them 100 percent support—that is, until the time comes that management clearly can't do the job.

Bragg adds that Day will take this support beyond mere words. At one point, the Bragg companies needed to raise money and were struggling a bit in the effort. Bragg had been thinking about a government program that would provide tax credits on funds invested. He thought about tapping investors through a bond issue.

Later, Bragg received a call from Day saying he and Ann had talked it over and were willing to put up some funds to buy bonds. Based on what they could borrow, their commitment would be about $250,000. An investment in a growing private company is not the most secure undertaking for a retirement-age couple, but they were sending the message: we are here for you. The money was not needed in the end—Bragg got his financing anyway—but he treasures the loyalty. "There was no fuss about it, just a private call and we never talked about it again."

It speaks volumes that, for a number of Canadian family companies, Day was either the first outsider, or among the first, on what had been a family-only board. He has played this role with companies as diverse as Acadian Seaplants, the Halifax-based pioneer in processing seaweed for human and animal use, and the Martin family's shipping firm, CSL. That requires a special tact and insight, but also the courage to tell it like it is. It is too easy for a director to take a laissez-faire stance and a passive advisory role in many private companies. Day, however, given an opening, can deliver a stream of questions and observations, drawing widely from his own rich experience. A CEO has to learn to sift through these comments and choose what works best for him or her and the company, but it is well worth the effort, say the CEOs who have worked with him.

Timid or tentative CEOs cannot thrive in the face of the Day bulldozer. They roll over too quickly. It is easy to assume that "Sir Graham knows best" because of his rich experience, but even Day concedes he is sometimes wrong, and faces up to it. It is better to express his opinion firmly than to let an issue die with no debate. For managers, the best approach, as with any strong director, is to challenge his thinking and adapt it—and come prepared to be interrogated.

Allan Shaw learned this lesson at Shaw Group, the private building materials and real estate development company whose board Day joined soon after returning from Britain. Like Sobeys Inc., but on a smaller scale, the company was contemplating a move beyond its familiar base. Shaw Group is a legendary Nova Scotia company with origins in the mid-nineteenth century. It was run for years by Lloyd Shaw, a lifelong social democrat and a major figure in the Co-operative Commonwealth Federation, the forerunner of the New Democratic Party. His daughter, Alexa McDonough, became national NDP leader in the 1990s.

By the late twentieth century, the company was owned by its management group, having made the transition from family control. The chairman was Lloyd's nephew Allan, the last family member with a stake in the company. Day joined what would become a powerhouse board, with towering personalities such as fish and telecom magnate John Risley and aerospace tycoon Ken Rowe.

For the company to grow, Allan Shaw was convinced it had to look outside the region, possibly beyond the continent, but it was a case of finding a comfort level. That set off a long journey into the global economy. Allan had good guides. Day and the board encouraged him to look around the world, including at the high-growth markets of China and Thailand. Allan did his Asian tour, came back, and told them what he had seen, and how Shaw Group could participate with local partners. Then the board asked: Are you prepared to fly over there every two weeks to manage that relationship? What if you are being exploited by offshore partners? What would you do? Shaw was unsure he could make those commitments, although he would try. The board suggested he look a little closer to home.

So he pulled his focus back to Central and South America, and went through the same process of visits and discussion. Again the board suggested he shift the focus even closer to home. By that time, Allan had reined in his global aspirations, but the company still had to grow. The board suggested looking at other sectors; indeed, Shaw's team had been thinking about the wood industry. It turned out that the big Swedish furniture retailer IKEA needed to buy pine furniture to supply North America. Shaw Group started negotiating with the company, and they put together a deal: IKEA would buy wood products from Shaw Group over seven years at ever-decreasing costs, as its business model dictated.

As that negotiation was going forward, Shaw Group was also investigating opportunities to get into the pipe coating business in Nova Scotia, feeding off offshore gas discoveries. Day helped open some doors, and Shaw Group made a connection with ShawCor (no family relation), a Toronto-based company involved in energy piping. The two contracts were signed the same week. It was a heady time for the old brick company.

The IKEA contract was a great relationship, but it could not survive IKEA's unrelenting imperative to drive down costs. After about five years, it was hard to make money, and by that time, IKEA was looking farther afield for partners. As the Nova Scotia plant became uncompetitive, the Shaw Group shut it down, having learned a lot. It didn't lose any money, and it helped many people who never before had permanent jobs learn skills to take out in the world.

It is a sad day when a plant closes. Allan was walking around the dark factory with a woman who was one of the lead workers.

There were just the two of them, and she said she felt so bad for his having to do this. Shaw said he felt bad for her: she was losing her job. Then "we both cried."

Global business stories do not all have a happy ending. Graham Day was part of that project and it was the right thing to do, just as it was right to diversify into modular housing, which has worked well for Shaw Group. "[Day] helped us figure out what we shouldn't be doing, and concentrate on what we were good at," Allan says. "We were always good at doing our homework, but he probably helped us narrow it down. And when we went after those things, we were convincing."

But Allan Shaw warns about the importance of being stalwart in the face of formidable directors. The directors once shot down a business proposal with one of them saying, in effect, "that's the stupidest thing I have ever heard, and we don't ever want to hear about it again." In retrospect, Allan wishes the company had looked at the idea more carefully first, but the board's pre-emptive rejection discouraged management from bringing new thoughts to the table. Nobody wanted to be part of the stupidest idea ever.

It gave him insight into the dynamics of a strong board, where one director, or several, can swing the debate. Then there is the danger of piling on. "I saw that the odd time with Graham. I don't think he ever meant to do it, but he had the stature to be able to end a debate by saying something very definitive." But that is also what you gain with a powerhouse director, "this kind of power and magnetic personality, charismatic, that other people want to follow." For Shaw and his team, it was part of their education in working with a strong board. Day, he says, was "absolutely a positive force."

Shaw also pays tribute to the board's tough-minded thinking in appointing a new CEO as his successor. Allan had backed the appointment of a long-time manager, but some board members, led by Day, thought the man lacked sufficient commitment. Still, the directors agreed to back his choice. Then, just days before he was due to take over, the CEO-in-waiting got sick and took leave. The board pondered the choice again and this time concluded the appointee was not the right person. When the man returned, Allan Shaw had to tell him the company had changed its mind. Day became part of the committee to pick another CEO, a methodical three-year process. Thanks to strong direction from the board, the company, albeit painfully, made the right choice.

It is another example of what one friend says is the essential attribute of Graham Day: "When Graham is in, he is all in." He will give it his all with unflinching loyalty and commitment, but he will also be unsparing in his opinions.

Derek Oland came to understand that. His family brewery, Moosehead, based in Saint John, New Brunswick, was unhappy with the American importer of its beer into the United States, the US branch of Guinness, but it could not decide how best to extricate itself from the relationship: negotiate an exit or just cut the cord.

The Olands did their legal work through Stewart McKelvey, where Day was now counsel. Oland had met Day on the Nova Scotia Power board and found him very impressive, a straight shooter who was good with numbers. Oland asked Day to help solve the US problem. It became evident that Moosehead should negotiate its departure. It was an expensive divorce, but it worked well for Moosehead. Oland was able to move its US business over to San Antonio–based beer distribution company Gambrinus Co. It was a great relationship for ten years, until Moosehead took control of its own channels in the United States.

Day's role with the Olands would widen beyond legal advice. Derek's father Philip Oland had died in 1996, and Derek, after being president for seventeen and a half years, was preparing to move into the chair's role. His father had resisted having a board of independent directors, but Derek knew he needed the support of knowledgeable outside people. Graham Day would be the first to join from the outside, followed by Courtney Pratt, an experienced executive from Toronto.

The decision was made that Derek should not stay on as president, but no one in the family or the company was ready to succeed him. Who should be the first non-Oland to run the Moosehead business, with its roots stretching back more than 150 years in the Maritimes? Oland and Day were working with a headhunter and saw a number of candidates, but were not happy with the choices. One day, they arranged to meet an experienced consumer goods executive named Bruce McCubbin, who had been working for the Montreal conglomerate Imasco. Oland knew that, when Day is bored, you need only look below the table and see his foot moving like mad. About ten minutes into the interview with McCubbin, "I looked down, and the leg had stopped. I knew Graham was interested, and I was, too."

McCubbin became an outstanding CEO who garnered the respect of Derek Oland's sons in the company and helped guide their development. One son, Andrew, would succeed McCubbin as president in 2008. Meanwhile, Moosehead further expanded the board, adding people such as John Bragg and Aldéa Landry. "Graham was a strong part of it," Derek says. "His motivation was he liked to see family companies do well in the Maritimes, and anything he could do as a director, he was prepared to do."

But there is a sad sidebar. Through much of his tenure on the board, Day watched the tension between Derek and the other holding company shareholders: his siblings Richard and

Jane. Philip Oland had chosen Derek over Richard to run the company, and the residue of resentment remained. It was an example of the toxicity that can surround a difficult succession in even the best family companies—and the best families. Day served on the board for nine years, until 2006, and he saw the business turn around and a development plan put in place for the Oland sons in Moosehead. Arrangements were made to buy out Jane and Richard.

But the story does not end there. On the night of July 7, 2011, Richard Oland was murdered in his downtown Saint John office, setting off a wave of gossip and speculation around the Oland family. More than two years later, Richard's son Dennis was charged with second degree murder, setting the stage for a closely watched and widely reported trial. On September 16, 2015, a jury found Dennis guilty, and he was sentenced to life imprisonment. In late October 2016, however, the New Brunswick Court of Appeal ordered a new trial, citing flaws in the trial judge's instructions to the jury.

Graham Day could only watch from the sidelines as this sad saga played out. His affection for the families he served continued long after he had left their boardrooms.

CHAPTER 19

Power Play

On an early June day in 2002, the directors of Hydro One were holding a meeting with a single agenda item: their own mass resignation. Chairman Graham Day was in on the conference call, knowing the board's relationship with the owner of the power utility—the province of Ontario—had reached the breaking point.

Day was the central figure in a potential $5.5 billion privatization IPO that had gone badly off the rails. Up to now, in privatizations where he had played a role, he had known only triumphs: British Shipbuilders, Rover, PowerGen, Nova Scotia Power. He had built an international reputation as a privatizer-at-large who could drive these projects like no one else. This one would be different.

The conference call ended quickly, because the board knew it was in an untenable position, having lost the support of the single shareholder. A dispute over executive pay had escalated to the point that the province was publicly slamming the board and overriding its authority. It was clearly a prelude to aborting the IPO and, as the plans became known, replacing the current board. In the view of some directors, they were victims of a public flogging by a government acting in bad faith. "We can't work in this kind of a situation," director Bernard Syron, chairman of the food services giant Cara Operations Ltd., later told the *Globe and Mail.* "It's a catastrophe. It's a tragic situation."

Day was frustrated, but he was also experiencing a familiar feeling. If he felt something wasn't fair, to him or the people he worked with, "I'd push back. I don't get pushed easily, and I won't roll over, and I've never rolled over. At Hydro One, I said 'I'm out of here' and all the board walked out with me."

How did it happen? This should have been the crowning cap to his impressive career. But here he was in a political firestorm, accused of, at worst, a serious governance lapse in enriching members of his team; at best, being tone deaf to the political and economic forces roiling Canada's largest province. That was not how he saw it. At sixty-nine, after four decades in the privatization wars, he was learning another lesson: never trust a government to keep its backbone in the midst of a contentious privatization.

He had signed on to the Ontario Progressive Conservative government's plan to privatize Hydro One, and he had worked with a highly capable CEO to make it happen. The initial public offering had been days away. There had been a court challenge, and the judge's decision had gone the other way, but that was fixable. Then the executive compensation scandal dragged in Day—although his own integrity was never seriously questioned, except as a politically motivated diversion. Now it was over, ending four of the most tumultuous years in Graham Day's life—and yet it had all started with such promise.

When the saga began in 1998, Day was sixty-five and had nothing more to prove in life. He had a knighthood, the gratitude of the UK government (particularly Conservatives), and was an inspiration not only to free market advocates everywhere, but also to anyone who respected integrity in business. He still was a very busy corporate director and a mentor to an impressive group of acolytes. The Thatcher privatization thrust had been influential around the world, and he basked in the reflection of its success. It was a heady time.

Privatization in Canada had not been as ambitious, but there had been progress: the federal Progressive Conservative government under Brian Mulroney had released Air Canada and Canadian National Railway from the government clutches. Day had admired the CN process and the work of two former public servants, Paul Tellier and Michael Sabia, in making it happen. He believed any privatization had to be a clean break, with no lingering government role. Then, on June 8, 1995, Ontario voted in a majority Progressive Conservative government and a new premier. Mike Harris, a former golf pro, was no Thatcher. He was not particularly impressive as an opposition leader, but he had seized on free market principles in his election pitch, and he rode them to victory. Harris and his followers promised a Common Sense Revolution. A group of conservative-minded party members had been meeting to develop principles to change Ontario utterly. Among the ringleaders was Bill Farlinger, the boss of the Canadian branch of the accounting firm Ernst & Young. Farlinger was a golfing buddy of Mike Harris, and became the prime mover behind the privatization push.

Once again, Day got one of those fateful phone calls, this time from Farlinger, now chairman of Ontario Hydro, asking him to join the board. Farlinger told him the Ontario PCs had plans to privatize the massive power utility. “Because of PowerGen, I thought I knew a little bit about electricity,” Day says. “I thought I knew more about the generation side than the transmission.

And I assumed that Farlinger wanted that knowledge and, quite frankly, that credibility." He also thought he understood how governments work. He dealt easily with public servants, and had flourished under the Thatcher approach: As the chief of a privatizing company, he valued that the government let him run the business while the politicians looked after the politics. Ministers never faltered in their support, and he never embarrassed them. "I was dealing with people who did what they said they would do, when they said they would do it. I had no experience at all from either [major British party] of bad faith." That would not be the case in Ontario.

Day was already familiar with Ontario Hydro because he had done consulting work for the utility. "I thought it would be fun." It would be another form of service, and the opportunity to work with such a country-building or, at least, province-building entity. As he told journalist Rod McQueen for *Financial Post Magazine* in March 2001, "Canada has always been very slow on privatization. As a nation with a lot of state involvement, Canada has always been well behind the curve." He blamed foot-dragging in the Canadian public service: "Do turkeys vote for an early Christmas?"

But it was clear that Ontario's vast electricity system needed a new idea. It was groaning under the weight of high costs, inefficiencies, and huge debt after a binge of nuclear power investment. Consumers were angry over hefty rate increases. But for all of Hydro's sins, privatization would meet strong headwinds. The utility was founded in the early years of the twentieth century by entrepreneur-turned-politician Sir Adam Beck, who left a legacy of faith in publicly owned power. Beck, a sharp-tongued autocrat from London, Ontario, was the closest thing to a saint in the province's pantheon of public service. But by the early 1990s, the Beck model was under pressure. Bob

Rae's embattled NDP government, reeling from an economic recession, reached out to Maurice Strong, environmentalist, wealthy capitalist, and big idea man, as Hydro's new chairman and CEO. Strong became an advocate of a new Ontario Hydro, privatized and engaged in competition, both in Ontario and on the global scene. Strong's financial advisors suggested a model that would break up the monolith into two or more pieces, separating the generation side from the transmission grid and the distribution businesses. "Restructuring of the industry on this basis would be clearly conducive to privatization," Strong said.

With the PCs rising to power under Harris, Strong departed and Farlinger became Ontario Hydro's chairman. When Day came on board, people inside Ontario Hydro knew what that meant: Day was a brand, and it stood for privatization.

As a Hydro board member, Day began to work with the utility's finance chief, Eleanor Clitheroe, a star in the Ontario public service. The holder of both an MBA and a law degree, she had been a banker and had gained expertise with bond markets. She joined the Ontario government and had risen to deputy minister of finance in the darkest hours of the early 1990s recession. Working with the Rae government, she won admiration for trying to keep the province financially afloat. Some observers, including Day's friends, suggest he was intellectually smitten by the idea of Eleanor Clitheroe. He had made a career of championing bright people, and he was famously gender blind. He was impressed by talented women such as Clitheroe, Frances Elliott, and Lydia Bugden because they typically possessed a stronger work ethic than their male peers and yet faced such formidable obstacles.

In the plan to split Hydro into a generation and a transmission company, Clitheroe was chosen to lead the transmission entity that would become Hydro One. Despite his deeper experience in generation, Day wanted to work with Clitheroe, and became chair of the transmission company. Farlinger would be chair of the generation side, which would become Ontario Power Generation (OPG). The transmission company would be the first to come to market through an IPO, potentially the biggest in Canadian history. To prepare the offering, Day and Clitheroe became a team. The goal was to mould a business that could operate in a competitive power market. The final result would be the end of monopoly and, according to their thinking, a path to lower rates. As the Day-Farlinger team saw it, Hydro One would assume some of the staggering debt of OPG, an amount which Hydro One could carry comfortably. So when the proceeds of the IPO came in, the government could apply a sizable chunk to improving OPG's generating operations, which should create a more stable power system for consumers—for generations, Day believed.

Clitheroe and Day looked at a range of things—the transmission grid, the retail system, the relationship between municipal and Hydro One systems—and which elements would come over to Hydro One and which would stay with OPG. Then began the process of selecting investment firms. "By the time Hydro One was actually established, we knew each other very well," Clitheroe says. "We worked together constantly and on a daily basis."

Day was reliving his British experiences, although this time he was only the chair, not the CEO. But he was an active chair. He was in Toronto a few days every week, doing what he does best: building a team. Once he had signalled his desire to join Hydro One, others wanted to follow. There was a feeling that this was the right side of the business to be on because Graham Day was involved. "He became a big draw for a lot of people," says Joan Prior, who joined as the chief counsel for the new company. Malen Ng felt the same way; she ran the financial side of the "de-merger" of Ontario Hydro, and became the chief financial officer of Hydro One.

Another close colleague was a bright assistant general counsel, Laura Formusa. Her story was impressive. She had come out of law school in the early 1980s recession looking for a legal job and found nothing. She became the lowliest typist in the secretarial pool, and rose through the ranks. Hydro was a male-dominated, engineer-run company, but she was able to climb the ladder. Under Day, the opportunities for women in leadership advanced dramatically. Formusa became one of his team, and he became her mentor. She says he inspired her to be all that she could be. Formusa was not in Day's direct reporting circle, but she saw him at work as a chair. Beyond the intensity of the company-design period, he maintained the proper balance of oversight. He was generally not an in-your-face chair, she says—he was "nose-in, fingers-off." Under his guidance, says Formusa, "we built a strong regulatory framework, made acquisitions, and integrated them." The company bought a bunch of small municipal systems, and it was well set up to make more capital investments, including a line into the United States.

Meanwhile, the premier was eager to accelerate the timetable. As Day recalls, "We pressed on—we were within just weeks [of going public]. Everything was go, go, go." But one thing Day did not see coming: "The Hydro One thing was all right up to the point the premier decided he didn't want to be premier anymore."

Harris's Common Sense Revolution had taken aim at the foundations of big government Ontario, including many institutions built by previous Progressive Conservative governments. It faced huge resistance from the people who felt targeted by its policies: welfare recipients, teachers, unions. With this constant upheaval, Ontario seemed to be a province in chaos. Like Thatcher, Harris was viewed in stark extremes: Mike Harris, revolutionary and liberator of Ontario; Mike Harris, bully and ideologue. But neither the Liberals nor the NDP were able to consolidate the considerable opposition. The PCs were re-elected in 1999, and the revolution seemed to roll on.

Then, on October 16, 2001, six years and two elections into his mandate, Harris unleashed a thunderbolt: he was resigning. He said the decision came while flying home to northern Ontario for Thanksgiving, during a period of calm reflection. He was quoted in the *Globe and Mail*: "I saw the leaves. I saw the land like I really had never seen it before. And I had the time on that flight and I had time over Thanksgiving weekend to stop and to reflect." That, of course, was not the whole story. Harris had been having a now highly publicized affair, and his marriage was in trouble. The government faced the prospect of more scandal, as well as increasing strife. And it was possible that he was just tired.

This is when the privatization of Hydro One ended, not with the court challenge, not with the compensation scandal that followed, not with the union and public relations battle. It ended with the departure of the political champion of privatization. In the ensuing leadership campaign, Harris's friend and former cabinet ally Ernie Eves was elected leader.

The IPO seemed, at first, to be still on track. The investment banking team, which included an impressive young Mark Carney at Goldman Sachs, had done its work. As spring proceeded, the initial public offering could be done any day, given the right timing in the markets. But the coalition against privatization was gaining force, and key players were members of the labour movement. Two unions, which actually did not represent Hydro workers, the Canadian Union of Public Employees and the

Communications, Energy and Paperworkers Union of Canada, launched a legal challenge against selling the utility under the terms of the province's power legislation.

On April 19, 2002, Laura Formusa was sitting in a courtroom on Toronto's University Avenue to hear the judgment in the Ontario Superior Court proceeding. Mr. Justice Arthur Gans started by invoking Sir Adam Beck, the father of public power: "Ontario Hydro was one of the defining characteristics of the Province, one with which its residents could identify. Its creation and basic foundation was the primary reason a knighthood was bestowed upon Sir Adam Beck in 1914. His sculpted image stands watch over University Avenue." Formusa knew what was happening, and she began to tap a message on her BlackBerry: "This judge is going to pull a Sir Adam Beck on us." At that point, "I knew we were toast." The decision stated the province did not have the authority under legislation to carry out the sale.

The momentum was clearly shifting. The Eves government no longer saw privatization of Hydro One as a cause to die for. It was watching the escalation of power rates, and was wary of any political risk. The government signalled it was looking at other options, possibly an income trust, a non-profit corporation, or a lease of assets to private companies. "Everything is on the table," Eves-appointed energy minister Chris Stockwell said. Eleanor Clitheroe, too, sensed the mood had changed. Mike Harris had been actively engaged, and she and Day had briefed him regularly. But after he left, "I spent very little, if any, time with the new premier, so I'm assuming that he was briefed by his advisors, not as much by the board or by the executive." Graham Day later said he or the board never met with Eves after he became premier.

And Clitheroe's compensation was about to grab centre stage. It proved to be a handy smokescreen for the wavering government. Some observers say her major flaw was that she was acting as if the IPO had already occurred, while in fact the utility was still in government hands. She had become the focus of a media campaign, she was the face of the IPO, and when her pay package became a cause célèbre, she was an easy target.

Compensation is a thorny issue in a privatization through the IPO process. As the offering approaches, the company is in a kind of limbo, still part of the public sector but preparing to act like a listed company on the stock market. It wants to retain its team, especially through the offering process. It was felt the Hydro One compensation packages had to be comparable to that of similar private sector organizations—and in Hydro One's case, to that of OPG's leader, Ron Osborne. When the compensation of the senior team was disclosed, it was high for public servants, but not for private power executives. But optics are important, and the optics were not good. Clitheroe was being paid $2.2 million a year, and if she lost her job she would qualify for a severance package of more than $6 million, as well as a pension of more than $700,000 a year. (Of course, the public would never have had to pay the severance—it would be the responsibility of the privatized company.) Other executives were well paid by public sector standards: more than $800,000 for some members of the leadership team.

Day had been there before. As chairman of Britain's PowerGen, the big privatized utility, he had faced withering criticism about compensation packages and accusations of greed. He defended the near-tripling of the salary of PowerGen's chief executive to £200,000 ($375,000 at the time)—small change compared with Clitheroe's haul. Then, as now, Day held firm, saying, "He is worth every penny we pay him." This time, the pay packages, while explained in the preliminary prospectus, seemed to be news to energy minister Chris Stockwell: "The compensation numbers we are seeing are outrageous." This statement, and others by the Eves government, violated Graham Day's privatization principle: the owner does not publicly criticize the board and the company, thus undermining the trust of employees and the public and the value of the company.

He absolves Clitheroe of any blame in the compensation affair. "I know that, in salary and allowances and everything, she had never asked for anything," he maintains. The board had taken advice on the pay packages from compensation consultants and investment advisors. It told the government that, as it prepared to go public, it would move salaries up to the bottom end of what was paid by comparable employers. The message to the government, Day says, was that the company was not going to wait till after the IPO to disclose pay. "It'll be revealed on the offering documents so everybody will know."

But public opinion had made its judgment: Clitheroe was a symbol of corporate greed. The outrage grew as details became public about some of her expenses: $40,000 in house renovations had been temporarily billed to the province, as well as a bunch of club memberships. The company's sponsorship of a racing yacht was seen as sinister—after all, Clitheroe was a weekend sailor, back when she had the time. The government seized on the fact that, as it mulled over whether it might undertake a trust or a non-profit solution, the board widened the severance terms to allow it to be paid in those circumstances as well. When Queen's Park voiced its disapproval, the company indicated it was willing to compromise, but there was no response from the politicians.

All of which led to that June day in 2002 when the board decided it had no choice but to resign. By then, the government was preparing to fire the directors and roll back compensation of the top executives. A month later Clitheroe, who had already quit as a director in the mass exit, would be fired with cause as CEO. The expenses became a club with which to beat her up. One detail stuck out: $330,000 in limousine charges billed to Hydro One by Clitheroe, who was already provided with a rich automobile allowance for a new car every twelve months. It was later revealed that the bill included eleven hundred trips during a three-year period for Clitheroe's family, her children, and her nanny.

In the aftermath of the board's exit, those expenses would later be explained by Dona Harvey, who had headed the human resources committee. It was a rare look into the harried life of a female executive who was trying to balance motherhood and executive duties. In a private company, it would be a footnote; in Hydro One it was a front-page headline. Harvey explained to the *Globe and Mail* that Clitheroe had used the limo as a way of avoiding maternity leave. It was usually a Dodge minivan, and many of the trips were intended to let Clitheroe work in the passenger seat, rather than drive the Mercedes-Benz station wagon she had bought with part of her $214,000 annual car allowance. Harvey told the newspaper that Clitheroe and her husband had become parents by adopting a son and daughter. The first adoption came in the fall of 1999, just as her first real vacation was beginning. Clitherone learned she could fly to Vancouver the next day and pick up a baby boy. As a new mother, she returned to work about two weeks later.

According to Harvey's account, the HR committee felt she was entitled to maternity leave. But Clitheroe indicated she would stay on the job—there was too much happening, and she feared her unplanned leave would be harmful to the company at that moment. So, the story goes, Day and Clitheroe worked out the limo arrangement to allow her to juggle her two roles, and in lieu of maternity leave. Most women can't avail themselves of such treatment, but Clitheroe had an understanding board—and a chairman sympathetic to the extra burden shouldered by working women in a marriage. Was that so terribly wrong?

After the board's mass exit, Day went home to Hantsport to lick his wounds. He stayed loyal to Clitheroe and quiet about the government that had hired him and then forced him out. As a reporter then for the *Globe and Mail*, I called him at home, and he expressed confidence that he would be vindicated: "All my life, I have endeavoured—and I believe with some success—to behave properly, honourably, to discharge my duties, and I'm confident nothing has changed." Only later, in an interview with *Canadian Business* magazine, did his anger come bubbling to the surface: "Clitheroe was screwed. And ratepayers and taxpayers were screwed, and screwed roundly, with her."

Whatever one's opinion of Eleanor Clitheroe, the incident affirmed Day's reputation as a chairman who could be counted on through thick and thin. "It was a dirty game," Peter Godsoe says, and, through all the controversy, "he never blinked." The famous Day technique—that blend of charm and firmness—had been effective in disarming politicians and civil servants in Thatcher's Britain, but it seemed to fail him in Ontario. Perhaps Canada's largest province was more alien to him as a Maritimer than the so-called foreign country across the ocean. Of course, in Britain, he had a leader who was secure in power and provided the necessary political cover. A senior executive at an Ontario Crown agency who knew Day told me at the time that he had a reputation as a fiercely independent and upright chairman: "His view was that he had been hired to run Hydro One, and he had no tolerance for interference from the government or politicians." As a result, the official said, "he didn't have many allies at Queen's Park."

Day believed in promoting women, but had he been too dazzled by Eleanor Clitheroe? If he had, so had the whole board and the government, which promoted her and built the IPO around her. In the midst of an IPO, when expenses were flying around, her people should have been more careful with receipts. The limo service perhaps should have been subject to second thoughts. The board should have paid more attention to optics, but, in a $5.5 billion privatization, the sums were a piffle. One can't help but note that the same level of scrutiny and outrage did not fall on Ron Osborne, the respected veteran male executive who headed OPG and who would make $2.3 million in the same year Clitheroe's $2.2 million pay package caused such an uproar.

The real issue was Ernie Eves's political calculation. But he got defeated anyway in the 2003 election, giving way to Dalton McGuinty, thus starting a long Liberal run in power in Ontario.

The Day team scattered and pursued new roles. At Hydro One, Day had sent Joan Prior to Harvard for an executive training program, because he knew the value of general business expertise beyond the legal area. Prior briefly ran an operating unit of the utility. After leaving Hydro One, it took her some time to find a new role that suited her, until she was hired as a lawyer with Bank of Nova Scotia. Malen Ng, the finance chief, was also nudged by Day into operating roles, and she too thrived. She left Hydro One to be the chief financial officer at Ontario's Workplace Safety and Insurance Board for six years. She also found a career as a director, taking roles on the boards of companies such as Sobeys, Empire, and Extendicare. Both Prior and Ng could see the invisible, and often visible, hand of Graham Day in their later careers.

Day watched the train wreck that ensued at Hydro One. When Clitheroe was axed, the Ontario government promoted Tom Parkinson, an experienced Australian power executive, to run the company. Parkinson resigned in an expenses scandal of his own, and walked away with a $3 million severance. When the dust settled, Hydro One was running out of CEO options. Laura Formusa was still in the company as general counsel, and she was appointed acting CEO. She liked the job, and was good at it. Graham Day had taught her well. She showed the board that she should stay on as the permanent CEO. She was steadfast, guiding the utility through difficult times, but the uncertainty eventually got to her. She did not know the path forward for the utility, and she too left at the end of 2012.

Hydro One remained a political hot potato, accosted for its rates and billing systems. The public had become cynical about any chance of improving Ontario's power system. The gas plant fiasco of the McGuinty era—cancelling two suburban Toronto natural gas plants for political reasons at a cost of over $1 billion—was just another example of the broken system, where politics had become the major driver. That system sat in limbo for fourteen years, divided into generation and transmission/ distribution arms. There were none of the efficiencies of a single company, but, privatization advocates argue, none of the potential benefits of competition or a private sector mindset. (One nod to privatization has been private ownership of the Bruce nuclear plant.) Ontarians are said to have paid many millions in higher power bills for this half-assed state of play. It seems such a waste.

The Liberals escaped severe electoral punishment for their gas plant sins. A new premier, Kathleen Wynne, came to power facing a fiscal challenge in an uncertain economy. Despite being painted by critics as a left-winger, she was pragmatic on power, and became convinced of the need for a significant selloff of Hydro One. The company would remain intact, as Day and Clitheroe had designed it, and the province would retain a 40 percent stake. The rest would be sold over time in a series of public share offerings. Day was sceptical. He didn't believe in partial privatization: the company should be moved entirely to the private sector. He also wondered about the aim to spend the proceeds on infrastructure outside the power system. There was just too much cluttering the agenda, he felt, while the goals should be to invest in the system and constrain rates.

Throughout his career, in Britain and Canada, Day's goal had been to take politics out of the business of the companies he privatized. But in Ontario, successive governments had failed to depoliticize electricity. By 2016, little had changed, and public anger over exploding power rates was rising to a crescendo.

It is summer 2016 at Canadian Forces Base Borden, north of Toronto. The Tim Hortons has a busy lunchtime crowd, a sea of olive green fatigues. It would be easy to miss the small figure striding through the door if not for Eleanor Clitheroe's confident gait and welcoming smile. She, too, is wearing fatigues—standard fare for a reserve chaplain doing duty at a military base while ministering as an Anglican priest to her church in the Niagara Peninsula.

After the Hydro debacle, Clitheroe, a person of faith, made a career change, went to divinity school, and kept in touch with Graham Day—there are Christmas cards—but from afar. The bond is still there, she says. "He was gender neutral, if you want to say that. He took talent as opposed to preferences. And so I loved working for him. I'd work for him again if he ever needed someone." Would she have done anything differently at Hydro One? "I might have left a little earlier, but that might be the only thing." What about her compensation? "It was what I was told to do, so I did it." In 2016, it is a different world. The new CEO of a partially privatized Hydro One is paid up to $4 million a year; at the time of this writing, there had been very little comment. He should thank Eleanor Clitheroe, who took the heat and paid for it with a career.

There remains bitter opposition to privatization. But Clitheroe believes that, as the power debacle has unfolded since she left Hydro One, consumers' attitudes have been shifting. "In the fourteen intervening years, they've seen rates go up significantly. And so they're saying to themselves, 'Well, I thought retaining government control of a monopoly was going to protect me, and it hasn't.'" She and Day had worked towards an integrated strategy that, in their view, ultimately would have upgraded the system, delivered more competition, and kept a lid on rates. That didn't happen, Clitheroe observes. But she feels that, as people become more and more frustrated, they will look back and say that maybe she and Graham Day had a better plan.

CHAPTER 20

Knee-Deep in the Rubicon

Anyone who wants to discover the picture-perfect Maritimes could do worse than head to Hantsport, a tidy mill town with white churches, frame houses, a Tim Hortons outlet and hardware store, and the peaceful feel of a place that has scarcely changed in a hundred years. It's not where you might expect to find a man who has walked the corridors of power, turned around global companies, and was knighted for services to a British prime minister.

Yet this is where Graham and Ann Day ended up after their British adventures, in the pewter-coloured Cape Cod they had built in the 1970s and to which they kept putting on additions. (Whenever a child left, Day likes to quip, they would add a room.) Looking downriver, they could see the ruddy banks of the Avon River as it flows softly out to the Bay of Fundy's Minas Basin. Upriver lay the Jodrey mill, the Jodrey factory, and a cluster of Jodrey company houses and family homes, a reminder of the clan that has dominated Hantsport since the 1920s.

These are the Days' roots, and with roots come responsibilities—and a sense of duty to the family of Roy Adelbert Jodrey, the tough old plutocrat who gave a young lawyer a chance. This became the scene of one of Graham Day's most daunting challenges, rivalling anything he tackled in Britain, and perhaps his most successful outcome. The Jodrey story is a case study in navigating a tortuous, emotional family-enterprise breakup while avoiding litigation and deep hostility.

Roy Jodrey was one of the most resilient entrepreneurs Canada has produced, a man who battled to the top of the pile, almost lost it all, and scrambled back up again. He was the descendant of French-Swiss immigrants to the South Shore, Nova Scotia. In the 1870s, an ambitious young man named Joseph Jodrey moved to the Gaspereau River, a beautiful arm of the broader Annapolis Valley. There he joined the established settlers, many descended from planter families from New England who were offered land in the fertile valley by the British after the shameful expulsion of the Acadians in the eighteenth century. Joseph owned a sawmill, but his son Roy was destined for bigger things. At the dawn of the twentieth century, Roy left school in the sixth grade and, as a born trader, was drawn to the Annapolis Valley's luxurious apple production. By age sixteen, he was transporting barrels of apples to the docks in Wolfville for shipping around the world. As his ambition swelled, he invested in power dams on the Avon River and a pulp mill in the river town of Hantsport, which became the base of the Jodrey empire. In 1927, Minas Basin Pulp and Power Company was born and became Roy Jodrey's core business.

Then, in 1933, Jodrey founded a company called Canadian Keyes Fibre, using a Maine company's process to turn pulp into moulded paper trays and plates. Canadian Keyes Fibre was also one of the first Canadian companies to seek shelter under the *Companies' Creditors Arrangement Act*, a now popular means of protecting an insolvent company against creditors, allowing time to reorganize. This was the Great Depression, and Jodrey was up to his neck in debt. His businesses were bankrupt, but he held on with the support of the Bank of Nova Scotia. The businesses recovered—including Canadian Keyes Fibre, later known as CKF, which prospered under vertical integration, using materials and power flowing from other Jodrey enterprises. Roy Jodrey went on to triumph after triumph, dying in 1973 at age eighty-four.

But by the time the twenty-first century dawned, inside the frame houses and mills of Hantsport a storm was gathering. It was part of the natural life of families. The Jodreys were in the third generation of the family enterprise, and they had evolved into three branches: the family of Roy's son John, still active in his nineties, and John's son Bruce, a top manager in the business; the family of Roy's daughter Jean Hennigar, now led by her investment banker son David; and the family of another daughter, Florence Bishop, led by her son George. The apple businesses had grown into a sprawling entanglement of assets worth more than half a billion dollars and controlled by a family holding company called Scotia Investments. The Jodrey name did not appear on supermarkets, gas stations, or frozen food packages. The companies were not household names. This was old, quiet money.

Some Jodrey companies were old-economy survivors in processing and manufacturing, now challenged in their markets and needing new investment. But change was hard. Various members of the family handled different assets: John and Bruce paid attention to the core businesses, Minas Basin Pulp and Power, and CKF; George Bishop oversaw the holding company and served in some of the core companies; the Hennigars tended to real estate, retirement homes (Extendicare in Canada, Assisted Living Concepts in the United States), waste management, and the family's controlling interest in High Liner, a fish-processing company based in Lunenburg. Roy Jodrey, like his friend Frank Sobey, had been an enthusiastic investor in Canadian public companies. George Bishop and Scotia Investments chief financial officer Archie MacPherson were stewards of a large portfolio of stocks, estimated by outsiders at $200–300 million, including Roy Jodrey's old position in Scotiabank. One of the prize assets was Algoma Central, a century-old rail company that had evolved into a Great Lakes shipper. It had even named a tanker after its illustrious shareholder. Alas, the *Roy A. Jodrey* sank in the St. Lawrence River shortly after the death of its namesake; fortunately, all hands were saved.

The Scotia Investments operating model—certain cousins in charge of certain assets—worked for a while. A constructive relationship existed among the four main personalities—George Bishop, David Hennigar, and the father-son tandem of John and Bruce Jodrey. But it was getting tense. As one group brought forward proposals about its business, it had to face the judgment of the entire family. It would walk away with the sense it could never get what it wanted. There was frustration all around.

Complicating this picture was a generational reality: the family was branching out, encompassing some cousins who worked in the company and some who did not, some well informed but others unknowledgeable. There were three children and twelve grandchildren and they were having children in turn. The shareholder group had widened to about fifty members in the second, third, and fourth generations. The consortium of cousins had no reason to be together except for an increasingly thin blood relationship. The board, consisting entirely of family members, was increasingly dysfunctional. It was a recipe for conflict—and it eventually pulled Graham Day into its stew.

George Bishop was concerned about what would happen in the next generation, if they did not get the companies on a stronger governance base. He proposed bringing in three independent directors. His uncle and cousins agreed. George suggested Moncton trucking magnate Wes Armour; David supported Toronto businessman Ken Cork. And Bruce Jodrey championed Graham Day. Over the next seven years, Day's mission would be to prepare the Jodrey family for the future while preserving asset values and avoiding lasting rancour. The man who had privatized great swaths of the British economy would later say, "The resolution of the differences, and the differing aspirations, of all the shareholders from the three branches of the Jodrey family was the most time-consuming, complicated, and demanding group of transactions in which I have ever been involved."

Ann Day says he did it for the right reasons. "This is our town, and we have some friends in the family. He said if he could help, he should." Help, he did. The role of director on the board of a private family company can be pretty simple. It often means rubber-stamping decisions and offering a bit of advice, with no real expectation it will be followed. But Day was taking on something much bigger: the role of mediator and problem-solver for a very diverse set of individuals.

George Bishop was a courteous man who loved operations and felt a deep responsibility to the Annapolis Valley and its people. His uncle John was widely respected for his business acumen. As he advanced into his nineties, he was still very smart, but feeble and losing his hearing. Bruce had been pulled along in the business by his father, but was increasingly distracted by health and philanthropic issues. David Hennigar was a chip off

Roy Jodrey's block, an outsized character with a colourful turn of phrase and a stockbroker's love of the deal. Now the board had to make room for new personalities, and none was bigger than Graham Day's. David Hennigar knew Day as "a kind of a shoot-from-the-hip guy." Hennigar's wry appraisal was that "sometimes I think he thought about things and sometimes I'm not so sure." According to Hennigar, "He was never short of opinions, usually bolstered by stories about something that had happened in his career."

Archie MacPherson watched as the new director settled in. There was never a sense of doubt in Day's words. "He wasn't there to sugar-coat but to say exactly what he thought, and that is what you need, especially in a family company. It's the idea that you don't pay me to agree with you, you pay me to say what I think. You can still do what you want."

Senior family members knew they needed someone of Day's authority. They had seen other families ripped apart by governance and succession disputes; the businesses suffered, and family relations were irreparable. In New Brunswick, there was the McCain story, and the memory of brothers Wallace and Harrison locked in bitter confrontation about who would succeed them, and the public spectacle of a legal battle. And New Brunswick also had the Irvings. K. C. Irving had built a sprawling family empire based on forestry, energy, real estate, shipbuilding, media, and retail assets, and as K. C.'s three sons moved into their eighties the family was splintering. One branch, the forestry side, didn't get along with the energy side. The Irvings managed to achieve a sweeping reorganization, but the family split was never repaired. Inside one branch, , there had been a very public falling out between Arthur, one of K. C.'s three sons, and his own son Kenneth, who had fallen from chosen one to outcast. There was, however, one model of success: the Sobey supermarket empire founded by Roy Jodrey's investing pal Frank Sobey and built by Frank's sons. There was the inevitable friction among cousins, but the Sobeys were developing strong governance practices. They also had publicly traded companies that allowed disaffected or uninterested family members to cash out their holdings.

The Jodreys could see the seeds of disaster. It was like a marriage on the rocks. They loved each other in many ways, but they couldn't really live together. So they had to consider divorce. George Bishop remembers his cousin David Hennigar coming to him and saying that his branch had an attachment to to some things, and Bruce and George's branch to others. The thinking was: why not go their own way? Roy Jodrey must have been rolling over in his grave, but the family agreed to give it a try. They were baffled, however, about how to start the process. By this time, John Jodrey had stepped down as chairman in favour of Graham Day, who was coming to the same conclusion as the family. He was the right man at the right time. George Bishop was impressed by how quickly Day sized up the situation and put together a team to carry out what would be an almost two-year process of reorganization.

As for Day, he loved the sheer challenge: "In a sense, it's not doing anything materially different than I did with Shipbuilders or cars or whatever. The pieces are different, but you've got this puzzle and the puzzle's not going to go away, and somehow you've got to make the pieces fit as best you can." Day knew he could call on people savvy in the world of business. First, he would put Jim Dickson, a Stewart McKelvey partner, at the centre of the negotiations among the family members. Dickson knew operational issues and he knew families, having worked with the Sobeys as both an outside counsel and a senior manager. On tax and valuation issues, Day would work with

John Roy, a partner with the accounting firm Grant Thornton in Halifax—and another veteran of the Sobey file. Lydia Bugden, the bright young commercial lawyer with Stewart McKelvey, would work with Scotia Investments, and other lawyers would help on key pieces of the file.

John Roy felt from the beginning that there had to be a way to hold the family conglomerate together. That was before he and Jim Dickson embarked on in-depth interviews in search of what the family wanted. After as many as twenty conversations, they were surprised. Some members didn't know what they wanted, and it took time to clarify their feelings. Others had a fierce attachment to certain assets, but were diffident about others. Some just wanted to escape. John Roy changed his view, coming to understand that, if the businesses stayed together, it could be destructive for the assets and the relationships.

The two men delivered their findings: some people wanted to own operating assets, others wanted cash and securities. The next challenge was getting it done. It came down to a long and complicated negotiation. Says John Roy, "It meant breaking up a family business of several generations, and it was and still is emotional." The Bishop and Hennigar branches clearly wanted to take assets, but one of the most surprising responses came from Bruce Jodrey. Coming out of university, he had worked side by side with his father John and his cousins, rising to vice-chair of the holding company and chair of CKF. But his life had taken a different turn. He and his wife Martha, a renowned educator with her own successful career, were passionate about improving the conditions in Nova Scotia for children with learning disabilities, a commitment that arose from family experiences.

In 1995, Martha almost died on the side of a road after a horrific auto accident. The Jodreys and their two sons were coming home from a Christmas concert when a woman, apparently bent on suicide, threw herself at their car. She came crashing through the windshield, striking Martha. The woman was dead and Martha was alive, but barely, and destined for a string of serious operations. "It changed everything," Martha says. The hitherto sacred family business was just a bit less hallowed. By the time the restructuring came, the couple were in their mid-sixties and their priorities had shifted. Health and travel loomed large in their lives, as did volunteering and philanthropy. Their two sons were on their own paths, with one working inside the family business. "We had a whole other life," Martha says.

So Bruce and Martha Jodrey went to Graham Day's house in Hantsport, and he listened. Bruce knew that, if he stayed in, he would never be able to retire: a family business does not provide an avenue for true retirement. He also knew his father John would be bitterly disappointed that their branch would not carry on. But he and Martha would always be wondering why they didn't seize the chance to devote themselves to what they cared about the most. Day told them it was okay to feel this way. "It was helpful to talk to someone somewhat at arm's length to give you the advice that makes sense," Bruce says. In the end, Bruce and Martha chose cash and securities. It was a major step in the unravelling of the Jodrey empire. Bruce has thought about it a lot since then, but, now in his mid-seventies, he knows he did the right thing.

Even though Day stayed out of the way of the team, he was constantly informed, never meddling, but interceding with a family member if he or she needed to talk. There would be aspersions that Day was favouring one side or that he personally wanted to take over the company. But he shrugged off the emotion and kept the outcome ahead of him. In the final analysis, Day says, "I believe I was trusted and I didn't have any skin in the game." George Bishop remembers Day would often take him aside and coach him quietly. "If you weren't being sensible, he'd be the first to tell you. It would come out in friendly conversation, a comment like, 'Maybe this is not a good idea because....'"

John Roy says Day did three things right. First, he was astute enough to know something had to be done to break the impasse. "Inertia is an awful thing sometimes," Roy observes. Second, he put a team together he had faith in. And third, he allowed that team to do its own thing. "He was intellectually several steps ahead of us, but allowed us to get there our own way. He is a pretty clever man." Day even coined a name for the project: Rubicon, the river of no return in Julius Caesar's advance on Rome to overthrow the republic. This was a Rubicon, because the Jodreys could no longer maintain the status quo.

Once Roy and Dickson knew there was going to be a negotiation, they shifted to making sure the right information got into everyone's hands at about the same time. Then the two men took on the role as facilitators, trying to get a deal.

There was another shadow looming in the background: a litigation against CKF regarding its use of trademarks, including its brands of paper plates called Chinet or Royal Chinet. The original Maine company with which Roy Jodrey had negotiated use of the trademarks in 1933 had become part of a Finnish group, Huhtamaki. The new owner wanted to enter the Canadian market by selling directly to retailers under the name Chinet. But CKF blocked the entry, asserting it had exclusive Canadian rights to the brand. It set off a complex intellectual property dispute in which Day played a pivotal role. He could see the potential threat to the reorganization of the Jodrey assets. When the lead lawyer at Stewart McKelvey was appointed to the Supreme Court of Nova Scotia, Day decided that a young lawyer, Daniela Bassan, should lead the CKF side. Another product of the Graham Day School of Championing Young People, she succeeded masterfully.

The Finnish company had sued CKF in Maine and Ontario, as well as in Nova Scotia, but the Canadian company got these other actions thrown out, arguing that Nova Scotia was the proper jurisdiction. After months of back and forth, the other side withdrew. The plaintiffs received no compensation, had to absorb their own costs, and were not able to enter Canada to manufacture or to sell. Day had spent a lot of time thinking about the litigation's potential effects, knowing a negative result could dramatically undermine valuations and distributions.

Meanwhile, the Great Jodrey Breakup was nearing the end. In the final marathon negotiation, the various interested parties were sequestered in six or seven meeting rooms at Stewart McKelvey's Halifax offices, with Dickson and Roy moving back and forth. Then they all came together in a big room to hammer out the deal. There were tears and cheers. The Bishop branch got the paper and manufacturing assets, led by Minas Basin and CKF, which remained the core of a newly reconstituted Scotia Investments. The Hennigars got real estate, nursing homes, and waste management. Perhaps the most serious sticking point was the fate of High Liner. Based on the valuations, it ended up in the Bishop camp, but the Bishops needed cash to pay off departing shareholders, and could not afford to keep it. They expected they would have to sell it to fishery players outside the family.

It was an emotional issue. High Liner—once called National Sea Products—is the heart and soul of Nova Scotia's fishery heritage; Roy Jodrey first invested in it in the 1940s. After Ottawa proposed nationalizing the company in a 1980s fishery bailout, David Hennigar, a passionate free marketer, stepped forward with a private sector control bid on behalf of the Jodrey family, with support from the Sobeys. Over twenty-five years, with Hennigar's stewardship and under capable management, National Sea Products weathered the collapse of the cod stocks and the lurching volatility of fish markets. The company made a wrenching decision to get out of fishing and focus on being a branded, value-added processor known as High Liner, with sharply fewer plants and employees. Headed by Henry Demone, the son of a fishing fleet captain, it made hard choices, and the company was rewarded with strong performance in a very tough business.

Now it was in danger of passing out of Jodrey hands, and Hennigar was intent on avoiding that. He felt the company was undervalued and he clearly loved the business. So he made a pitch for High Liner, and he was given a tight deadline to arrange financing. The deadline rankled a bit, but Hennigar had prepared for this eventuality. "I had already started with financing a couple of months earlier and we had a bank ready to say yes," he recalls. So he bought the control stake. It was a good move: the stock took off, and Hennigar made immediate paper profits before the price slipped back a bit.

"Who deserves it more than David? Because he was the guy who saved it," George Bishop says, adding, "we couldn't afford to keep it." In the end, Hennigar takes a realistic view of the outcome of the negotiation. "Everybody was equally unhappy, which is probably not bad," he says. Although he still has some issues with Day, he admits: "I don't think without him there it would have happened." Hennigar personally thanked Day for his role in getting an outcome. "I give him full marks for doing things; I didn't always agree with how he did them."

Archie MacPherson remembers that, at the end of the transaction, there was a get-together dinner. Everybody got a bottle of wine labelled Rubicon. But Day knew the painful odyssey of the Jodrey family was not over. When the two-year reorganization exercise ended in 2011, he felt only a handful of shareholders truly grasped the reality of what they had done. Now the split-off businesses faced the next stage of family ownership as investors.

Day had been paid the director's fee of $50,000 a year—nothing extra as chairman or for his work on the reorganization. However, when some business friends were setting up a scholarship program in Day's name at Dalhousie's school of management, a number of the Jodrey and Bishop families made meaningful contributions.

One of Day's hopes was that George Bishop would give up his CEO's duties at Scotia Investments and hand them over to Archie MacPherson, the very capable chief financial officer. Bishop agreed, but he wanted Day to stay around a while longer on the board. The older man demurred. Bishop remembers his words: "I don't want to be reading another annual report on the way to my funeral." Day was pulling back a bit. His three grandsons—Mike's two boys, Zachary and Harrison, and Deborah's son Alastair—were growing up. He and Ann were enjoying life in their Cape Cod, with his vast, book-lined basement study.

Day resigned from the Scotia Investments board on March 31, 2011. He left behind a board of eight: four independent and four family members. As of this writing, Bishop is chair, but he does not have a vote. He has persuaded his daughter Kristen to take his voting place on the board. One of Bishop's first acts in the post-reorganization world was to preside over the closing of Minas Basin Pulp and Power's board plant in Hantsport, with the loss of 140 jobs: after eighty-five years, Roy Jodrey's little mill had become uncompetitive. Bishop made the unusual decision to help a local photographer put together a book paying tribute to the mill, its people, and history. It is rare for a company closing a plant to pick so publicly at the scab of failure, but the Jodrey family felt a reverence for the business, which had meant so much to the Annapolis Valley. The book, with its employee photos and memories, does not pull punches—there are some remarks about questionable investments—but underlying it all is a tone of mutual respect and regret.

For George Bishop, it is part of the stewardship of a business family in its community. Meanwhile, the CKF business is thriving: the company has diversified into medical supplies and has a broader national presence, with plants in Ontario and British Columbia. David Hennigar has been busy since the breakup. His family sold the waste management and nursing home assets, and ended up focusing most intently on real estate and High Liner, the decision to scale back reflecting David's sombre view of the world and its economic prospects. George and David are no longer partners in business, but as family they are linked forever. Their acceptance of that reality, combined with a determination to move on, is Graham Day's achievement.

CHAPTER 21

One Man, Four Acts

> All the world's a stage,
> And all the men and women merely players;
> They have their exits and their entrances,
> And one man in his time plays many parts.
>
> —*As You Like It*

Act One: London, late October 2015. Fall's shadow descends on the city as the days get shorter and the wind blows more fiercely. But in Westminster Abbey, there is only colour and pageantry as 2,200 people gather to commemorate the six hundredth anniversary of a battle in a mucky French field.

Graham Day is here on this day, celebrating the Battle of Agincourt in 1415, one of the moments in history that crystallize the survival instincts of the English people.

Dunkirk. The Somme. The Spanish Armada. Agincourt.

The man who so proudly wears his status as a Canadian knight is drinking it all in as the sword of the English commander, Henry

V—his bones buried in this very building—is carried through the abbey. Graham Day listens to ninety-year-old actor Robert Hardy, whose signature roles are as Winston Churchill and a country vet, read from Shakespeare's *Henry V*, describing the "creeping murmur and the pouring dark" on the night before the battle.

Day is attending as a member of the council of the Imperial Society of Knights Bachelor, the order of knighthood to which he belongs. The Knights Bachelor can be traced back at least as far as the thirteenth century. "Theoretically, our forbearers were at Agincourt," he says later, explaining why the council members are present in their robes as part of the procession.

Sir Graham Day, Knight Bachelor, did not earn his honours on a soggy field of battle, but in the shipyards and car factories of urban Britain—and in the parlour of a prime minister, just steps away from this abbey. But he loves being part of the thread of history extending back to a bloody battle in northern France. Like many assembled in the old abbey—even someone with proud Canadian roots, and so modern in his thinking—Day has the capacity to live in the present and the past at once. It is the English way, and he feels it deeply.

Act Two: 180 miles to the northwest. Tourists are clustered on the ferry that will transport them over the Mersey estuary. As they move away from the Liverpool docks, the sweet voice of Gerry Marsden streams from the loudspeaker, crooning the 1960s megahit "Ferry 'Cross the Mersey." The boat leaves behind the cultural hothouse of downtown Liverpool, whose museums mix memories of the glorious maritime past with tributes to the British rock and roll explosion of the 1960s and 1970s.

On the other side, truly 'cross the Mersey, the passengers' eyes are drawn on the left to a big grey box structure with two wide openings. This is the modern production hall of Cammell Laird, and it dominates much of the Birkenhead shoreline, just as the shipyard's cranes and sheds have dominated that shore since 1828. But the production hall is a recent addition, hailing from the 1970s. It is another piece of the legacy of Graham Day, one of the tangible reminders of his impact as a transatlantic business figure. In Liverpool, his story is that of a modernizer who tried to liberate the shipyard from its past. In this and his other big British jobs, Day strove to save an economically besieged country. No Canadian has ever had such impact in Britain as a force of nature who helped lead a revolution, who saved companies and jobs in diverse industries—not without controversy—and retained his lustre as a capitalist hero.

Act Three: Halifax, Nova Scotia, a week later. Three thousand miles west of Liverpool, the mastermind behind the Cammell Laird production hall sits in the sleek offices of Stewart McKelvey, with a view of another ferry, the one that transports commuters across the harbour between Halifax and Dartmouth, the birthplace of his beloved Ann. Graham Day thinks about the twists of fate—the serendipity—that carried him from a boyhood in this town, on to Montreal, Toronto, Tokyo, Liverpool, and London, and now back to this boardroom, an hour away from his house in Hantsport.

Around him, Stewart McKelvey lawyers march about with a sense of purpose in their serious strides. They stop occasionally to pass the time of day with their elder statesman, now eighty-three and still a storehouse of stories and epigrams. He tells them of his latest trip to London to see the Agincourt ceremony. The tone is respectful and warm. These young men and women of a giant law firm are among Day's most enduring legacies, but there are other people, too. Looking beyond these offices to nearby Dalhousie University, and beyond that to Stellarton, Toronto, and Montreal, his impact is reflected in the next generation of leaders in classrooms, boardrooms, and executive offices.

"Leaders in business are judged by the people they leave behind," Day would often say. And he will leave behind an ocean of talent, whose impact will long survive the great grey production hall.

Act Four: A boardroom in Toronto. Any fan club for Graham Day would be headed by Michael Donovan, who runs DHX Media, a company that has burst out of Halifax to become the largest independent holder of digital children's content in the world outside the major studios. Still based in Halifax, but present everywhere that kids watch shows—*Teletubbies* and *Caillou* are part of its stable—this business would be the last of Day's public company boards.

Donovan is a serial entrepreneur who, with his brother, founded one of the pillars of Canadian TV, Salter Street Films, the producer of comedic icons *This Hour Has 22 Minutes* and *Codco*. After he sold Salter Street in 2001, he found an international vision for his next venture: to become a go-to source of children's viewing for the digital age. But he needed capable directors. When Day was invited to join the board of the new company, he said he knew nothing about the digital content business, let alone children's programming. But Donovan insisted he would grasp the big picture of the entertainment world—after all, he had worked on *Singalong Jubilee*.

Day came on the board, serving as lead director to Donovan's executive chair. He understood the vision; more important, he understood how to be a mentor and friend. He has the qualities of character that transcend technical knowledge. Day was the person Donovan could go to with confidence that he knew the business's risks and potential, and could stand firm in the face of hard choices. "Not infrequently, he was the difference that made a difference," Donovan says, interviewed in DHX's offices on Toronto's harbourfront.

Donovan believes Day epitomizes the best of Canadian business leadership. Canadian businesses often shrink from thinking beyond their borders, Donovan believes. But with their small markets and distance from other North American centres, Maritimers are forced to look farther afield internationally, more so than do other regions of Canada. But the Maritimes are also bereft of financial capital, and Day understands that dilemma, too. He has straddled the two worlds of Maritime enterprise: the old families and the new technologies that must thrive if the region is to have a chance.

At one point, after a decent stint, Day wanted to leave the DHX board, but Donovan urged him to stay. Later they came to an agreement: Day would leave the board at the end of 2016. "He is irreplaceable," Donovan laments. "He is somebody I could confide in, and always has been disinterested and discreet. He is truly one of the most interesting and original people I know."

Indeed, he is—like the guy in the beer ad, but without the beer and the blonde. He is the real thing.

In most of his British jobs, Graham Day was at the helm, the centre of the action, with talented sweepers coming up behind him. In Canada, he has been the epitome of director, mentor, and friend—the wise presence standing at the shoulder of the leader. He plays both roles with aplomb, and would continue to do so into his eighties, displaying the vitality of a much younger man while coping with prostate cancer and a bout of pancreatitis.

A number of years ago, still in his seventies, Day happened to take the ferry across the Bay of Fundy from Saint John to Digby. It was a boat Day knew well: the *Princess of Acadia*, whose construction he had once contracted for as a young lawyer with Canadian Pacific. It was now an aging workhorse in the fleet of Bay Ferries and Day's friend Mark MacDonald. The *Princess*'s captain had heard about Day's marine background, and invited him up to the bridge. At one point, it was suggested that the passenger guide the vessel out of its berth, with Day playing the captain and the captain the helmsman. The location was tricky, the harbour busy, there was the force of the Fundy tides—and the captain could always override Day's instructions. But Day flawlessly directed the ship's movement as it left the berth and headed out of the port.

It was a reminder of past adventures, past ports, past shipyards. It was also a classic Graham Day kind of moment in his Canadian period: the guiding intelligence working with a steady helmsman. The captain was impressed. He concluded that, among his other talents, Graham Day was one fine ship handler.

ACKNOWLEDGEMENTS

To write a biography of Graham Day is a challenge. There are so many sides to the man, and he has always defied being pigeonholed. So I have to thank Graham himself for patiently guiding me through his remarkable career and for his prodigious memory of people, events, and dialogue. Ann Day was also a warm and insightful navigator through the adventures of their life together, and Michael Day shed important light on the man who is his father and friend.

The idea for this book began more than a decade ago with Don Mills, who suggested a biography of Graham Day and tirelessly supported the project. Thank you, Don. Peter Fardy, vice-president of advancement at Dalhousie University, has my appreciation for leading the university's participation; Dalhousie has been a great sponsor and partner, and I am grateful for the support of its president, Richard Florizone. Thanks also to Peggy Cunningham, former dean of the Rowe School of Business, and to Kim Brooks, former dean of the Schulich School of Law. Elizabeth Thompson was invaluable in assembling the photos.

Among the people who contributed, I must single out Roger and Val Vaughan for being such kind hosts in England as I chased down part of the Graham Day story. This book is, in fact, a collaboration with all the people who sat down with me, either by phone or in person in Britain and Canada: Steve Acker; Marg Ashcroft; Catherine Bell; Jim Bennet; George Bishop; Colette Bowe; John Bragg; Mary Brooks; Lydia Bugden; Dominic Cadbury; Blaise Cathcart; Eleanor Clitheroe; Louis Comeau; Jim Dickson; Michael Donovan; Laura Formusa; David Gardiner;

John Gardiner; Peter Godsoe; Costas Grammenos; David Hennigar; Bruce Jodrey; Martha Jodrey; Aldéa Landry; Greg Maddison; Mark MacDonald; Archie MacPherson; Paul Martin; Bill McEwan; Malen Ng; Peter Mills; John Monks; Derek Oland; Geoffrey Owen; David Parker; Helen Parker; Gillian Perry; Joan Prior; John Roy; David Sobey; Donald Sobey; Allan Shaw; Peter Thompson; and Rick Waugh.

Len Waverman, dean of the DeGroote School of Business at McMaster University, has been a supporter of my work, and I enjoy my role as the school's business writer in residence. He was very understanding as I focused on this book. Through my valuable association with DeGroote, I gained access to the McMaster University Library, allowing me to tap into online databases. That opened up the resources of British and Canadian newspapers, most notably the *Financial Times*, the *Times* of London, the *Financial Post*, and the *Globe and Mail*. Particularly useful were two feature articles on Graham Day at the peak of his British period: one by Hazel Duffy in the *Financial Times*; the other by Valerie Grove in the *Sunday Times*.

Also, a word on the books I mined. I am in particular debt to George Bishop for giving me a copy of the story of the Minas Basin paper mill, *We Wanted It to Last Forever* (South of the River Publishing, 2015), with photos and interviews by Dick Groot. Harry Bruce's books are always good companions, and I avidly read *RA: The Story of R. A. Jodrey, Entrepreneur* (McLelland & Stewart, 1979). I am also indebted to that guide through the internal politics of Canadian Pacific, *Lords of the Line*, by David Cruise and Alison Griffiths (Viking, 1988). Stephen Kimber's *Sailors, Slackers, and Blind Pigs* (Anchor Canada, 2003) opened up the world of wartime Halifax. I found great value in Kimber's books and magazine pieces, as I did in the work of my friend

John DeMont. *The Chocolate Wars* by Deborah Cadbury (Douglas & McIntyre, 2010), was a revelation. Anne Murray's memoir *All of Me* (Knopf Canada, 2009), co-written with Michael Posner, provided important context.

My agent, Dean Cooke, is a friend and unflappable supporter in all my projects. Once again, Nimbus has been a fine publishing partner and freelance copy editor Barry Norris a tireless and skilled collaborator. Leah Handler has been astute and timely in transcribing my often rambling interviews. Emily MacKinnon brought endless patience and kindness to her role as copy editor.

The biggest thank you goes to my family, led by Elaine, who is my first reader and staunchest ally through the anguish and joy of producing yet another book.

DALHOUSIE UNIVERSITY ACKNOWLEDGEMENTS

Dalhousie University acknowledges generous financial support from these from these individuals and organizations:

The John & Judy Bragg Family Foundation
The Donald Sobey Foundation
David Sobey, CM
Archie MacPherson
Stewart McKelvey
Peter Godsoe, OC
Hector Jacques, OC
Halifax Port Authority

APPENDIX

Sir Graham Day's Awards and Honours

Legal

Graduated, Dalhousie University Law School, May 1956
Admitted to Nova Scotia Bar, November 1956
Admitted to Ontario Bar, February 1967
Queen's Counsel (NS), December 2011

Honours

Knight Bachelor, January 1989, "dubbed" July 1990,
Arms granted November 1990
Order of Nova Scotia, 2011
Officer, Order of Canada, 2014

Military

Commissioned, Canadian Army, September 1961
Appointed Honorary Colonel, The West Nova Scotia
Regiment, May 2005
Appointed Colonel Commandant, Legal Branch, Canadian
Armed Forces, May 2011

Medals and Decorations

Queen Elizabeth II Diamond Jubilee Medal
Canadian Forces Decoration (CD)

Honorary Doctorates

CANADA
Dalhousie University, 1987

United Kingdom
The City University, 1989
The Council for Academic Awards, 1990
Cranfield Institute of Technology, 1991
University of Aston in Birmingham, 1991
University of Warwick, 1991
University of Humberside, 1992
South Bank University, 1992

Other Award
Honorary Fellowship, University of Wales, 1995

Recognitions
Freeman of the City of London, 1985
Companion, Chartered Management Institute, United Kingdom, 1991
Fellow, Institute of Corporate Directors, Canada, 2000
Member of the Nova Scotia Business Hall of Fame, 1996
Member of the Canadian Business Hall of Fame, 2006

Livery Companies
Worshipful Company of Shipwrights, 1985
Worshipful Company of Coach Makers & Coach Harness Makers, 1987

INDEX

Y